RACE AND THE ANIMATED BODYSCAPE

RACE AND THE ANIMATED BODYSCAPE

Constructing and Ascribing a
Racialized Asian Identity in *Avatar* and *Korra*

Francis M. Agnoli

University Press of Mississippi / Jackson

The University Press of Mississippi is the scholarly publishing agency of the Mississippi Institutions of Higher Learning: Alcorn State University, Delta State University, Jackson State University, Mississippi State University, Mississippi University for Women, Mississippi Valley State University, University of Mississippi, and University of Southern Mississippi.

www.upress.state.ms.us

The University Press of Mississippi is a member of the Association of University Presses.

An earlier version of "Background Design and Painting" in Chapter Four was originally published as "Building the Transcultural Fantasy World of *Avatar*" in *Animation Studies* (Special Issue, 2019).

Copyright © 2023 by University Press of Mississippi
All rights reserved

First printing 2023

∞

Library of Congress Cataloging-in-Publication Data

Names: Agnoli, Francis M., author.
Title: Race and the animated bodyscape : constructing and ascribing a racialized Asian identity in Avatar and Korra / Francis M. Agnoli.
Description: Jackson : University Press of Mississippi, 2023. | Includes bibliographical references and index.
Identifiers: LCCN 2022051872 (print) | LCCN 2022051873 (ebook) | ISBN 9781496845085 (hardback) | ISBN 9781496845092 (trade paperback) | ISBN 9781496845108 (epub) | ISBN 9781496845115 (epub) | ISBN 9781496845122 (pdf) | ISBN 9781496845139 (pdf)
Subjects: LCSH: Avatar, the last airbender (Television program) | Legend of Korra (Television program) | Animation (Cinematography) | Race on television. | Asian Americans on television. | Animated television programs. | Fantasy television programs. | Human figure in art.
Classification: LCC PN1992.8.A78 A46 2023 (print) | LCC PN1992.8.A78 (ebook) | DDC 791.45/72—dc23/eng/20230210
LC record available at https://lccn.loc.gov/2022051872
LC ebook record available at https://lccn.loc.gov/2022051873

British Library Cataloging-in-Publication Data available

AUTHOR'S NOTE

For Korean names, this book uses the same spelling and ordering as they appear in the series end credits or in behind-the-scenes material. This results in some stylistic inconsistencies.

CONTENTS

Acknowledgments ix
Introduction 3
Chapter One: The Visual Components of the Animated
    Bodyscape 20
Chapter Two: The Aural Components of the Animated
    Bodyscape 49
Chapter Three: The Narrative Components of the Animated
    Bodyscape 68
Chapter Four: Visual Worldbuilding and the Animated Bodyscape . . . 85
Chapter Five: Aural Worldbuilding and the Animated Bodyscape. . . . 115
Conclusion 133
Notes 145
Bibliography 173
Other Sources 187
Index 195

ACKNOWLEDGMENTS

There are a few people I wish to thank, without whom this book would never have come to be. Rayna Denison, for her mentorship during the beginnings of this project. Emily Snyder Bandy, for her guidance through the publication process. Everyone who has read my early drafts and provided feedback, for pushing this book to be the best possible version of itself. And, finally, all of my family and friends, for their love and support over the years.

RACE AND THE ANIMATED BODYSCAPE

INTRODUCTION

Race does not exist in animation. It must instead be constructed and ascribed. Yet, over the past few years, there has been growing discourse on the intersection of these two subjects within both academic and popular circles. In 1982, Irene Kotlarz published one of the first pieces of scholarly writing on race and animation. Her article, "The Birth of a Notion," examines Black representation in US cartoon shorts from the 1930s and 1940s.[1] For her, animation is more clearly "constructed" or "crafted" than live-action productions, meaning that these shorts display corporate racism in embarrassing clarity.[2] Over the decades, subsequent publications have continued the trends set by Kotlarz, with a shared focus on Blackness, on the golden age of cartoons, and on how animation begets exaggerated caricatures.[3] Across these writings, visuals take priority, with only a few touching on aural elements, such as music or vocal performances.[4] When discussing more recent animation, scholars still tend to focus on Blackness, such as in Sarah Banet-Weiser's book on Nickelodeon, where she discusses how the network's brand identity relied on the commodification of Blackness to signify an "urban" "coolness" in the 1990s and 2000s.[5] Even in an article purportedly about all racial minorities, Hugh Klein and Kenneth S. Shiffman ultimately focus on the depictions of Black characters in US animation.[6] On one hand, this emphasis makes a certain amount of sense. As Klein and Shiffman conclude in their quantitative study, Black characters are the most commonly depicted racial minority in US animation from the 1930s to the 1990s.[7] Furthermore, as observed by C. Richard King, Mary K. Bloodsworth-Lugo, Carmen R. Lugo-Lugo, Christopher P. Lehman, and Nicholas Sammond, the history of US animation is heavily intertwined with nineteenth-century minstrelsy as well as swing-era racist caricatures.[8] Regardless, such a narrow focus has only revealed part of the picture. While writings on non-Black racial representation in US animation are rarer, they still offer insight into how this filmmaking method can produce meaning. Writings specifically on Asian representation in animation, for example, have often emphasized the importance of vocal performances.[9] The concepts of "brown voice" and "yellow voice," as defined by Shilpa Davé, Alison Reiko Loader, and Hye Seung Chung, are discussed in greater depth in the second chapter of this book.

In contrast, nonacademic discussions have centered on celebrities in high-profile US animated television series and feature films—including *The Simpsons* (FOX, 1989–present) and *BoJack Horseman* (Netflix, 2014–20) as well as *Kubo and the Two Strings* (2016) and *Isle of Dogs* (2018).[10] During summer 2020, in response to civil rights protests against police brutality, *The Simpsons*, *Family Guy* (FOX, 1999–present), *Big Mouth* (Netflix, 2017–present), and *Central Park* (Apple TV+, 2020–present) all announced that they would replace white voice actors who had been portraying Black characters with Black voice actors.[11] Within a few months, Emmy Raver-Lampman was cast as Molly Tillerman on *Central Park*, Ayo Edebiri as Missy Foreman-Greenwaldon on *Big Mouth*, Alex Désert as Carl Carlson on *The Simpsons*, and Arif Zahir as Cleveland Brown on *Family Guy*, taking over roles originated by Kristen Bell, Jenny Slate, Hank Azaria, and Mike Henry, respectively.[12] This moment of apparent self-reflection has not completely stopped the casting of white celebrities as nonwhite characters in animation. As of this writing, Lizzy Caplan continues to voice Reagan Ridley, the biracial Japanese American protagonist of *Inside Job* (Netflix, 2021–present), for example. Character design, in contrast, is often sidelined in popular discussions, only emerging when a work explicitly references the racist caricatures of the past, such as with the videogame *Cuphead* (Studio MDHR, 2017), later adapted into an animated television series, *The Cuphead Show!* (Netflix, 2022–present).[13]

The analysis of race and animation calls for a holistic approach, one that can be applied to any racial group, one that treats both the visual and the aural as intimately connected. Furthermore, such an approach must recognize animation as a distinct filmmaking practice, something that depicts race in a fundamentally different manner than live-action productions do. After all, someone in front of a camera is not the same as someone in front of a microphone. Due to its illusory and constructed nature, animation affords untapped opportunities to approach the topic of race in media, looking beyond the role of just the character designer or actor and taking into account the various factors and processes behind the production of racialized performances. This book, therefore, offers a blueprint for how to approach the analysis of race and animation, looking specifically at the US television series *Avatar: The Last Airbender* (Nickelodeon, 2005–8) and its sequel, *The Legend of Korra* (Nickelodeon, 2012–14; nick.com, 2014). Set in a high fantasy world with almost exclusively human characters, all rendered in a hyperrealist aesthetic, this television franchise is an ideal candidate for such a study. But first, before continuing, we must determine the meaning of "race" as well as what animation specifically offers that live-action does not.

What is race? According to sociologists Matthew Desmond and Mustafa Emirbayer, race refers to a "a symbolic category, based on phenotype or ancestry and constructed according to specific social and historical contexts, that is misrecognized as a natural category."[14] With this description in mind, we see an emphasis on physical appearances (e.g., skin color, hair, and facial structure) and that race itself is socially constructed. Of course, if that is the case, then it must have been constructed by someone, specifically someone with an agenda. Since the species commonly known as humans first evolved in what we now call East Africa, they spread across the world. Those with genetic traits best suited for their new environments lived long enough to reproduce, passing those genes down to their offspring. Thus, over the course of thousands of years, people who lived in separate parts of the world grew recognizably distinct in appearance. For millennia, individuals who traveled great distances for trade or exploration were well aware that the further they were from home, the more different people looked to them. While one could study these variations in phenotypes to trace ancient migratory patterns, cataloguing different groups of people cladistically, such categories could not be confused for commonsensical or folk understandings of race. Any scientifically rigorous attempt to divide and label humanity in such a manner would beget thousands of "races," none of which would line up with modern definitions.[15] Those were not developed until relatively recently.

As popularly understood, race is, first and foremost, a pseudoscientific system of categorization developed during the Age of Enlightenment in defense of European colonialism; it has persisted to modern times as a continued justification of certain social, economic, and political status quos, including ongoing Euro-American imperialism. The taxonomies developed by physicians and scientists, such as François Bernier, Carl Linnaeus, Johann Friedrich Blumenbach, Georges Cuvier, Joseph Arthur de Gobineau, and Robert Knox, proposed hierarchies that justified the exploitation, genocide, and enslavement of their presumed inferiors. Of these three, Linnaeus's system of classification has had the most influence on contemporary definitions of race. For the tenth edition of *Systema Naturae*, the Swedish botanist devoted a few pages to four varieties of *Homo sapien*: *Homo sapien americanus*, *Homo sapien europaeus*, *Homo sapien asiaticus*, and *Homo sapien afer*. He also included an entry for *Homo monstrosus* or cryptids. In his descriptions, he treated geography, physical appearance, and personality traits based on the four humors as intrinsic characteristics for each subspecies. The American race was red, choleric, and virtuous; the European race was white, sanguine, and brawny; the Asian race was sallow, melancholic, and rigid; and the African race was black, phlegmatic, and easygoing.[16] These categories and their associated qualities have persisted into contemporary definitions of race: Indigenous or Native American, white, Asian or Pacific Islander, and Black. Depending on a country's foreign policies or immigration laws, additional ethnic, religious, or national groups may also become "racialized" Others, even if they are, according to the above categories, "European" or "white."

The ideological descendants of Linnaeus and his contemporaries continued to invent pseudoscientific fields to defend indefensible policies and practices. Phrenology justified the enslavement and later segregation of Black Americans as well as the over-policing of Irish immigrants in the United States; eugenics mandated the forced sterilization of those deemed "undesirable"; and intelligence quotient (IQ) tests are still cited as grounds for cutting social welfare programs that might benefit minority communities. Over time, the validity of race as a system of classification has eroded, in part due to the discoveries of blood types and DNA but also largely due to social changes. Those who critiqued scientific racism were motivated by the widespread lynching of Black Americans following the Civil War, by the appointment of Adolf Hitler as chancellor of Germany in 1933, and especially by revelations about the Holocaust after World War II. Upon seeing the end result of scientific racism in their own metaphorical backyards, a new generation of writers were overtly motivated by the mantra of "Never again." Henceforth, dominant accounts of race would treat it as a social construct rather than as a biological reality.[17]

With this history in mind, race can be understood as a system of constructed categories into which individuals are forced, erasing or flattening differences, usually in the service of the agenda of those in power. In other words, race as a concept exists in order to define and defend whiteness through the designation of non-white Others. As such, it is tempting to disregard those who continue to utilize and police racial definitions as the disciples of European imperialists. However, at the same time, individuals within marginalized communities have invoked shared racial identities as a means of uniting and organizing diverse diasporas, such as when civil rights activist and historian Yuji Ichioka coined the term "Asian American" in the 1960s. Whether they come from the top or the bottom of the social ladder, whether they erase differences in an act of dehumanization or of solidarity in the face of white supremacist systems, racial categories are here to stay, at least for the foreseeable future. Therefore, attempts to understand how and by what means racial definitions are formed and enforced are warranted and justified.

Artistic depictions, such as those rendered in animation, codify and perpetuate such definitions of race, and the "stereotype" can be a useful tool for discussing how. This concept was first developed by American writer and journalist Walter Lippmann in 1922 to describe how the human brain functions. We, as a species, are incapable of truly conceptualizing billions of unique individuals. So, instead, we develop categories based on our lived experiences, on what we have been taught, and on what we have seen and heard in the media. Whenever we encounter someone, we automatically interpret visual and aural stimuli in order to place them into these constructed categories.[18] By the 1930s, scholars had already started to implement this concept in their studies of discrimination against racial and ethnic minorities.[19] Media studies has also utilized the idea of stereotypes for analyses of artistic depictions of such groups. After all, the dominant narrative mode of cinematic and televisual storytelling necessitates some degree of stereotyping. These formats allow time and space to develop just a few characters, to give the impressions of only a few fully lived lives. For the vast majority of on-screen roles—those without the suggestion of interiority and that exist in relation or in service to the main characters—artists employ visual, aural, and narrative shorthand. Audiences are expected to recognize these cues and to fill in the gaps based on their presumed lived experiences, their education, and their exposure to other pieces of media. As one may guess, these circumstances can result in a feedback loop, where stereotypes are perpetuated almost exclusively through media representations, independent of the lived experiences of those who produce or consume them. These depictions exist at a cross-section between the two types of "representation" of which Gayatri Chakravorty Spivak has written. They are "representations" in the political sense, where one stands in for an entire community. Furthermore, they are "re-presentations" in the artistic sense, where someone or something from the real world is re-created for and within a work of fiction.[20] Media portrayals of a community, especially of a marginalized or minority community, tend to focus on one or a few figures who, either by accident or by design, stand in for the larger group, in a sense operating as substitutes for reality. The result is what Donald Bogle has described as "square boxes" into which even actors from those communities must force themselves in order to fulfill white expectations.[21] Thus, any artistic depiction reveals more about the group doing the depicting than of the group being depicted.

Perhaps, instead of thinking in terms of race, we should think in terms of "racialized identity." With this reframing, I intend to emphasize the constructed-ness and arbitrariness of the above definitions. In many ways, my approach mirrors that of Anne Anlin Cheng, who has written about the "yellow woman" as a fabricated figure within the Euro-American imagination.[22] Such a framework proves especially beneficial when considering works of animation, which grant artists extensive control over images, as well as works of fantasy, which deviate the furthest from the real world. In addition, with this term, I acknowledge the tendency to collapse geographic, ethnic, religious, and national groups into whatever categories benefit those in power while also recognizing the various factors behind their constructions. Cultural markers, including clothing, hairstyles, accents, language, music, and food, contribute to the "writing" and "reading" of racialized identities. At the same time, while "racialized identities" can suggest a break from reality—as though they were just an alternative to "real" racial identities—these definitions still need to be tethered to historical and cultural contexts in order to be legible. Components that ground a work of media, especially one that is animated or fantastical, to the real world therefore contribute to the construction and maintenance of these identities, and they should be taken into account. This includes not only elements that evoke specific real-world communities or other works of media but also reality in general. Therefore, by discussing racialized identities, this study considers a combination of visual signifiers that emulate real-world phenotypes and ancestries, cultural markers that evoke real-world contexts, as well as supporting elements that mimic reality in general and ground the above components. As a result, this study looks at how every production process contributes to the construction of these racialized identities. For the analysis of the *Avatar* franchise, one racialized identity stands out as especially relevant, and it requires more precise unpacking.

The world of *Avatar* clearly emulates Asian—specifically, Chinese—cultures from our reality, and this fantasy world is populated by figures clearly meant to emulate real-world Asian peoples. Therefore, before continuing with our analysis of the *Avatar* franchise, it is worthwhile to address what precisely "Asian" or "Asianness" means as defined by US media as well as how that identity is an inherently racialized one. Any singular definition of Asia or Asian should be impossible, as it would erase innumerable national, regional, ethnic, linguistic, and cultural distinctions. However, within the Euro-American popular imagination, a monolith has formed, even in the face of a pluralistic and diverse reality. Again, it is this fabricated image that I am addressing and seeking to define rather than any real-world diasporic communities. Within this context, the "Asian race" can be most neatly summarized as the "perpetual foreigner."[23] Their innate exoticism renders full assimilation—something available to white, European immigrant communities—impossible. Even despite their "model minority" status—a designation used to pit racial and ethnic groups against each other—the Asian American can never become fully American.[24] This attribute can manifest in various ways, reducing Asians to a threat, a sexual fetish, a joke, or some combination of the above.

This racialized identity has been defined and codified through popular culture, most plainly through the "yellowface" performances of the nineteenth and twentieth centuries.[25] White actors would use makeup to give themselves sallow skin, buck teeth, and slanted eyes in order to perform "Asianness" for a white audience. However, while these visual elements were certainly defining characteristics of yellowface performances, they were not the only ones. In addition to makeup, these actors would affect pidgin English and plain gibberish as substitutes for the various real-world accents of immigrants who had adapted the idiosyncrasies of their native languages to English. I address the function of accents in works of media at greater length in chapter 2. These visual and aural imitations are further complemented with cultural markers. Along with makeup and accents, Krystyn R. Moon identifies clothing and hairstyles—black or blue tunics and the queue, to be precise—as key components of early yellowface performances.[26] Indeed, racialized identities are more than just phenotypes or ancestry; they are perpetuated and conveyed through such cultural markers. In addition to non-Western clothing and hairstyles, simulated religious practices and beliefs, medical treatments, cuisine, and martial arts can all mark a figure as foreign, as Other, as another race. Works of media, even ones that do not technically qualify as "yellowface," have continued to stress the exoticism of the perpetual foreigner, placing the Asian in opposition to the default Euro-American. Over time, this singular "Asian race" has supplanted the disparate and diverse diasporas of numerous real-world Asian countries in the Western popular imagination. While *Avatar* and *Korra* both take many steps to avoid falling into these patterns, as discussed throughout the following chapters, they still exist as part of this history of representing or re-presenting a fantastical racialized Asian identity. In order to understand how and by what means, we need to look at these shows holistically, recognizing the significance of each and every production process. We also need to understand how animation differs from live-action filmmaking practices.

Animation is notoriously difficult to define, as various scholars have emphasized over the years. Nichola Dobson notes that the "very fluid nature of the form" precludes the establishment of a singular, agreed-upon definition.[27] In the first chapter of her book *Art in Motion: Animation Aesthetics*, Maureen Furniss references Charles Solomon, who identifies two qualifications—"(1) the imagery is recorded frame-by-frame and (2) the illusion of motion is created, rather than recorded."[28] She also cites Norman McLaren, who writes: "Animation is therefore the art of manipulating the invisible interstices that lie between the frames."[29] After acknowledging this shared focus on movement, Furniss ultimately proposes a continuum between mimesis, the reproduction of reality, and abstraction, the reduction of visuals to their purest form, on which both animation and live-action could exist.[30] Paul Wells and Samantha Moore undergo a similar journey in *The Fundamentals of Animation*. They reference a widely circulated quote by animator Gene Deitch, who describes cinematic animation as "the recording of individually created phases of imagined action in such a way as to achieve the illusion of motion when shown at a constant, predetermined rate, exceeding that of human persistence of vision."[31] While imperfect, these definitions, especially with their common emphasis on the illusory and constructed nature of the medium, are helpful for understanding how and by what means animation produces and ascribes racialized identities. This book also highlights these attributes. As a filmmaking practice, animation is "non-indexical," "iconic," and "plasmatic." It is wholly constructed, defined by a tenuous connection to the real world; although this quality is up for debate, as animation can incorporate elements of indexicality. It is streamlined, with extraneous details elided to abet reproducibility. Finally, it is fluid in both form and identity. The ramifications of these traits on racialized identities in animation are explored more fully in the first chapter.

In order to analyze how racialized identities are produced and ascribed within animation, I have adopted and adapted the concept of the "bodyscape" as coined by art historian Nicholas Mirzoeff. In the book *Bodyscape: Art, Modernity, and the Ideal Figure*, he utilizes this term to describe re-presentations of the "ideal figure" as well as of the "Other" in Western art, although he does not use Spivak's discerning hyphen. He defines the bodyscape thusly:

> The body in art must be distinguished from the flesh and blood it seeks to imitate. In representation the body appears not as itself, but as a sign. It cannot but represent both itself and a range of metaphorical meanings, which the artist cannot fully control, but only seek to limit by the use of context, framing and style. This complex of signs is what I shall call the bodyscape.[32]

Rather than think of a body within a work of art as a singular, monolithic entity, with a similarly immutable identity, we can instead view it as a sea of various intersecting components, each created via distinct production processes and potentially by different artists. Instead of the lone painters,

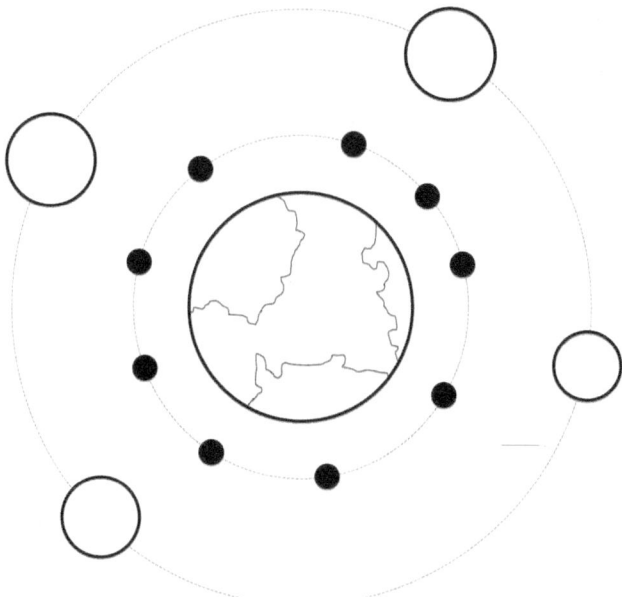

Planetary Production Cultures Model.

sculptors, and photographers behind Mirzoeff's case studies, animation—especially television animation—is produced via an intricate web of collaboration and delegation. Their cumulative creative decisions bring into existence the meanings contained within these complexes of signs, sometimes in ways beyond their control or knowledge. We can visualize these interlocking production cultures as a "planetary model." There is a central planet or primary site of production, itself divided into separate continents or departments. There are orbiting satellites—executives, consultants, freelancers, and remote workers—that contribute to but are not integrated into those communities. Finally, there are lunar bodies or geographically distinct secondary sites of production, such as overseas animation studios. Different components travel between locations, taking on additional signification as new sets of personnel adapt or modify them. While Mirzoeff focuses exclusively on appearances, mainstream contemporary animation is principally an audiovisual and narrative medium. Therefore, the animated bodyscape is composed of visual components that combine into an "animated figure," of aural components in the form of a "vocal performance," as well as of narrative components that make up the surrounding diegesis. These individual elements travel between locations as represented in the planetary model as new sets of personnel adapt or modify them before they are assembled and incorporated into the animated bodyscape. Once part of these complexes of signs, individual components intersect and interact with one another, creating additional meanings. With this context in mind, I present a definition of the "animated bodyscape": a complex of signs, composed of visual, aural, and narrative components, created via distinct production processes, assembled to create the impression of a unified whole. Furthermore, animation and thus the animated bodyscape possess their own set of distinct qualities, the aforementioned nonindexicality, iconicity, and plasmaticity.

Armed with the concept of the animated bodyscape, this book asks: How and by what means are racialized identities produced and ascribed in animation, specifically in and for the *Avatar* television franchise? The most direct way to answer this question is to ask those responsible. I have formulated a contextually driven and interview-based study that was tested against textual analysis. This approach is not quite production studies, although I was influenced by scholarship from that field, in particular that of John T. Caldwell. He and others consider producers of media to also be producers of culture through the creation of production communities.[33] Indeed, in order to track the development and assemblage of visual, aural, and narrative components, one should understand the formation and operation of the relevant departments. How were they formed? How are they structured? What is their relationship with the other departments? This approach privileges interviews while also cautioning against relying too heavily on them.[34] To mitigate the risk of spin and faulty memories, these scholars recommend using a variety of sources for cross-referencing.[35] In keeping with these methods, this book also prioritizes original interviews with above- and below-the-line personnel involved in various stages of production. Doing so emphasizes the role of the individual artist, their choices, and their actions within a complex of production communities. These testimonies are complemented by additional sources, namely, preexisting interviews available through studio-produced paratexts, third-party publications, and personal social media posts. However, production studies is designed for the analysis of contemporary or ongoing subjects, allowing the researcher to engage in direct observation of the production processes. By using the *Avatar* television franchise as a case study, this book introduces a historical component that requires unpacking and contextualizing. Therefore, scholarly writings that weave together original and preexisting interviews to create production narratives and uncover hidden histories, especially for television animation, are more applicable.[36]

As examples of 2000s and early 2010s US television animation, *Avatar* and *Korra* are the products of specific historical and industrial trends. Accounting for this background allows for greater understanding of these two series as well as how they construct and ascribe racialized identities. Following the antitrust case *United States v. Paramount Pictures, Inc.* (1948), commonly referred to as the "Paramount Decision," theatrical animated shorts were no longer economically viable, encouraging an industry-wide change in exhibition strategies. Generally, animation scholars and historians view the subsequent decades as a dark time for the medium. Tom Sito describes this era from 1952 to 1988 as a "lost generation" for what appeared to be a dying industry.[37] According to Paul Wells, with the rise of television, the dominating view became that animation was no longer an art form but was instead something exclusively for children.[38] Similarly, both Jason Mittell and M. Keith Booker see the shift from primetime animation, as represented by *The Flintstones* (ABC, 1960–66), to "Saturday morning cartoons" as one of becoming exclusively children's programming.[39] In part because of this change in audience demographics, some writings on race and television animation tend to focus on the effects of media depictions—be they in the form of negative stereotypes or positive representation—on child development.[40] This book does not make such qualitative judgments, instead focusing on how the tools and processes of animation are implemented to create meaning, including racialized identities.

Television animation's reputation did not improve in the 1980s, when US president Ronald Reagan and FCC chairman Mark Fowler oversaw the deregulation of the film and television industries. Cable soon became saturated with animated shows that were essentially toy commercials. Within and in reaction to this environment, Nickelodeon—the future home of the *Avatar* television franchise—was established. According to accounts of the cable channel's history by Heather Hendershot and Sarah Banet-Weiser, network president Geraldine "Gerry" Laybourne wanted to create a library of original animation programming with long-term rerun potential instead of licensed, toy-based ephemera.[41] Linda Simensky, a former Nickelodeon employee, recounted how Laybourne appointed Herb Scannell to lead the newly established animation department and to foster a creator-friendly development process.[42] Rather than adapt existing properties, the studio invited pitches for original ideas and produced short pilots to be audience tested, an expensive practice then unique in television animation.[43] Out of the eight original pilots, three were developed into full shows—*Doug* (1991–94), *Rugrats* (1991–2004), and *The Ren & Stimpy Show* (1991–95).[44] From 1996 to 2006, Scannell succeeded Laybourne as president and—according to Banet-Weiser—continued expanding the animation department.[45] His tenure saw some of the network's biggest successes, including *SpongeBob SquarePants* (1999–present), *The Fairly OddParents* (2001–17), and *Avatar:*

The Last Airbender. The next two presidents, Cyma Zarghami (2006–18) and Brian Robbins (2018–present), shifted focus to maintaining, reviving, and acquiring intellectual properties through their animated programming. Under their watch, Nickelodeon has aired tie-ins with DreamWorks features films, such as *The Penguins of Madagascar* (2006–15), *Kung Fu Panda: Legends of Awesomeness* (2011–16), and *Monsters vs. Aliens* (2013–14). They have also produced spinoffs and sequels to previous Nicktoons, including *The Legend of Korra*, *Planet Sheen* (2010–13), *Kamp Koral: SpongeBob's Under Years* (2021–present), *Rugrats* (2021–present), and *The Patrick Star Show* (2021–present). Also, Nickelodeon has ironically become the home of the *Teenage Mutant Ninja Turtles* television franchise, one of the archetypical cartoons-as-toy-commercial from the 1980s, with *Teenage Mutant Ninja Turtles* (2012–17) and *Rise of the Teenage Mutant Ninja Turtles* (2018–20).

Returning to the 1990s, Banet-Weiser identifies diversity as part of Nickelodeon's brand identity under Scannell, tying in with themes of inclusivity and empowerment.[46] She positions Black and Latino characters in supporting roles in the channel's animated programming as signifiers of an urban coolness in a supposedly postracial economy.[47] With their quasi-Asian fantasy setting and characters, *Avatar* and later *Korra* were also part of that mandate for diversity, one less interested in confronting and dismantling systemic inequality than in commodifying racial differences. Instead of contemporary urbanness, the evocation of an Asian identity in the *Avatar* franchise recalled another media trend from the era. These two shows are the results not only of decades of US animation but also of a then-recent anime boom. There has been a long history of cross-pollination between the animation industries of the United States and Japan. Many scholars—including Giannalberto Bendazzi, Susan J. Napier, Rayna Denison, Tze-yue G. Hu, Brian Ruh, Jonathan Clements, Ian Condry, Michal Daliot-Bul, and Nissim Otmazgin—have already written on the subject.[48] Ruh provides a helpful timeline of this influence by dividing the importation of Japanese animation to the United States into a series of "waves." The first was in the 1960s and was disseminated through broadcast television; the second appeared in the 1970s and 1980s and was spread by home video; the third took place in the 1990s and was defined by early Internet fandom and cable syndication; and the fourth one featured distribution via downloads and torrents.[49] The recent rise of official streaming services—including Hulu, Netflix, Funimation, and a legitimized Crunchyroll—coproducing and distributing Japanese animation suggests the emergence of a fifth wave. Following these designations, *Avatar* was pitched and developed in the aftermath of the third wave, which had introduced US audiences to *Sailor Moon* (TV Asahi, 1992–97) in 1995,

Dragon Ball Z (Fuji TV, 1989–96) in 1996, and most notably *Pokémon* (TXN, 1997–present) in 1998.

These syndications had a noticeable impact on US television animation in the late 1990s and 2000s, specifically in the form of what Daliot-Bul and Otmazgin call "anime-inspired cartoons." The authors define this type of programming as "an effort by a non-Japanese studio to produce an animated show that refers to, reproduces, and even emulates that particular (rather elusive) something found in anime."[50] Sometimes, these products imitate generic and aesthetic anime conventions while still centering primarily white or white-coded characters, as seen in *The Powerpuff Girls* (Cartoon Network, 1998–2005) and *Teen Titans* (Cartoon Network, 2003–7). Other times, these shows feature East Asian content and leads while mostly retaining US stylistic norms, as seen in *Jackie Chan Adventures* (Kids WB, 2000–5), *Samurai Jack* (Cartoon Network, 2001–4), *Xiaolin Showdown* (Kids WB, 2003–6), *Hi Hi Puffy AmiYumi* (Cartoon Network, 2004–6), and *American Dragon: Jake Long* (Disney Channel, 2005–7). Nickelodeon, however, did not jump on this particular bandwagon until *Avatar*. The franchise's emulation of the stylistic and narrative conventions of anime affected how it produced and ascribed racialized identities to animated bodyscapes.

The world of *Avatar* is divided into four nations—the Water Tribe, the Earth Kingdom, the Fire Nation, and the Air Nomads. Select individuals have the ability to manipulate or "bend" their nation's respective element through fantastical martial arts. Only the Avatar, a mystical being reincarnated every generation, can control all four elements. After a hundred-year war in which the Fire Nation wiped out the Air Nomads, Water Tribe siblings Katara and Sokka discover the new Avatar, a young airbender named Aang, frozen in an iceberg. Across three seasons and sixty-one episodes, the last airbender and his new companions travel the world as he masters the four elements in order to defeat Fire Lord Ozai and restore balance to the world. Over the course of the series, they are accompanied by earthbender Toph and are pursued by the banished Prince Zuko, his uncle General Iroh, and eventually Princess Azula from the Fire Nation.

Cocreators and executive producers Michael Dante DiMartino and Bryan Konietzko were joined by other creative voices for this production. Aaron Ehasz was head writer, overseeing a fluctuating writing staff. A duo known as the Track Team—consisting of composer Jeremy Zuckerman and sound designer Benjamin Wynn—handled much of the show's soundscape. Andrea Romano served as voice director. The series also hired outside consultants to both ensure and signal cultural authenticity. As the calligrapher and translator, Siu-Leung Lee has been consistently framed as an expert in his field. In the end credits, his name is accompanied by a PhD, and the official art book spotlights his work in a way that stresses his range of knowledge.[51] He is presented as possessing both the native knowledge of a first-generation Chinese American and the acquired expertise of an academic. The involvement of cultural consultant Edwin Zane functioned differently. The former vice president of the Media Action Network for Asian Americans (MANAA) was hired to provide feedback on production artifacts, such as concept art and scripts. Rather than an expert in Asian culture, he functioned as a representative of a prospective Asian American audience. However, out of all of these cultural experts, the martial arts consultant, credited as "Sifu Kisu of the Harmonious Fist," was the most prominent, at least within studio-produced paratexts. A Black American born in Morocco, Kisu does not have an ancestral claim to an Asian culture like Lee and Zane do, yet he has also been positioned as an expert. Behind-the-scenes material highlight his knowledge of various Chinese martial arts, and the end credits include the title "Sifu."[52] Finally, the animation was completed overseas by the South Korean studios JM Animation, DR Movie, and Moi Animation, whose involvement on *Avatar* was likewise highlighted in promotional materials.[53] As with the three consultants, their presence signaled authenticity. In addition to these people, various below-the-line crew members made impactful creative decisions.

Set seventy years after its predecessor, the sequel series follows the next reincarnation of the Avatar, the eponymous Korra. For four seasons and fifty-two episodes, she contends with and questions her role in a rapidly modernizing and fractured world. Whereas *Avatar* centered on a single conflict, *Korra* has a new antagonist each season. First, she—along with Mako, Bolin, Asami Sato, and her mentor Tenzin—face off against the anti-bender terrorist Amon in the cosmopolitan Republic City. In the second season, she finds herself in the middle of a conflict between the Northern Water Tribe ruled by her uncle Unalaq and the Southern Water Tribe ruled by her father, Tonraq. In the third, she begins rebuilding the Air Nation while being hunted by a group of anarchists led by Zaheer. For the final season, she confronts the military dictator Kuvira, who has seized power in the Earth Kingdom and seeks to forcibly reintegrate the United Republic into her Earth Empire. Across these four seasons, Korra questions the role of the Avatar in a modern world that always seems to be in crisis as well as her ability to fulfill that role.

This fragmented structure was in part due to the show being originally developed as a twelve-episode miniseries, before it was renewed while they were storyboarding the finale. As a result, *Korra* started with a smaller stateside crew than *Avatar* had. Cocreators and executive producers DiMartino and Konietzko returned, this time entrusting oversight of the directing and storyboarding to a team of producers—Joaquim Dos Santos, Lauren Montgomery, and Ki Hyun Ryu. Without Ehasz, DiMartino and Konietzko cowrote every episode of the first season, and they were subsequently joined by *Avatar* veterans Tim Hedrick, Joshua Hamilton, and Katie Mattila. The Track Team, Romano, and Lee returned to their previous positions. Kisu's role was more limited, and his work was supplemented by that of other martial arts consultants, most notably stuntman Jake Huang. The overseas animation was handled almost entirely by Studio Mir in South Korea, with a few episodes being animated by Studio Pierrot in Japan. Even with a smaller crew, *Korra* was the product of numerous less-visible workers.

This book looks at these individual artists and their production communities in order to trace how they created and modified the visual, aural, and narrative components that comprise the animated bodyscape. It explores how crew members infused these elements with meaning, including with racialized identities. Each chapter traces the development of a different kind of component before its incorporation into the animated bodyscape. The first covers the production of visual components and the formation of an animated figure, the most obvious way to convey racialized identity in these texts. It focuses on how these figures differ from their live-action equivalents, exploring the impact of their nonindexicality, iconicity, and plasmaticity on the construction and ascription of meaning. The chapter also traces the development of the animated figure through specific production processes, from character design to storyboarding to animation, with special attention paid to the development of both form and color. Along the way, I explore how individual artists forged and mediated connections between their work and the real world as well as how their decisions impacted what significations are introduced into the animated bodyscape.

The second chapter considers the development of aural components, specifically of vocal performances that are sutured to animated figures in order to produce "animated performances." Akin to the preceding chapter, this one tracks the creation of these aural components through multiple departments and processes, from casting to recording to editing to synchronization. At each stage, the choices and actions of individuals had repercussions down the production line, illustrating the interconnectedness of these seemingly separate production communities. This chapter also explores how sounds—in particular, the voice—can be implemented to construct racialized identities, especially through the performance of accents and dialects. Furthermore, this chapter examines how sound functions as an agent of mimesis within animation, tethering the fantastical and abstract to reality, through the evocation of a physiological body as well as of specific historical and social contexts. Even after an animated figure and a vocal performance combine to form an animated performance, the animated bodyscape is not yet complete.

The remaining chapters broaden their scope to explore how the three types of components contribute to fantasy worldbuilding, to the construction of a diegesis that, in turn, projects additional meanings into associated animated bodyscapes. These significations can complement or contradict those produced by the animated figure and vocal performance. The first of these chapters focuses on the development of narrative components via the writing process. It begins by examining this stage of production through the theoretical lenses of fantasy and cultural appropriation. Via the "fantasification" process, artists modify a chosen real-world referent in order to transform it into its fantastical counterpart as well as to integrate it into an established diegesis. These decisions, in turn, impact the ascription of racialized identities through the introduction of new connotations. The second half of this chapter stresses how the formation and function of production communities, such as the writers' room, can impact these processes. These ideas carry over into the final two chapters.

The fourth chapter asks: How do animation productions build fantasy worlds visually? Like with the writing process, individual artists selected and adapted real-world referents for integration into an established diegesis. In addition to aspects of character design (e.g., clothing, hairstyles, and jewelry), the art department plays an important role in evoking and constructing cultural identities that are then incorporated into animated bodyscapes. Each section focuses on a separate production process—background design and painting, fight choreography, and calligraphy—interrogating how the drive toward authenticity manifested across the different departments. The use of real-world referents creates both intentional and unintentional significations. This pattern repeats in the fifth and final chapter, which asks: How do animation productions build fantasy worlds aurally? As with the voice, we see how music and sound effects also function as agents of mimesis within animation, grounding the fantastical and abstract to the real world, supporting and validating the other significations. This chapter also interrogates how production narratives frame the fantasification process. For the transference of meaning between reality and fantasy to occur, the audience must be aware of how the two are connected. Sometimes they are presumed to know and recognize it. Other times, they must be educated.

By tracking the development and assemblage of the different types of components, we can see the range of processes and personnel that goes into the production of an animated television series as well as into the formation of racialized identities. While the idea that mainstream animation is inherently collaborative is neither new nor radical, the animated bodyscape offers a helpful tool for contextualizing and conceptualizing disparate production narratives and histories. How and by what means does animation produce and ascribe racialized identities? It does so through the construction of visual, aural, and narrative components that are assembled and incorporated into an animated bodyscape. Thus, this book provides a blueprint not only for understanding how *Avatar* and *Korra* construct and ascribe racialized Asian identities but also for exploring how any animated text produces identity.

Chapter One

THE VISUAL COMPONENTS OF THE ANIMATED BODYSCAPE

Before proceeding, one must understand that animation and live-action are two distinct filmmaking practices, resulting in different types of bodyscapes. The core qualities of animation—and, thus, of the animated bodyscape—impact the construction and ascription of racialized identities across the different production processes. Live-action filmmaking practices are "indexical," recording some element of a profilmic, if highly manipulated, reality. In front of the camera, there exists a physiological body, one with its own phenotypes and ancestry beyond its implication in a specific text. These qualities persist even when steps are taken to obscure them, such as through hairstyling, makeup, costuming, and lighting. In regards to race and ethnicity, much has been written about the various "faces" donned by theatrical, cinematic, and televisual performers over the past centuries.[1] However, while such writings can offer a helpful starting point, they are not fully applicable to animation. An alternative approach should be considered.

When created through animation, the bodyscape is wholly constructed and is therefore "nonindexical." This, however, can be subject to some debate, and not only because definitions of "indexicality" are rooted in predigital filmmaking. Certain animation techniques and practices challenge my claim concerning the quintessential non-indexicality of animation. Rotoscoping and motion-capture both record the movement of bodies while generating their visual appearances; stop-motion records the visual appearances of real-world objects while simulating their movement; and, of course, many pieces of animation incorporate audio recordings.[2] However, while an animated text and thus an animated bodyscape may possess indexical elements, it is not itself wholly indexical, does not constitute a recording of reality. The animated figure, in contrast to its live-action counterpart, is entirely the product of artists. Thus, Rudolf Arnheim could praise animation as being more artistic than live-action because it affords greater control.[3] Thus, Paul

Wells could claim that "animation may be viewed as the most auteurist of film practices" regardless of degrees of collaboration because it requires the greatest amount of intervention on the part of the artist.[4] And, thus, Jane Batkins could open her book by saying: "The animator gives life to the animated—the two surely cannot be separated."[5] The artists' choices and actions should therefore take precedent when addressing how and by what means identities are constructed and ascribed through this filmmaking practice. Whereas visual signifiers behind racialized live-action figures are forged by actors, makeup artists, hair stylists, and costume designers, those incorporated into their animated equivalents are instead the products of character designers, storyboard artists, animators, and colorists. This chapter traces how their actions contributed to the creation and assemblage of the racialized visual components of an animated figure. In doing so, it illustrates the three core qualities of animation: its nonindexicality, its iconicity, and its plasmaticity.

CHARACTER DESIGN AND ICONICITY

Character design broadly refers to the production of model sheets for each animated figure that appears on screen. These include ones for main, guest, and background characters. Under the supervision of a producer or art director, these model sheets are created by character designers with colorists assigning "local colors" for skin tone, hair, and clothing. Of course, model sheets are far from the final stage of production; these images themselves do not appear in the finished animation. Character designs are instead reproduced and reinterpreted by various personnel at various stages of production (e.g., storyboarding, key animation, and in-between animation). Therefore, as a logistical necessity, they must be both specific enough that viewers can easily recognize individual characters and simplistic enough that subsequent crew members can efficiently recreate them. For television productions, like *Avatar* and *Korra*, with limited budgets and tight schedules, the latter concern is foregrounded. Cocreator and art director Bryan Konietzko noted another deterrent to producing more elaborate designs within this system: "If something's too realistic, people get scared to do expressions with them, and they end up looking too stiff."[6] Therefore, creative decisions—made by character designers and colorists as well as approved by their supervisors—must be made about which visual elements to preserve and which to streamline. These choices have repercussions.

In finding this balance between specificity and simplicity, the character design process unveils a second core quality of the animated bodyscape. In addition to being nonindexical, it is also "iconic." Extraneous details have been elided, leaving only essential visual elements. "Iconicity" can be understood in terms of the relationship between an image and reality. As stated in the introduction, Maureen Furniss proposed a continuum for all filmmaking practices between mimesis, the representation of reality, and abstraction, the reduction of visuals to their purest form.[7] Animation, especially mainstream television animation, tends toward the latter. With this model in mind, one should remember two things. First, every text, regardless of how mimetic, is not reality. Second, every text, regardless of how abstract, exists in relation to reality. Iconicity may enlarge the distance between the image and reality, but those connections are never fully severed. If they were, if the image had absolutely no relation to the real world, then it would hold no meaning for either those who made it or for those who see it. Instead, by manipulating these connections, artists can manage the transference and incorporation of meanings derived from real-world identities as well as from historical and cultural contexts into animated bodyscapes.

For *Avatar* and *Korra*, the art department mediated this relationship by adopting a "hyperrealist" animation style. Borrowing the term from Umberto Eco, Paul Wells uses "hyper-realism" to discuss how classic Disney features echo the "realism" of live-action films.[8] The term describes a drive within some schools of animation toward verisimilitude of the real world or, more specifically, of how a film camera records it. Such conventions can ground or normalize the fantastical and abstracted elements of an animated text. By incorporating relatively realistic visual elements, *Avatar* and *Korra* character designers strengthened their designs' connection with reality as well as counterbalanced the more cartoonish flourishes. In other words, these animated figures are more recognizably "human"—a category with which both artist and viewer have had real-world experience—than more abstracted cartoon ones would be. In other words, they exist in closer relation to a shared perception of reality. As a result of these reinforced tethers, racial and ethnic identities derived from the real world were more easily ascribed to these animated bodyscapes. Nevertheless, the character designs remain iconic, and their production still involved streamlining, which impacted the development of racialized identity.

The removal of details can have curious effects. Imagine, for example, a stick figure—a circle atop a set of five lines, a head atop a torso with two arms and two legs. It is as iconic as a design can get while still being recognizably human. However, unlike the hyperrealist characters of *Avatar* and *Korra*, the stick figure is harder to place within other real-world categories, those stereotypes as defined by Walter Lippmann in the introduction. Now, imagine two lines coming down from either side of the stick figure's head. It has become a woman with long hair. Among simplified visual elements, the remaining details—no matter how small—are amplified. It is, in the words of comics scholar Scott McCloud, "amplification through simplification."[9] Similarly, as Wells writes, animation has the power to either "dilute" or "amplify" meaning.[10] However, there remains much to unpack about this scenario. If long hair is a signifier of womanhood, then its absence functions both as a signifier of manhood and as a sign of neutrality. If long hair is an aberration on the nondescript stick figure, then it would follow that womanhood is an aberration of manhood. This pattern repeats with other layers of identity. As comics scholar Jared Gardner observes, simplified designs risk reducing characters to caricatures.[11] There is a long history of illustrators and animators utilizing exaggerated facial features (e.g., large ears, low brow, narrow eyes, long noses, board noses, thick lips, and buck teeth) as signifiers for real-world racial and ethnic groups. Such design elements function similarly to blackface and yellowface makeup being applied onto a white live-action performer. They likewise position these groups not only as racialized Others but also as deviations from the default (i.e., white, able-bodied, neurotypical, heterosexual, and cismale) human body. Therefore, when working with iconic character designs, artists should be aware of this historical and cultural context as well as of the connotations of various visual elements.

We can interrogate the example with the stick figure further. Why is the default a white man? Why are additional design elements required to mark it as anything else? Along with amplifying select visual details, iconicity begets the absorption as well as the projection of meaning into the animated bodyscape. Later chapters address the former phenomenon; the latter calls for more immediate unpacking. In addition to sundry teams of artists, viewers and readers participate in the production of meaning within a text. In other words, they can project identities—including but not limited to racialized ones—into the animated bodyscape. According to Scott McCloud, the more iconic a face is, the more universal it is. He writes: "When you look at a photo or realistic drawing of a face—you see it as the face of another. But when you enter the world of the cartoon—you see yourself."[12] Building on this claim, Annabelle Honess Roe cites a neuroscience study indicating that the human brain responds more emotionally or empathetically to iconic animated images than to live-action recordings of real people.[13] Writing about comics, Derek Parker Royal also argues that iconicity encourages a reader to empathize with a figure who would otherwise be the Other.[14] After all, they are likely to be seeing more of themselves. Character designers can manipulate this phenomenon to their own ends. As McCloud notes, some Japanese comics utilize more detailed designs for antagonists and more simplified ones for protagonists.[15] Therefore, readers would see the villains as Other and the heroes as themselves. In *Avatar* and *Korra*, the child protagonists typically have more streamlined designs than villainous or secondary adult characters, creating such a distance. For example, the heroes are regularly rendered with large, expressive, cartoonish eyes, while other characters are more realistically proportioned.

One repercussion of the above phenomenon can be Own Race Projection (ORP). You can find examples within the popular discourse around various animated properties. Consider how some Black fans of *Looney Tunes* (1930–69), *A Goofy Movie* (1995), and *Dragon Ball Z* have read nonhuman characters (i.e., Bugs Bunny, Goofy and Max, as well as Piccolo, respectively) as Black, regardless of the intentions of the relevant artists. These audiences projected their own racial identities onto these iconic animated bodyscapes. Other animated texts, such as *Avatar* and *Korra*, center around unambiguously human characters with greater visual details than the average stick figure. How, then, does ORP occur under these circumstances? To answer, let us consider the concept of *mukokuseki* (無国籍) and how it applies to the Western consumption of Japanese animation.

Sociologist Koichi Iwabuchi defines *mukokuseki* as meaning "something or someone lacking any nationality."[16] On one hand, the term can refer to something having multiple national origins. In regards to Japanese animation, this application can refer to the dominant style's various influences and receptions, a dimension that interests animation scholars Rayna Denison and Jane Leong.[17] Alternatively, *mukokuseki* can suggest erasure, especially of physical signs of race or ethnicity.[18] This latter definition is of greater relevance for discussions of iconicity and ORP. When *mukokuseki* is brought up in Western discourse around Japanese animation, it is often in reference to white viewers questioning why these canonically Japanese characters look "white." For a short answer, they do not. For a longer answer, the audience members in question are projecting their own racial identities onto iconic animated bodyscapes. Amy Shirong Lu conducted a study confirming the existence of ORP among white consumers of Japanese animation.[19] However, there is something more complicated going on here.

One could argue that white viewers are reading the absence of explicit racial markers as indicators of whiteness because, as they have been conditioned by Western media, they view whiteness as the default. However, those familiar with anime will note that non-Japanese characters are often rendered with greater visual details than Japanese ones. Contrast the specificity of the majority of character designs in *Attack on Titan* (MBS TV, 2013–17; NHK

G, 2018–23) with the relative simplicity of Mikasa Ackerman, the one Asian character in the main cast. This disparity is even more apparent in the *chibi* parody spin-off *Attack on Titan: Junior High* (MBS TV, 2015). Still, characters in manga and anime are rarely rendered as stick figures. There are specific visual cues (e.g., light-colored hair, large eyes, and pale skin tone) that certain audiences interpret as signifiers of whiteness, even while they ignore anything that would contradict that reading. Terry Kawashima has interrogated these tendencies, writing that any decoding of visual markers to determine race is "a culturally conditioned, trained act" and that to read race is to produce it.[20] For example, Ueno Toshiya theorizes that light-colored hair was the product of visual exaggerations meant to differentiate characters in black-and-white manga rather than an attempt to convey a particular racial or ethnic identity.[21] Michal Daliot-Bul and Nissim Otmazgin also write that such features were used "to convey feelings rather than mark ethnicity."[22] Of course, when a text is read, the intentions of the artists are not always respected. Nevertheless, *mukokuseki* can be a helpful concept to keep in mind when addressing how character designers can intentionally or unintentionally construct and ascribe racialized identities to iconic animated bodyscapes—and not only within Japanese animation.

Looking at the animated figures of *Avatar* and *Korra*—or of any animated text, for that matter—there are a series of questions to consider: (1) What are the connections between the character designs and the real world? (2) How do artists mediate those connections through the elision and retention of certain details? (3) What resulting meanings are incorporated into the animated bodyscape? Consider, as an example, the series of creative decisions that resulted into the initial character design of Prince Zuko. Zuko is the primary antagonist for the first season of *Avatar* before he eventually joins the heroes. He is the first member of the Fire Nation shown on screen and therefore becomes representative, in the political sense, of that fantasy culture. As relayed by the cocreators, the idea for the character came from Nickelodeon executive Eric Coleman, who thought that the series could use a recurring villain.[23] From the initial sketches by Konietzko and Yoon Young Ki, character designers ascribed meaning onto this animated figure.

In order to mark the character as Asian, original concept sketches adapted Japanese—more specifically, samurai—referents for Zuko's armor and hairstyle. Doing so visually distinguished the Fire Nation from the more Chinese-inspired Earth Kingdom.[24] Thus, direct links were cultivated between the fantastical and animated Zuko and the real-world nation and culture of Japan. However, connotations can go both ways. By marking the villains as Japanese and the heroes as Chinese, Japan is marked as villainous and

Zuko's first appearance. Still from "The Boy in the Iceberg" (Avatar S1E01). Blu-ray release of *Avatar: The Last Airbender—The Complete Series* (2018).

China is marked as heroic. As cultural consultant Edwin Zane warned Nickelodeon upon seeing these designs: "This might be interpreted or translated as 'Japanese are bad, and all other Asian people are good.'"[25] As a result, the art department shifted to utilizing more Chinese referents for Zuko's and thus Fire Nation armor. In other words, in an act of fantastical distancing, the tether connecting this character design to reality was altered to transfer a general Asianness rather than a specific Japaneseness.

For other instances, the character designers sought to conceal the connection between design and referent. Konietzko recalled early feedback from Coleman: "Eric said, 'You know how skinheads are scary? But when you see a thirteen-year-old skinhead, it's somehow scarier?' So, that's what he said, and I just said, 'Can he have a scar?'"[26] In this recounting, Coleman tasked the character designers with transforming a real-world referent, the shaved scalp of a young skinhead, into a signifier of scariness and intensity. However, an unmediated connection between character design and reality would have similarly conveyed real-world racial and cultural connotations—namely, the hairstyle's link with white supremacist movements. By including additional visual elements, both the scar and topknot/ponytail, Konietzko sought to mitigate the severity of these significations. Thus, a design element could be mined for general connotations while being divorced from real-world contexts.

While Zuko's hairstyle changes over the course of the series and of the franchise, his scar remains a consistent identifying mark. If all other facial features were abstracted away and Zuko rendered as a stick figure, that burn scar over his left eye would be sufficient to identify him. While, according to Konietzko, the scar was originally intended to counterbalance the character's shaved head, Zane had a different reading. He told me:

> I remember giving them the note that there's actually a genetic trait in the Asian population . . . There's a lot of Asian people that have this really big birthmark . . . on parts of their faces that they can't hide or they can't cover . . . I did point out to them that there is a significant Asian population—especially if there's children watching this—that can easily identify with not being able to hide a certain shame, even though . . . his was a scar and theirs was a birthmark.[27]

Zane appears to be referring to port-wine stains (*nevus flammeus*), congenital vascular malformations caused by permanently dilated blood vessels, most commonly on the face. According to the Vascular Birthmarks Foundation, this reddish birthmark is nonhereditary, affecting all racial groups equally.[28] That said, most common removal treatments were still designed for lighter skin tones.[29] Regardless, Zane saw port-wine stains as signifiers of Asianness, and he saw Zuko's similarly colored and positioned scar as carrying the same connotation. Even though the artists had full control over the means to mediate the relationship between the character designs and the real world, they were not in full control of the meanings that were transferred between the two.

The above accounts demonstrate how artists forge, exploit, and mediate the connections between character designs and reality in order to construct and ascribe meaning to an animated bodyscape. By transforming referents from the real world, they link Zuko with East Asian cultures as well as with skinheads. They further manipulate these connections by removing specificity and by introducing other design elements. As a result of their creative choices, Zuko is explicitly marked as Asian and as intimidating. However, as Zane's testimony reveals, the decision making behind iconic designs leaves room for audiences to project supplemental identities. Through the added details of the armor, hairstyle, and scar, an iconic character design was able to incorporate a racialized Asian identity into an animated figure. This core pattern repeats across character designs.

Throughout *Avatar* and *Korra*, character designers used the physiological bodies of other crew members, friends, and family as models. The pirates from "The Waterbending Scroll" (*Avatar* S1E09) were based on the animators from JM Animation in South Korea, June the bounty hunter from "Bato of the Water Tribe" (*Avatar* S1E15) emulated postproduction supervisor Lisa Yang, and Joo Dee from "City of Walls and Secrets" (*Avatar* S2E14) was modeled after line producer Miken Lee Wong in "design and personality."[30] In the sequel series, the Equalist doorman from "The Revelation" (*Korra* S1E03) was based on martial arts videographer William Rinaldi, Ryu from "Rebirth" (*Korra* S3E02) on producer Ki Hyun Ryu, and two Kuvira supporters from "The Coronation" (*Korra* S4E03) on designers Angela Song Mueller and Christine Bian.[31] While personnel of different racial and ethnic backgrounds were all transformed into Asian-coded characters, the use of Asian and Asian American models was often highlighted. When *Avatar* animatic editor Dao Le condemned the casting for the live-action film, she specifically wrote that "some of the characters were even modeled after Asian members of the crew."[32] This statement suggests that the employment of Asian models can be cited as proof that these characters are likewise Asian, that the racial identity of the former was transferable to the latter. She does not address whether the presence of non-Asian models had an equivalent effect for other characters. Still, some aspects of a model can be incorporated into an animated bodyscape, especially when viewers are made aware of the connection between the character design and real world. In the following examples, the character designers for *Avatar* and *Korra* used specific models or referents because of their association with some sort of Asian identity, which they intended to convey in their character designs.

The Pirate Barker introduced in "The Waterbending Scroll" and the Warden introduced in "The Boiling Rock, Part 1" (*Avatar* S3E14) share the same model, Seung Hyun Oh, an employee of JM Animation and later a supervising director at Nickelodeon.[33] A comparison of the two designs reveals which facial features were considered most representative of Oh and therefore worth retaining or exaggerating. Both characters have prominent lips, downward eyebrows, epicanthic folds, and long faces. By the third season, the designs for guest characters had become relatively more detailed. As a result, Jae Woo Kim's design for the Warden has more pronounced nasolabial folds, whereas those in Konietzko and Woo Sung Gu's design for the Pirate Barker barely pass his nostrils. The Warden's nose and chin are also less pronounced, and his cheekbones are more defined, clearly rendered as black lines. For the character designers, these facial features were enough to represent and re-present Oh. The creators and crew members have not

The Pirate Barker. Still from "The Waterbending Scroll" (*Avatar* S1E09). Blu-ray release of *Avatar: The Last Airbender—The Complete Series* (2018).

The Warden. Still from "The Boiling Rock, Part 1" (*Avatar* S3E14). Blu-ray release of *Avatar: The Last Airbender—The Complete Series* (2018).

offered a clear rationale for modeling these particular characters after this person. Because neither character shares a personality, Oh's likeness does not appear to signify any internal qualities. Perhaps they thought he looked interesting, with his long face and pronounced lips. Regardless, this choice of model carries connotations related to identity. If nothing else, recalling Le's earlier statement, it helps mark these characters as racially Asian.

"Sokka's Master" (*Avatar* S3E04) introduces the character of Piandao, a master swordsman and teacher, modeled after the show's martial arts consultant, Sifu Kisu. Alterations were made between model and design. The latter is aged and given facial hair, although Kisu has claimed to still being able to recognize himself.[34] By using their martial arts consultant as a model for this guest character, Konietzko and Mueller were marking him as a master in Chinese martial arts. Here, the Asianness ascribed was not through Kisu's racial or national identity—that of a Black American—but instead through his acquired and widely publicized expertise. It is a cultural Asianness being ascribed rather than a racial one. Nevertheless, such a connotation would only be possible for those with behind-the-scenes knowledge, those who would have likewise recognized Kisu in Piandao.

Piandao. Still from "Sokka's Master" (*Avatar* S3E04). Blu-ray release of *Avatar: The Last Airbende— The Complete Series* (2018).

Baraz (*left*) and Ahnah (*right*). Still from "Reunion" (*Korra* S4E07). Blu-ray release of *The Legend of Korra—Book Four: Balance* (2015).

What happens when the model is not a specific physiological body? First featured in "Reunion" (*Korra* S4E07), Baraz is a firebender who has escaped from an Earth Empire reeducation camp. Because his design was not yet finalized, the storyboard artists rendered him as a mixture of Spike Spiegel from *Cowboy Bebop* (TXN, 1998) and Mugen from *Samurai Champloo* (Fuji TV, 2004–5), sharing their triangular faces, messy hair, and thin eyebrows.[35] This appearance persisted into the final animation. For those familiar with the referents, the emulation of these iconic anime characters connotes facets of Baraz's identity. Despite the character's brief appearances, he is marked as a rough rogue, in imitation of both Spike and Mugen. The connection is further reinforced by the casting of Steve Blum, who voiced the two anime characters in the US English dubs of their respective shows. Furthermore, through their sketches, the storyboard artists positioned this animated figure in relation to Japanese animation, therefore to Japan, and therefore to Asia. Thus, through their use of referents, the storyboard artists were able to signify both this character's personality and his Asianness.

Across the above examples, character designers and other personnel explicitly connected their designs with the real world—with specific people, with sources of cultural knowledge, and with national industries. Through the use of these models and referents, they sought to convey and ascribe certain qualities to guest characters with limited screen time. Specifically, they intended to mark these characters as Asian, either racially or culturally. While this process involved some degree of mediation, audiences would still have had to recognize the referent in the final design, which would often require some behind-the-scenes knowledge. The associations then enhance rather than wholly constitute the characterization of these animated figures. That all said, animated bodyscapes are not static illustrations on model sheets but are instead bodies in illusory motion. These character designs still had to be rendered and interpreted by episode directors, storyboard artists, and animators.

STORYBOARDING AND PLASMATICITY

The transformation of static images into fluid ones is fundamental to the medium of animation. In addition to being nonindexical and iconic, the animated bodyscape is also "plasmatic." Early film scholars have recognized and underlined this instability. Sergei Eisenstein writes of animation's "rejection of one-and-forever allotted form, freedom from ossification, the ability to dynamically assume any form. An ability [he would] call 'plasmaticness'" and that I simplify as "plasmaticity."[36] As a result, the animated bodyscape is, according to Wells, "a form constantly in flux" and therefore one that subverts traditional understandings of identity.[37] For Batkin, it is "an elusive 'thing'" that complicates the application of a likewise fluid identity.[38] From the production of storyboards to final animation, the animated figure reveals itself to not be a singular object but instead is a series of still images projected in such a manner as to create the illusion of a single entity. It is plasmatic in nature, and its significations are similarly malleable. While an appealing concept in theory, these writers might be overstating matters. After all, Eisenstein wrote during a specific era of US animation, and the hyperrealist aesthetic of *Avatar* and *Korra* is a far cry from the "rubber-hose" animation of the 1920s and 1930s. Furthermore, certain animation techniques—such as some forms of stop-motion or computer-animation—involve the puppetry of singular objects.[39] Nevertheless, one should consider how additional meanings can be introduced in later stages of production. As these components travel between different production communities, new visual elements can complement or complicate a racialized identity.

For *Avatar* and *Korra*, upon completion of a script, an episode would be assigned to a director and team of storyboard artists. *Avatar* storyboard artist Juan Meza-Leon described his job as to "interpret" the script in order to tell the "visual narrative of the story."[40] The storyboards would, in turn, be interpreted by yet other groups of personnel. As *Korra* assistant director Olga Ulanova noted, they were not tasked to create the final animation but instead "to create an animatic that we could send overseas to be animated."[41] *Avatar* director Giancarlo Volpe and *Korra* director Melchior Zwyer both discussed how they would divide the script into sections for each member of their team of storyboard artists.[42] Their work still received extensive feedback and underwent extensive revisions, even after they had moved to another episode. Due to this degree of collaboration, Joaquim Dos Santos—director and storyboard artist on *Avatar* as well as producer and director on *Korra*—has frequently commented on the difficulty of assigning credit to one person for a single section or even for a specific element in a storyboard.[43] There were innumerable interpretations of both scripts and character designs. While storyboards and animatics do not make up the final product, as a synthesis of ideas from various individuals, they can still incorporate additional significations into the animated bodyscapes by altering a character's visual appearance as well as by ascribing meaning through movement.

Across repeated recreations of the character design by different personnel, variations are introduced either by accident or with intent. While, ideally, the character remains recognizable across all iterations, inconsistencies open up space to insert and incorporate additional significations. Given this type of animation, plasmaticity was inevitable. Too many people were involved to preserve the specificity of original designs, regardless of streamlining. As Konietzko phrased it: "Dozens of storyboard artists and animators all take turns drawing the same characters, and their interpretations can vary widely. And we just don't have the time, money, or energy to have every inconsistency corrected in retakes."[44] Sometimes, these deviations are minor, such as in one shot in "Enemy at the Gate" (*Korra* S4E05) where Baatar Jr. buttons his cufflink, a feature of his uniform absent in the model sheet created by Konietzko and Mueller.[45] Whether the action originated in the script or the storyboards, this image is the result of someone reinterpreting a character design, adding details and attributes that did not previously exist. Other deviations are more significant.

According to Volpe, by the storyboarding stage, the art department would often still be creating the designs for new locations, characters, and props.[46] Meza-Leon and Ulanova both confirmed having worked with rough approximations or non-finalized versions.[47] For example, Meza-Leon recalled using a blank mannequin as a placeholder for Piandao. Knowing that the character would be modeled after Kisu, he drew the figure as tall and lean but otherwise nondescript.[48] Other times, these placeholders would contain details that survived to final animation. This was the case with Baraz, where an unidentified storyboard artist drew Spike from *Cowboy Bebop* in lieu of a new character design. Konietzko recalled making some alterations, such as adding a receding hairline, to lessen the resemblance. However, he noted that "you change it too far from the board, then the expressions get watered down in translation."[49] Storyboard artists exercise immense power over an animated figure and thus over an animated bodyscape. Their interpretations of or substitutes for a character design introduce elements that can persist into final animation. One of the more prominent examples of a character permanently altered by a storyboard artist is Varrick, introduced in "Rebel Spirit" (*Korra* S2E01). Because this eccentric Water Tribe entrepreneur was a recurring character for the new season, a design by Ryu was finalized ahead of storyboarding. Nevertheless, that model sheet still needed to be interpreted by storyboard artists, including Lauren Montgomery. Her off-model renderings of Varrick were lankier than Ryu's, and they ultimately supplanted the original in subsequent appearances.[50] While these changes did not directly impact any racial or cultural significations, they did mark the character as more visually comedic, impacting his characterization.

For the third season of *Avatar*, Meza-Leon recalled that supervising director Oh instructed the storyboard artists how to draw anime-style.[51] Despite its supposed statelessness, anime and its conventions are often associated with national and cultural identity, with scholars such as Susan J. Napier describing how it captures aspects of Japanese society.[52] Rayna Denison also recounts how writers such as Antonia Levi and Gilles Poitras have treated this kind of animation as representative of Japan and Japanese culture on a global stage.[53] Approaching the topic from within an East Asian context, Tze-yue G. Hu refers to anime as a form of cultural imperialism, as the dominant form of animation in the region and the only type to reach global audiences.[54] Through the appropriation and imitation of stylistic elements of anime, the directors and storyboard artists of *Avatar* and *Korra* positioned their show in relation to Japan and more broadly to Asia.

In his list of recognizable "anime-esque" traits, Stevie Suan includes "common conventionalized facial/body expressions."[55] Other writers have identified some of these visual components as *manpu* (漫符) or "manga notations," iconic symbols that indicate and amplify emotional or mental states.[56] According to Suan:

> The most common citational acts are not of specific instances from other anime, but of more formal elements such as the figurative acting of characters in their conventionalized facial and bodily expressions, each expression citing previous instances of that expression. These expressions are generally slower changing and some of these gestures have been almost inseparable from the image of anime, integral acts

of the anime-esque. Each re-performance of every anime-esque act, by its very nature as a conventional act, will be citing prior anime performances.[57]

Through the appropriation and imitation of *manpu*, *Avatar* and *Korra* storyboard artists directly linked animated bodyscapes not to specific texts but to anime in general, in turn signifying Japaneseness, in turn signifying Asianness. At numerous points in the franchise, an on-model rendering of a character is comically juxtaposed with an exaggerated or "super-deformed" version, frequently accompanied by *manpu*.

In "Lake Laogai" (*Avatar* S2E17), Aang yells at Joo Doo. To convey the character's extreme frustration, storyboard artist Kenji Ono incorporated a set of visual icons emphasized by Aang's enlarged head.[58] The most prominent *manpu* are the "veins" or "blood vessel mark" in his left temple. Koji Aihara, Kentaro Takekuma, and Thomas J. Wallestad identify this symbol as indicative of anger.[59] Amplifying the effect, steam nondiegetically shoots out from behind Aang's head, another *manpu*.[60] As with all instances, such exaggerations in this franchise, the reaction functions as a comedic contrast to his usual appearance and demeanor. For a similar example, guest character Chan has a particular reaction to Azula's attempt to flirt with him in "The Beach" (*Avatar* S3E05). He is shocked, nervous, and intimated by her but awkwardly tries to hide it before excusing himself. To achieve this effect, storyboard artist Ono simplified the design and added a distinctive *manpu*.[61] A single drop runs down the right side of Chan's face. Wallestad writes about the versatility of this icon. In addition to sweat, it can represent tears, saliva, or mucus, each indicative of different emotions or states. Here, the symbol is a manifestation of a "psychological cold sweat."[62] Against more iconic features, the *manpu* and its signification are amplified.

Such extreme reactions are tempered in *Korra*. When the characters do acquire *manpu*, their appearances do not drastically deviate from the model sheets. They do not indulge in their plasmaticity as much as their predecessors. In "When Extremes Meet" (*Korra* S1E08), when Ikki is frustrated after Korra shuts a door in her face, episode director Ryu storyboarded her eyes glowing and her face darkening.[63] In "Darkness Falls" (*Korra* S2E13), Tenzin undergoes a similar transformation after he is surprised by Kya's sudden scream. The art book credits Dae-Woo Lee as the storyboard artist for this sequence.[64] While Suan views them as emblematic of "comedic shock and despair," the blank white eyes that define these instances act as multipliers for the characters' existing expressions: Ikki's anger and Tenzin's alarm.[65] Ono also included this element as part of Aang's aforementioned outburst.

Aang, angry. Still from "Lake Laogai" (*Avatar* S2E17). Blu-ray release of *Avatar: The Last Airbender—The Complete Series* (2018).

Chan, concerned. Still from "The Beach" (*Avatar* S3E05). Blu-ray release of *Avatar: The Last Airbender—The Complete Series* (2018).

Ikki, upset. Still from "When Extremes Meet" (*Korra* S1E08). Blu-ray release of *The Legend of Korra—Book One: Air* (2012).

Tenzin (*center*), surprised by Kya (*left*). Still from "Darkness Falls" (*Korra* S2E13). Blu-ray release of *The Legend of Korra—Book Two: Spirits* (2014).

While they are relatively subtle embellishments, those blank white eyes still position these animated bodyscapes in relation to Japanese animation, to Japan in general, and more broadly to Asia.

In both *Avatar* and *Korra*, episode directors and storyboard artists exploited the plasmaticity of the animated bodyscape to associate them with anime and therefore to construct and ascribe Japaneseness and Asianness. As Suan writes, these expressions and *manpu* connect these characters not with specific texts but with anime in general. Through anime, they are linked with Japan and, more generally, with Asia. The discourse around these reinterpretations of character design also highlights their Asian origins, with the cocreators primarily crediting Asian and Asian American personnel—Ono, Ryu, and Lee—for these flourishes. According to production narratives, these individuals brought their specific perspectives to their renderings of these character designs. Thus, *manpu* become part of the animated figure and are incorporated into the animated bodyscape.

Like character designers, storyboard artists also transformed real-world elements to block and choreograph performances and actions. In our interview, Meza-Leon recounted being directed to use preexisting acting references, specifically of Jennifer Aniston for Katara and of the child protagonists of various 1980s US films for Aang. He also described how some of his colleagues would film themselves acting out assigned scenes. These expressions and movements would be polished during the cleanup stage, especially if the voice actors had not yet been recorded.[66] This practice appears to have been largely abandoned for *Korra*, with Ulanova saying: "We didn't really need reference for [acting] . . . Honestly, there's not a lot of complicated stuff like that in the show that would need additional reference for the animation studio."[67] There were exceptions, such as when episode director Colin Heck acted out a scene from "The Ultimatum" (*Korra* S3E11) where Bolin reacts to meeting an elderly Zuko.[68] Elements of these cinematic and live performances were selected and integrated into the storyboards and then into the animation. This practice highlights two main facets of the ascribed identity. First, it represents a drive toward mimesis as the storyboard artists imitated the naturalistic body movement and expressions of actors or of themselves. The second point conjures questions about the selection of models. The actors cited by Meza-Leon are overwhelmingly white and American, yet elements of their performances were transcribed to characters who are neither. How much of their identities was transferred to these newly constructed bodyscapes? How do they intersect with the other signifiers? The use of these performances as models was apparently regarded as neutral. The meanings that these elements conveyed relate to mimesis rather than something explicitly racial or cultural. Nevertheless, these referents operate as unintentional signifiers of an American identity. The use of reference footage can also place *Avatar* and *Korra* in relation to other texts, genres, and national industries. In addition to references to anime throughout the franchise, the climactic fight in "The Waterbending Master" (*Avatar* S1E18) ends with Pakku retraining Katara with long spikes of ice, resembling a scene from the *wuxia* film *House of*

Flying Daggers (2004), where characters are likewise trapped by bamboo shoots. Similarly, in "The Crossroads of Destiny" (*Avatar* S2E20), Katara holds a lifeless Aang in a pose emulating the *Pietà* (1498–99), a famous statue by Michelangelo Buonarroti depicting Mary cradling the dead body of Jesus. In both cases, through intertextual references, meanings are transferred to these images and to the characters involved.

Animation is inherently nonindexical, iconic, and plasmatic. These qualities reveal themselves in the production of model sheets, storyboards, and animatics, where we see individual artists intervene in the development of meaning. The iconicity of the character designs highlights how the selection, simplification, and amplification of details heighten the ascription of racialized identities. Furthermore, the plasmaticity of the storyboards creates space for personnel to introduce new connotations. However, the animated figure is not a series of black-and-white line drawings, and the journey of these visual components are far from other. We see the core qualities of animation persist into the next stages of the production process: animation and the application of color.

OUTSOURCING ANIMATION

The visual components of these animated bodyscapes traveled far before being assembled into the final product, bouncing between multiple production communities on the central planet of our model and then being sent off to an orbiting lunar site. Most of *Avatar* and *Korra* were animated at studios in South Korea. After the pilot was completed with Tin House, the first series was animated by JM Animation, DR Movie, and Moi Animation. For *Korra*, most episodes were handled by Studio Mir, which was aided in-house by Studio Reve for the third and fourth seasons. Studio Pierrot in Japan animated half of season 2, and computer animation for the vehicles in season 1 was outsourced to Technicolor India in Bangalore. For *Avatar*, the Korean studios were spotlighted in the art book and on home video releases, and the creators would credit specific animators by name when discussing the series.[69] For *Korra*, production narratives focused on Studio Mir over Studio Pierrot and Technicolor India.[70] Across interviews, Konietzko has repeatedly criticized how US productions traditionally treat overseas animators.[71] In his words, "We don't think they're using those artists like artists," and "They weren't allowed to actually be animators."[72] With this language, he positioned the *Avatar* television franchise as an opportunity to revise that system and allow for greater creative input and collaboration.

As the first major deviation from the conventional relationship between US animation productions and overseas studios, DiMartino recalled ceasing to make exposure or timing sheets and instead only sending over the storyboards and animatics for an episode. Even though scene lengths were set, this amendment decentralized production and provided the animators more freedom to "figure out the best way to execute it."[73] In the art book, DiMartino had elaborated: "The goal was to put some creative control and decision making into the hands of the Korean artists, and give them the freedom to make the best animation they could."[74] Konietzko repeated this view regarding the production of *Korra*: "We give [the animators] room to figure out a lot of the timing. They always do great embellishments and augmentation to what we've plotted out in the storyboards."[75] While animation always involves a degree of adaptation and modification at this stage, the production narratives put forth by DiMartino and Konietzko emphasize the extent of input that these particular animators have when adapting the storyboards and animatics.

Yoo Jae-myung, an animation director for JM Animation for *Avatar* and the president of Studio Mir for *Korra*, recalled this change from the early days of working on *Avatar*:

> In the animation industry, we have what's called an indication. An indication contains information on each scene, giving instructions on every fine detail, including the movements of characters as well as how and when they should move. This actually makes the animated characters' movements appear robotic. So, when we were asked to work on the pilot film of "Avatar: the Last Airbender," we asked the producers to scrap the indication because it'd prevent us from making the movements appear natural. I explained that following an indication makes the characters appear stiff and typical. Brian [*sic*] and Michael relayed our message to Nickelodeon, who rejected the idea at first. So, we argued with them, saying that this was an essential matter for this animation series. We finally got their approval to eliminate the indication and our studio had more freedom in choosing how the characters should act and move depending on the scene.[76]

Yoo challenges the more paternalistic framing put forth by Nickelodeon and the cocreators. Instead of DiMartino and Konietzko granting them more opportunities for artistic expression, Yoo and his colleagues insisted upon receiving that freedom. A similar formulation appears when he describes working on the sequel series:

As a [subcontractor], we are supposed to get things done as we are told. But Konietzko was different. While working on Korra, I asked him to allow us to present our ideas and he allowed us to do so. We were able to create characters and design backgrounds that required an artistic approach and innovative thinking.[77]

While he remains deferential, Yoo again presented himself as an instigator for change rather than as a passive recipient.

Regardless of who instigated the push for this change, the removal of exposure sheets afforded South Korean animators greater freedom in adapting the storyboards and animatics into animation. Seung Hyun Oh—then a timing director at JM Animation—described the animation process thusly: "By the time we finished season one we were pretty used to it. As we got better at it we were able to become more creative. Not only did we improve our skills but the acting became more free and enjoyable."[78] His colleague, animation director Hong Kyoung Pyo said: "I was very happy about not having set timings, because that opened up the flexibility of what we do . . . We had a lot of freedom."[79] Fellow animation director Jeong Hoon added: "In the beginning, it was difficult but after a while we began to see it as a really joyful animation. It almost felt as if we were actors doing all the action. We thought of ways to make our work better too. That way, we could enjoy work together."[80] In-between checker Lee Joo Ri recalled: "There were no timings attached to the original drawings, so I could do as I wanted. Sometimes that made it difficult to connect with other parts."[81] During his segment, Oh spoke of the gap between the US and Korean sides of the production, specifically regarding video references. He was translated saying: "In the case of acting, I became concerned about the difference between what Koreans think of acting and what Americans think of acting . . . Having such references . . . especially for facial expressions, helped me greatly."[82] Whatever creative leeway these animators had, they were still adapting and modifying the visual components produced by stateside character designers and storyboard artists.

From early in the production, overseas animators had a recognizable and recognized impact on *Avatar*, which is most evident in the figure of Foaming Mouth Guy. In the episode "The Warriors of Kyoshi" (*Avatar* S1E04), Aang performs an airbending trick in front of the denizens of Kyoshi Island. As the crowd cheers, one person has an extreme reaction. His arms flail about, he foams at the mouth, and his eyes roll back in his head before he finally collapses. DiMartino recalled this moment, how the storyboard had initially depicted a figure merely fainting before Ki Hyun Ryu—then an employee

Foaming Mouth Guy. Still from "The Warrior of Kyoshi" (*Avatar* S1E04). Blu-ray release of *Avatar: The Last Airbender—The Complete Series* (2018).

at JM Animation—improvised the action within the confines of the scene length. He had radically adapted the storyboard and added a distinctive flair, something that the stateside crew had not considered when blocking the scene. The cocreator remembered thinking: "This new system might work."[83] Ahead of the series premiere, an article in the *New York Times* called attention to this moment, describing it as the result of the Korean animators being given more creative freedom.[84]

Across these accounts, two seemingly contradictory threads dominate. First, stateside elements, such as Western-style acting, were prioritized. The production remained centralized at the Nickelodeon Animation Studio, with the overseas studios operating as secondary sites of production, a lunar body orbiting a planetary one. Second, these animators emphasized that they were not automatons, that they were collaborators who produced something new and unique. Yoo repeated the latter conceptualization:

> If I were to do simply what I was told without a sense of ownership, then I'd be labeled as a "subcontractor." But if I add my own ideas to the materials I receive to make them my own, then I'm contributing to the planning process, and it becomes a "new creation." The definition

of subcontractor is very loose, and it's you who decide on its meaning. I've never considered the projects I've undertaken as someone else's. As soon as I undertake a project, it becomes my own. And I try to make a creative approach with a sense of ownership.[85]

Through their participation and contributions, artists like Yoo and the various crew members at JM Animation, DR Movie, Moi Animation, and Studio Mir transformed this franchise into a "new creation," into something to which they can lay claim. Such an act holds great significance. Since the 1960s and especially going into the 1990s and 2000s, as the animation industry became increasingly globalized and reliant on international outsourcing, animation studios in South Korea have been defined by their role as subcontractors for Japanese and US productions.[86] As a result, individual studios and Korean animation in general have struggled to form their own brand identity. In the mid-2000s, Joon-Yang Kim chronicled the history of original Korean animation to the best of his ability, noting how it has had difficulty finding a receptive audience domestically and distribution abroad.[87] Within this context, by claiming figurative—if not literal—ownership over *Korra*, Yoo and Studio Mir are trying to establish a clearly defined brand identity, allowing the studio to stand out and thrive in a competitive marketplace. In doing so, as Grace Han notes, they are also making the globalized animation pipeline more transparent, are highlighting the transmission of components between production communities and across borders.[88] The visual components of the animated figure continued along their production paths, returning stateside for correction and retakes before being completed.

COLOR AND ICONICITY AND PLASMATICITY

Due to iconic facial features, skin tone is of heightened importance for the production and ascription of a racialized identity to animated figures and thus to animated bodyscapes. As previously addressed, color is first introduced when producing a model sheet, with the colorist selecting the "local colors" for the various components of a character design. For the sake of visual and logistical simplicity, only one or a few hues are selected to represent a character's skin tone at this stage. The resulting visual depicts the character under an imitation of neutral lighting conditions. However, over the course of a production, the colorist will be asked to assign a range of alternative hues or "dials" to give the impression of different lighting conditions.[89] Within a hyperrealist animated show with a dynamic range of realistic and fantastical scenarios, the scope of this task is compounded. *Korra* colorist Sylvia Filcak-Blackwolf detailed the level of precision required for the show:

> TV is a super fast-paced schedule. You got to kick out like a show every two weeks. It doesn't matter if there's 200 characters . . . And you have to do all the tones and the highlights and all that stuff, and you got to get that approved first. And then, after that, you got to pop everything on the background and do it for every single piece of lighting. So, a lot of times, there would be 500 what we would call "dials." So, you would just have to crank it out fast.[90]

The ink-and-color method utilized to render skin tones illustrates both the iconicity and the plasmaticity of these animated figures. In both the model sheets and the finished episodes, they lack the texture or gradient of real-life skin. Barring special lighting effects, usually only one or two colors would be utilized at a time. In addition, in order to integrate characters into different environments, these skin tones can and do change between scenes and even between frames.

While most examples of dials do not deviate far from the local color, these animated figures always possess the capacity for extreme change. Konietzko discussed two types of lighting conditions that make a significant impact: "Any time you add green, it really makes the characters' skin just look bizarre. Green and blue. They all react differently."[91] These distortions are so "bizarre" because they drastically break from the warm and naturalistic tan and brown hues usually utilized. In isolation, such dials do not appear to follow hyperrealist animation conventions; they are not mimetic of physiological bodies or of how a film camera would record them. However, such hues help integrate these characters into their surroundings, still having a grounding effect. Consider how Katara's skin tone changes throughout the first series. In "The King of Omashu" (*Avatar* S1E05), the green light of King Bumi's throne room results in a sickly green hue, reminiscent of mold. In "The Waterbending Master," the cold polar light of the Northern Water Tribe banquet hall turns the character dark blue. A comparison of these scenes to her model sheet reveals just how wide a range of skin tones an animated bodyscape can possess, from hexadecimal #bd916f as the local color to #6a8938 and #383c68 as the dials. These hues are not imitative of the human body, appearing to break away from the hyperrealist aesthetics of the franchise. Nevertheless, in addition to integrating Katara in specific settings, they also do not break the illusion of a unified bodyscape. Across these renderings, Katara remains recognizably Katara, despite the visual disparity. Korra, in the sequel series, undergoes a similar procedure as she approaches a spirit portal in "The Southern Lights" (*Korra* S2E02). Due to the otherworldly and Antarctic setting, the character's local color is replaced with a cyan-green tint, from hexadecimal #a08365 to #61aba5. Again, the difference between the two is great, revealing how these figures are plasmatic not only in form but also in color.

Once again, these bodyscapes passed along the chain of production, with overseas studios utilizing the dials selected by the color stylist before returning the final animation to Nickelodeon for postproduction. Once back, these animated bodyscapes underwent one more major step: color correction. Konietzko has framed this process as a refining of the work of the original stylists. When discussing a scene featuring Zuko from "The Siege of the North, Part 1" (*Avatar* S1E19), he recalled:

> Hye Jung Kim, the color supervisor, and I tried to do this difficult lighting situation where there was cooler color coming from outside, from the nighttime, and this warmer color coming from the gas lamps inside this bay. That was pretty complex, and Kevin [Kirwan] kind of wrapped it all together nicely.[92]

According to this description, the colors used for Zuko's skin tone in this scene were the products of multiple individuals. Kim supplied the local colors and dials before Kirwan smoothed out the rough edges.[93] The resulting pinkish gray integrates the character into his surroundings without appearing incongruous with his other appearances. Zuko remains recognizably Zuko. In turn, the creative choices and actions that resulted in this appearance complicate but do not erase the ascription of racial and cultural identity from previous renderings of the character.

At each stage in the production process, individuals affected and built on each other's work. Their use of color underlines the iconicity and plasmaticity of these animated bodyscapes, complicating the ascription of a singular identity based on complexion. Their choices were motivated largely by a desire for internal consistency without sacrificing mimesis, to make the characters look like they were in fantastical environments while remaining recognizably themselves and recognizably human. Within this window, these hues could vary widely from both the local colors of model sheets and real-world physiological bodies. Given how pivotal skin tone is to the definition and ascription of race in the real world, failure to navigate these elements could mitigate or compromise the supposed Asianness of these animated bodyscapes, as seen in the online discourse around the character of Kya from *Korra*.

Ahead of the second season of *Korra*, Konietzko posted a series of pictures from a screening of early animation. One image was a photo of the monitor showing the characters Bumi, Kya, and Tenzin—the three adult children of Aang and Katara—in the episode "Darkness Falls."[94] Later that night, episode director Colin Heck responded to an anonymous Tumblr "ask" that has since been deleted but was screenshot and reposted by Konietzko. The unnamed individual simply wrote: "None of katara and aang's kid share katara's complexion."[95] The complaint and subsequent reply focus on the character Kya, who has the darkest skin tone of the three. According to the art book, initial design and color concepts for this character were drawn up by Montgomery, with Ryu and Konietzko finalizing the design.[96] Heck's response was terse and somewhat dismissive:

> Look—I know that complexion of cartoon characters is a fraught issue these days, but I'd ask you to not put too much stock in an iPhone photo of a non-color-corrected tv. Especially when the lighting situation that those characters are in might be different from normal lighting. Actually, look up color theory and then light theory and get back to me.[97]

A few days later, Konietzko expanded on the topic, going through the stages of applying color to the characters.

In his Tumblr post, Konietzko noted that Katara in *Avatar* and Kya in *Korra* actually do have the same local color—hexadecimal #bd916f, to be precise. Multiple factors contributed to the appearance of different skin tones. First, the art director explained color theory and the contrast effect: "In simple terms, colors are pushed lighter, darker, warmer, and cooler based on what other colors are next to them."[98] Kya's gray hair makes her skin appear lighter than had it been contrasted with Katara's darker hair. Furthermore, for this shot, Kya is in front of a light source in the Spirit World. Therefore, the dial for her skin tone is lighter than the local color on her model sheet. Konietzko also noted that this image was from before retakes or color correction. While scheduling does not always permit drastic revision of finished animation, the art director claimed to have done so when characters looked "too light."[99] Finally, the cocreator wrote about how this photo is of a monitor and thus the colors are distorted. All these elements combined to create Kya's skin tone for this image.

No character from *Avatar* or *Korra* retains the local color of their model sheet. Over the course of their respective series, personnel at different stages in production made creative decisions that impacted the application of color.

As seen with Kya as well as Katara and Korra, dials were implemented to integrate a character into fantastical settings. During postproduction, another round of personnel refined the final animation to ensure coherence and consistency, a step that the shot of Kya had not yet reached when Konietzko published the initial Tumblr post. However, it is ultimately dependent on those consuming these images to decode their meaning. As demonstrated by the response to this image as well as the cocreator's defense of it, the synthesis of these factors does impact the construction and ascription of racialized identities to the animated bodyscape.

CONCLUSION

By looking at the creation and assemblage of visual components of the animated figure, this chapter has detailed how the core components of animation—nonindexicality, iconicity, and plasmaticity—impact the ascription of racialized identities to the animated bodyscape. The animated figure is wholly the creation of artists, distinct from reality. Nevertheless, it remains tethered to reality through the use of models and referents. Artists can manipulate those connections, evoking real people, cultural knowledge, and national industries. Due to the limitations of television animation productions, character designs must be reproducible by episode directors, storyboard artists, key animators, and in-between animators, across departments and national borders. This iconicity opens these animated bodyscapes up to additional signification. The artist is not in full control of these complexes of signs. Audiences can project their own meanings, including their own identities, onto simple designs. Thus, Edwin Zane was able to interpret Zuko's scar as a sign of Asianness.

Furthermore, the animated bodyscape can absorb meanings produced by other departments and processes. Once incorporated into these complexes of signs, new components collide with the visual elements of the character design, creating additional meanings. After all, the model sheet is not the final version of the animated figure or of the animated bodyscape. The design must be adapted into storyboards, animatics, animation, and finally corrections. Along the way, artists from different departments interpret and adapt what came before, introducing new connotations to the animated figure, as seen in the storyboarding of *manpu*, the animation of Foaming Mouth Guy, and the various dials for Kya's skin tone. Even within a hyperrealist animation aesthetic, fluid bodies beget equally fluid identities. While this chapter has covered the creation of the animated figure, that should not be confused for the entirety of the animated bodyscape. As stated in the introduction, mainstream US television animation is an audiovisual and narrative medium. Therefore, additional components are incorporated into these complexes of signs, further developing their racialized identities. The following chapter turns to a less visible production process, the construction of the vocal performances that are sutured to animated figures.

Chapter Two

THE AURAL COMPONENTS OF THE ANIMATED BODYSCAPE

Aural components of racial and racialized identities have been historically and academically undervalued, especially in comparison to visual markers. There have been attempts to remedy this disparity, as seen across various accounts on blackface and yellowface performances.[1] Also, within the field of linguistic profiling, researchers have conducted studies to determine how accurately participants could identify the race of native English speakers, with varying results.[2] As an audiovisual medium, animation—and, more specifically, contemporary television animation—utilizes both visual and aural elements in the creation of meaning. Any account of the construction and ascription of a racialized identity in animation should then address (a) the role of sound as well as (b) how sound operates differently in animation versus live-action productions. This chapter, therefore, examines the role of the voice in the animated bodyscape by tracing the production of vocal performances across multiple production processes and communities.

To take a step back, what is sound, specifically? More relevant, what is the voice? A symphony of body parts coordinate to create pressure that temporarily reverberates through a three-dimensional space, most commonly air.[3] While something could exist and be observed without it generating sound, the inverse is impossible. Therefore, these ephemeral and intangible vibrations indicate the presence of whatever created them. A voice therefore signals a body, even if the listener must imagine one. This observation is not new. Roland Barthes has written on *le grain* of the voice, emphasizing the materiality of a body generating sound.[4] Vocal coaches have repeatedly stressed the physicality of voice work to acting students.[5] In both live-action and animation productions, this relationship is complicated by the technology that records, edits, and ultimately projects the voice. This chapter looks at three key stages in that production process, wherein a vocal performance is created and incorporated into an animated bodyscape. First, casting personnel selects voice actors with racial and ethnic identities that may or may not complement those conveyed by the character design.[6] Second, recording sessions generate line readings, or aural building blocks. Finally, sound editing manipulates and reconstructs the recorded audio to assemble coherent dialogue tracks. The result is a vocal performance, which is sutured to an animated figure in order to produce an animated performance as well as be incorporated into an animated bodyscape.

THE CASTING PROCESS

Recalling the casting process, actors from both *Avatar* and *Korra* have shared similar experiences. They often begin with submitting an audiotape of their audition. Jennie Kwan told me about how her agent sent her "sides" for her audition for Suki.[7] Johanna Braddy recounted recording her audition for Princess Yue at her agency and that she was hired based on that tape.[8] Zelda Williams also recalled recording her audition for Kuvira at home.[9] From this initial step, vocal performances are severed from the actors' physiological bodies, with casting personnel potentially unaware of their racial and ethnic identities. Regarding the aforementioned actors, Kwan is Asian American, Braddy is white, and Williams is white and Filipina American. Such circumstances would not apply to actors already known to the casting personnel or other decision makers. While they still submitted auditions, the cocreators were already familiar with actors Jessie Flower and Seychelle Gabriel prior to their being cast as Toph Bei Fong and Asami Sato, respectively.[10] They were already aware that Flower is white and that Gabriel is Latina. The same applies to "celebrity voice actors," whether they were offer-only or were asked to audition. In some cases, ahead of being hired, the voice actor was invited for "callbacks." Kwan recounted: "They had me come back for a callback, which was in-studio, where I got to work with the [voice] director and the creative team."[11] As Janet Varney, voice actor for Korra, recalled:

> I had already done some work for Nickelodeon, so they called my voiceover agents to invite me to audition for the role. If I remember correctly, there were a couple of different phases to the process. I think I read just for Nickelodeon casting first, and then for Mike [DiMartino] and Bryan [Konietzko], and then in a chemistry test with a handful of other actors in consideration for the roles, and they did a kind of mix-and-match with people.[12]

As soon as these voice actors were in the same room with casting personnel, the cocreators, and other decision makers, their racial and ethnic identities would have become factors, even if they were unspoken ones.

Across various production narratives, those involved in casting for *Avatar* and *Korra* generally did not discuss the role and impact of race unless directly asked. Regardless of intention, both series had predominantly white casts. Throughout the television franchise, only three main voice actors—meaning, those who worked on over half of the episodes of their respective show—were people of color. Dante Basco, who is Filipino American, voiced Zuko in *Avatar*; Mako Iwamatsu, who is Japanese American, voiced Iroh in the first two seasons of *Avatar*; Seychelle Gabriel, who is Latina, voiced Asami Sato in *Korra*. These are the irrefutable results of the casting decisions. So, how does such an outcome happen?

It is tempting to look at the above accounts and assume that the casting process was more or less "colorblind" and that only the best people were hired. After all, casting personnel made initial decisions based on audio-only auditions. However, that would be a mistake. In her book, *Reel Inequality: Hollywood Actors and Racism*, Nancy Wang Yuen denounces "colorblind racism" as a veneer of neutrality that allows "white decision makers and creative personnel to divest themselves of social or moral responsibility while maintaining hegemonic control of the industry."[13] While Yuen goes through and dismantles a series of refrains employed in defense of "colorblindness," the one most relevant to this discussion is "blame the talent."[14] There simply are not enough actors of color in Hollywood, would bemoan an agent or executive. However, as Yuen notes, such decision makers are often unwilling to look beyond their own preexisting networks. She writes: "The 'best' person is really the most convenient."[15] Within this system, Yuen identifies talent agents and casting directors as "gatekeepers." "Though they do not have the final decision on casting, they serve a filtering purpose."[16] Returning to the above testimonies of *Avatar* and *Korra* actors, one can see this phenomenon in action. Without their agencies, Kwan, Braddy, and Varney would not have been able to audition in the first place, never would have been a part of the talent pool. Because this system historically disadvantages actors of color, they are often excluded from any consideration long before final casting decisions are made. In order to avoid such a scenario, one needs to actively seek out underrepresented talent.

While the talent is out there, finding it often requires some extra legwork. Such efforts can be curtailed due to logistical and financial concerns, especially for a television animation production, with its tight schedule and limited budget. Decision makers must choose how to best allot their time and money, must pick which aspects of the production are the most important. In an interview, Andrea Romano, voice director but not casting director on *Avatar* and *Korra*, presented a hypothetical scenario to illustrate how it could be more efficient to assign an already-cast actor an additional minor role than it would be to devote the time and resources to auditioning and casting someone new. She said: "It makes financial sense for me to use that Caucasian actor who's already doing two other characters as that third character."[17] When a show—or an entire industry—already centers whiteness in characters or casting, then we can observe its effects on depictions of peripheral characters. Hank Azaria as Apu does not happen just because the casting personnel refused to seek out South Asian talent but also because it is easier to ask an actor already in the room to record a few extra line readings. Returning to *Avatar* and *Korra*, Romano does note that the Screen Actors Guild (SAG) required reports for every episode to ensure that they were not deliberately excluding "minority actors."[18] However, as demonstrated by the lead actors for both *Avatar* and *Korra*, these guidelines were not especially effective for promoting diversity.

Nevertheless, Romano has noted the importance of expanding one's figurative rolodex as a voice director and, for other productions, as a casting director:

> I often go out and teach seminars to various different communities. For example, maybe two months ago, I went and spoke to the East West Players, which is an Asian theatrical group in downtown Los Angeles, and said, "Please, train, you guys. We need you. We need Asian voice-over actors. I need them all the time." There are very few Asian voiceover actors who work consistently in animation, only because they just haven't trained in it and they don't have the experience yet. And in working on *Avatar the Last Airbender* for Nickelodeon, which I'm very very proud of, it was filled with Asian characters. I worked really hard with the casting director at Nickelodeon, Maryanne Dacey, in finding Asian voice-over actors, but after the first season of 20 episodes, we had used almost every Asian voice-over actor that we know of.[19]

As Romano said, the US animation industry is not supportive of actors of color. To combat it, one must act deliberately, as Romano claimed to have done for *Avatar*. The talent is out there, but the will to pursue it often is not. Romano, even when operating outside of her job description for *Avatar*, appeared to have reached her limit after the first season. She also passes responsibility to rectify this situation to the actors, a gentler form of "blame the talent." Furthermore, while the first season of *Avatar* does feature some exemplary Asian and Asian American voice actors, they are largely limited to guest roles. Looking at this environment, there remains a key question. Is the extra effort even worth it for animation?

Does it actually matter that the majority of these characters are voiced by white actors? Simply put, yes. If it did not, then *Avatar* cultural consultant Edwin Zane would not have been "very happy and pleased" about the hiring of Basco and Mako or would not have stressed the importance of "instill[ing] the Asian American voice acting community into [the] product as much as possible."[20] Romano would not have boasted about the number of Asian and Asian American voice actors in guest roles during the first season of *Avatar*.[21] Regardless of contributing factors, the decision to cast a white actor to voice a character of color always denies a rare opportunity for a marginalized artist within an already white-dominated industry. Furthermore, their continued exclusion prevents them from being able to have input, however limited, on how their communities are portrayed. This has been the dominant way that popular discourse has understood race and animation. This should continue to be the focus for discussions of race and voice acting. For *Avatar* and *Korra*, the majority of casting decisions excluded Asian, Asian American, and Indigenous voice actors, be it consciously or unconsciously, even when the character designs overtly evoked those communities. Again, this is the irrefutable result of their creative choices.

However, does the race of the voice actor actually affect the development of identity within an animated bodyscape? Not necessarily. Hiring a white voice actor does not erase racialized visual signifiers. Janet Varney's voice does not inherently make Korra less Asian or less Indigenous. Yet, whiteness is not neutral either. Each actor contributes something to their performance, even if that quality is not explicitly racialized. They all make creative choices as actors about how to deliver their line or how to interpret feedback from the voice director, based in large part on their own lived experiences. In our interview, Varney stressed how "Korra's humanity, her vulnerability, and her strength" had a bigger impact on her vocal performance than the character's skin tone, even while stating that she would have understood and supported the hiring of a different actor.[22] She did not discuss how the character's proximity to real-world groups, such as Indigenous or immigrant communities, could have influenced her portrayal. Of course, the analysis of a vocal performance cannot be reduced to casting decisions; otherwise, countless examples of cross-gender or cross-generational voice acting would have been failures from the start. Still, choices made at this stage of production have repercussions that echo throughout the other processes. During recording sessions, those invited into the room can have an impact on the creative process, although I do not want to overstate the influence of one actor working within a large corporation. Furthermore, by managing audience awareness of the physiological body that produced the voice, additional meaning can be transferred into an animated bodyscape.

THE RECORDING SESSIONS

Once the requisite voice actors have been cast, they are gathered in a studio, either alone or in a group, to record the dialogue for a given episode, going through the relevant scenes line by line. Throughout her career, Romano advocated "ensemble recording," meaning having as many actors in the same session as possible. The voice director has promoted this method across interviews, podcasts, and commentary tracks, citing the benefits of actors being able to react to each other.[23] She specified that ensemble recording tends to lead to the best improvisation, typically involve fewer takes, and is less likely to require retakes at a later date.[24] Actors from both series have echoed this system's benefits. Basco has spoken about his time with Mako during the first season of *Avatar*, recounting: "We really established that foundation of who we were and our relationship with each other as the characters and just as actors."[25] His costar and the voice of Sokka, Jack DeSena recalled the "freedom" and "playfulness" the format allowed.[26] Varney likewise praised "the dynamic of the group reading together."[27] As Kwan said: "You bring different energy to each other as actors."[28] In these production narratives, ensemble recordings encouraged naturalistic line readings and interactions that audiences would recognize from their lived experiences, helping ground the most abstract and fantastical elements of these series.

Whether they are composed of one or many voice actors, recording sessions are overseen by the voice director, with input from other personnel, and they can take place before or after storyboarding. One should not credit the results of these sessions solely to the actor. Their line readings are the products of both their instincts as performers as well as the guidance of the voice director and of other decision makers. As an actor, Kwan spoke about how she would go over her lines and assign intentions to each one. However, she stressed the importance of the mantra "Commit to everything, but marry nothing."[29] As a voice director, Romano also prepared for recording sessions by forming a mental track of line readings as well as being open to contributions from the talent.[30] Once at the studio, they would go over the episode, recording multiple readings for each line, collaborating to produce the best takes. Kwan recalled: "We would just go through it . . . and, if they needed to make any adjustments to [my performance], then the director would give me some direction and I would go back and do the line."[31] Voice actors Crawford Wilson, Flower, DeSena, and Varney all concur that their takes were finessed by feedback and direction from Romano as well as other sources.[32] In addition to the voice director, Kwan identifies DiMartino, Konietzko, and some execs from Nickelodeon as regular presences in the recording sessions for *Avatar*.[33] This collaboration also allowed room for improvisation, as the adlibbing skills of DeSena and John Michael Higgins have been cited as pivotal to the development of their characters, Sokka in *Avatar* and Verrick in *Korra*, respectively.[34] However, there remains a caveat. According to Romano, her job was to get the takes that the writers, producers, and directors wanted.[35] Kwan agreed: "They have their vision. I have to leave room for that."[36] Recording sessions do not create complete vocal performances but instead generate line readings, or aural building blocks, to be selected and assembled by other personnel at a later date. Voice directors may express a preference, but they are not ones making that final decision. Regardless, creative choices made at this stage by both the voice actors and voice director contribute to the construction and ascription of racialized identities, and they should be taken into account.

As previously stated, racialized aural components are not as highlighted as visual ones. However, when the subject is not completely ignored, references to the role of the voice in the establishment and maintenance of racial categories tend to focus on the role of accents in defining out-groups.[37] For the purposes of this chapter, accents refer to how people learn to enunciate certain words, how they move their mouth, hold their tongue, breathe, and so forth. Accents describe when someone speaks a nonnative language, and dialects describe when someone speaks their native language. However, the two terms are often used interchangeably. As seen in *Avatar* and *Korra*, both accents and dialects are implemented to aid in characterization, including the development of racialized identities.

The aural building blocks produced via the recording process tether characters to the real world, not only through their association with a physiological body but also through their evocation of real-world historical and cultural contexts. For the *Avatar* television franchise, North American English is the default across character types, from heroes to villains, from authority figures to clowns, even when it was not the actor's natural speaking voice.[38] Jason Isaacs, who voiced Zhao in the first season of *Avatar* and had a cameo as the character in the second season of *Korra*, is one of the few voice actors from this franchise to voluntarily discuss how considerations of race impacted their performances. When asked about the then-upcoming live-action film adaptation of *Avatar* and the possibility of him reprising his role, the British actor responded:

> I can't imagine they'll [live action producers] be coming to me, because as far as I'm aware, I'm the only Caucasian actor that does a voice for it. It was very odd, the first time I went to record. I looked around, and it was like I was in the wrong studio. I said, "Do you guys want me to do an Asian voice or something?" They said, "no, no, no. Just be yourself." And then after we started recording, they went, "Okay, just to slightly clarify that. Be yourself, but be your American self." I said, "Okay, fine." But you can't help but be influenced by the fact that all the other actors are Asian."[39]

Based on this quote, Isaacs apparently has limited interactions with the rest of the cast. The other actors to whom he was referring were most likely Basco and Mako, with whom he shared all of his scenes in his first episode, "The Southern Air Temple" (*Avatar* S1E03). Their presence influenced Isaac's instincts as an actor. However, instead of mimicking an "Asian" accent, the British actor was directed to adopt an American dialect. Whether consciously or unconsciously, this creative decision positioned the vocal performance and the character in relation to a real-life context. Regardless of intention, North American English does not neutrally convey information but instead signifies Americanness. Specifically, it signifies the lived experiences of the target audiences, children in the United States, in turn grounding the fantastical elements.

Having primarily American voice actors performing in American English impacts the construction and ascription of a racialized Asian identity in more direct ways as well. Konietzko has discussed the creation of proper names in the *Avatar* franchise: "Some of the names Mike [DiMartino] and I make up, some we derive from real names in our world, and some are just straight names . . . from our world and from different cultures."[40] In other words, proper names in this franchise came from a mixture of fantastical, hybrid, and real-world conventions. For both series, actors were required to recite proper names derived from Asian and fantastical sources, resulting in the Anglicization and Americanization of notably non-Anglo and non-American words to fit how those actors habitually pronounce English. Konietzko commiserated: "It doesn't matter what name—what the origin is—whatever it is, the actors say it differently than we've decided it's going to be said."⁴¹ Sometimes, ensuring established pronunciation required special effort. Williams jokingly recalled undergoing "a Bolin boot camp" after repeatedly failing to say that name.⁴² On other occasions, the crew elected to be more lenient. They chose not to correct actors Mark Allan Stewart and Rick Zieff when they pronounced Mako as *may-ko* instead of *mah-ko*, reasoning that their characters—Lu and Gang, respectively—were impertinent and incompetent enough to make such an error.⁴³ When recording for the episode "After All These Years" (*Korra* S4E01), guest actor Robert Morse pronounced the state of Yi as *yai* as opposed to *yee*. Because the venerable actor had said it "with such authority," the mistake was not remedied during the recording session, and Morse was not brought back for a retake.⁴⁴ The art direction makes the error apparent by incorporating the logograms 夷國京師 (Yí guó jīngshī) on a sign marking the entrance to the Yi state capital. These incongruities are the result of casting actors unfamiliar with the relevant languages as well as hiring staff who either did not notice or did not care about such discrepancies. Decisions made in one stage of production affect those made in others. The live-action film adaptation attempted to correct such inaccuracies by introducing more "Asian" pronunciations of the proper names. However, these efforts were ultimately rejected by fans of the original series and were even mocked in *Korra*.⁴⁵

Within this franchise, those who speak anything other than North American English are notable exceptions. In "The Swamp" (*Avatar* S2E04), Carlos Alazraqui and William H. Bassett voice members of the Foggy Swamp Tribe with a southern twang, marking them as the *Avatar* equivalent of "hillbillies"—as rural, unintelligent, and comedic Others. Throughout *Korra*, Jeff Bennett and Anne Heche approximate mid-Atlantic dialects to position their characters—Shiro Shinobi and Suyin Beifong, respectively—and their setting in relation to the United States in the 1920s and 1930s, or at least that era as presented in Hollywood films from those decades. However, the most prominent deviations from American English fall under the category of "Asian accents." Given their rarity in this fantasy world, such vocal performances distinguish these speakers.

Before continuing, there are a few matters that need to be clarified regarding the function of accents and dialects in media and of "Asian accents" in particular. Across artistic depictions, performances of accents and dialects are utilized to create distances either between characters or between characters and presumed audiences. For examples of the former, consider recent animations that use accents and dialects to convey generational divides between parents and children. In *How to Train Your Dragon* (2010), the progressive kids with North American dialects are at odds with the traditional grownups with Scottish brogues.[46] Similarly, in *She-Ra and the Princesses of Power* (Netflix, 2018–20), Queen Angella's clipped British pronunciations put her in conflict with the brash Princess Glimmer.[47] More commonly, though, accents and dialects are used to create distances between certain characters and the assumed audience. In these cases, unfamiliar pronunciations mark the speaker as dangerous, funny, erotic, or otherwise exotic. In short, they are the Other. Writing about Disney films, Rosina Lippi-Green observes that characters speaking with accents and dialects associated with marginalized groups were overwhelmingly depicted either negatively or at least as possessing limited narrative agency.[48] Identification and empathy are reserved for the characters who sound like the presumed audience. Returning to the earlier examples, the Scottish and British dialects in *How to Train Your Dragon* and *She-Ra and the Princesses of Power* distance the speakers not only from their children but also from the intended viewers. In *Avatar* and *Korra*, child characters uniformly speak with generic North American dialects, encouraging target audiences to identify with the heroes and to Other those speaking with unfamiliar voices.

As noted by those who study linguistic profiling, accents and dialects play an important role in marginalization and discrimination, obstructing assimilation, classifying people as perpetual aliens, and denigrating intelligence.[49] Performances of accents and dialects serve the same function. The mimicry is just another act of dominance, another form of violence.[50] Cynthia Kwei Yung Lee explores this very exercise of power in artistic depictions of Judge Lance Ito from the O. J. Simpson trial. While the real-life figure spoke with a North American dialect, parodies universally gave him a Japanese accent as a means of discrediting the judge and of casting him as a perpetual foreigner.[51] These are ultimately the main functions of the "Asian accent" in media. Exaggerated vocal performances, with their "broken English" and grammatical errors, mark the speaker as unassimilable, justifying strict immigration laws and continued marginalization. Of course, the "Asian accent" is not real. It is as much of a construction as the "Negro dialect" of minstrel shows. As a continent, Asia contains far too many nations, regions, ethnicities, and languages to ever produce a uniform accent in any language. Instead, such diversity is flattened into a singular identity for consumption by a presumed white audience. A range of accents and dialects are thus transformed and reduced into "brown voice" and "yellow voice" performances, to borrow terms used by Shilpa Davé, Allison Reiko Loader, and Hye Seung Chung.[52] Asian actors are often expected to squeeze into these linguistic boxes, from the Golden Age of Hollywood to contemporary US sitcoms. In animation, where the actor is hidden from view, white artists can exert even greater control over these signifiers, pushing them to their extreme, without interference from potentially distracting makeup. Chung stresses this aspect of Trey Parker's vocal performance as Kim Jong-il in *Team America: World Police* (2004), and it holds true for numerous other examples.[53] With this background in mind, how do "Asian accents" in *Avatar* and *Korra* function?

For her recording sessions, Romano has had a policy against directing certain actors to perform certain accents. To continue an earlier quote:

> It makes financial sense for me to use that Caucasian actor who's already doing two other characters as that third [Hispanic] character. However, I will not ask him to put on a Hispanic accent. I don't want to have a Caucasian actor pretending to be a Hispanic actor with an accent. I typically will just have him do that voice straight-ahead.[54]

This proclamation requires some unpacking in regards to her work on *Avatar* and *Korra*. Replace "Hispanic" with "Asian," and the sentiment largely tracks. The white actors may have been playing Asian-coded characters, but they were not mimicking "Asian accents," were not performing "yellow voice," with one notable exception. For season three of *Avatar*, white voice actor Greg Baldwin officially became the new voice of Iroh, approximating the late Mako's distinctive Japanese accent. When Asian and Asian American actors did employ an "Asian accent," their vocal performances did not resemble the broken English often found in other media. No one mixes their r's and l's, omits articles, confuses verb tenses, or makes any of the other grammatical mistakes that Chung considers indicative of a "yellow-voice" performance.[55] Instead, their vocal patterns fall closer to an affect, more akin to Phil Lamarr's performance as Jack in *Samurai Jack* than Tara Strong's as Omi in *Xiaolin Showdown*. They are different but not entirely unfamiliar.

These vocal performances still mark the speakers as Other. However, rather than mark them as inherently comedic, threatening, or erotic, they instead signify wisdom and knowledge. This connotation operates much like the archaisms of which Susan Mandala writes, evoking a distant past that clashes with the more modern line readings of the child protagonists.[56] Furthermore, by tethering these characters to a real-life Asian context, even a largely imagined one, the content of their dialogue is legitimized and authenticated. This pattern repeats with Mako as Iroh throughout the first series, Sab Shimono as Monk Gyatso in "The Southern Air Temple," James Hong as an unnamed Air Nomad in "The Storm" (*Avatar* S1E12), Tsai Chin as Aunt Wu in "The Fortuneteller" (*Avatar* S2E14), Keone Young as Jeong Jeong in "The Deserter" (*Avatar* S1E16), Takayo Fischer as Lo and Li in "The Avatar State"

(*Avatar* S2E01), and Paul Nakauchi as Guo in "Old Wounds" (*Korra* S3E06). Each of these figures gives advice, trains, or explains different concepts to the heroes. Their accented deliveries, provided by Asian or Asian American voice actors, mark them as authorities of a given subject, so long as that subject is likewise coded as "Asian." Within this framework, Brian George's vocal performance as Guru Pathik in "The Guru" (*Avatar* S2E19) requires more consideration. An Israeli-British actor of Iraqi, Lebanese, and Indian descent, George is famous for his "brown voice" performances, especially as Babu Bhatt on *Seinfeld* (NBC, 1989–98). In *Avatar*, he portrays a character wholly unique to the franchise. No one else looks, acts, or talks like Guru Pathik. No one else even claims the title of "guru," preferring "master" or "sifu." In contrast to the predominantly East Asian and Chinese cultural influences on display throughout the series, Pathik—in appearance, voice, and narrative function—evokes a South Asian, specifically Indian, identity. This section just focuses on George's vocal performance. While another type of "Asian accent," "brown voice" does not have the same connotations as "yellow voice." The precise grammar gestures more to the "model minority" archetype rather than to that of the "perpetual foreigner."[57] In the case of Pathik, the vocal performance also alludes to the figure of the "guru," as described by Davé.[58] This signification then supports and is reinforced by the character's dialogue, as discussed in the next chapter.

At other points in the first series, primarily comedic characters are portrayed by Asian American actors utilizing "yellow voice." Shimono and Hong return in the second season of *Avatar* as new characters. The former voices Master Yu, a parody of strip-mall martial arts teachers in "The Blind Bandit" (*Avatar* S2E06). The latter voices the anti-Avatar Mayor Tong in "Avatar Day" (*Avatar* S2E05). While, for his initial appearances, Guru Pathik is depicted as a source of spiritual wisdom, his final appearance—a cameo in "Nightmares and Daydreams" (*Avatar* S3E09) where Aang briefly hallucinates a six-armed Pathik singing and playing a *veena*—is played for laughs. Even if the comedy is not explicitly derived from their accents, these characters are still Othered. Similarly, the show uses "yellow voice" for midlevel Ba Sing Se bureaucrats, performed by Asian American voice actors. Karen Maruyama portrays an unnamed official who blocks refugees from securing safe passage to the city in "The Serpent's Pass" (*Avatar* S2E12), and Lauren Tom voices Joo Dee, the heroes' handler in "City of Walls and Secrets." Both figures obstruct Aang's quest, with either a frown or a smile but always with "yellow voice." Those with actual power in the city—Long Feng and the Earth King, voiced by white actor Clancy Brown and Black actor Phil Lamarr, respectively—speak with North American dialects. Once again, the journey of the voice does not end with the recording session. Those aural components must still travel throughout the planetary production model. Those aural building blocks, severed from their physiological source and teeming with signification, still need to undergo sound editing and synchronization. The resulting interaction between aural and visual components is key to the construction and ascription of racialized identities into the animated bodyscape.

SOUND EDITING AND SYNCHRONIZATION

The 1970s and 1980s saw a new generation of French and US scholars addressing the nature of cinematic sound, its relationship with the cinematic image, and the primacy of the voice. Jean-Louis Baudry hears an authenticity in the aural that he believes the visual lacks.[59] After all, whereas a 3D profilmic reality has to be flattened for 2D screens, recordings of sound retain their dimensionality.[60] Nevertheless, cinematic sound is just as much a reproduction as the cinematic image. The processes of recording, editing, and projecting—which, to be fair, Baudry does acknowledge—manipulate sound too heavily for it to be considered equivalent to the original.[61] The result is a "cyborg" voice, a product of both physiological bodies and mechanical apparatuses. For this generation of scholars, the role of technology is paramount.[62]

The visual and aural are separate at every stage of filmmaking. Even if an actor recites lines in front of a camera and some version of that audio is ultimately synchronized with their likeness, the instruments and techniques for recording the two are fundamentally different. They only appear as one when projected together. Digital filmmaking practices have altered this dynamic somewhat but not in a fundamental way; even if a single device records or plays both audio and visual, it does so by using separate apparatuses. For Michel Chion, this is the "audiovisual illusion," "the spontaneous and irresistible weld produced between a particular auditory phenomenon and visual phenomenon when they occur at the same time."[63] For Mary Ann Doane, this is the "fantasmatic body," "the body reconstituted by the technology and practices of the cinema."[64] According to Doane, there is a drive in the audience to connect cinematic sound with a cinematic source, even if they must imagine one off-screen.[65] In this regard, Rick Altman likens sound cinema to ventriloquism. Akin to a dummy, images are subservient to sounds and distract from their true source, the loudspeaker.[66] William Johnson and Edward Branigan caution against overvaluing sound, and there are additional oversimplifications to address.[67] Unlike reality, the cinematic world can support sounds independent of diegetic sources. Johnson, for example, cites "imageable" cinematic sounds such as "room presence."[68] Omniscient narrators, nondiegetic scores, and fantastical elements round out the list. Regardless, for the majority of these texts, the cyborg voice is both severed from its source and sutured to an on-screen figure.

These theorizations impact the analysis of cinematic performances. For Gianluca Sergi, it means that there are technical aspects of a vocal performance outside of an actor's control, that any performance containing a vocal element is a collaboration with sound editors.[69] For Pamela Robertson Wojcik, it means that any discussion of film acting must account for these technological mediations.[70] For Starr A. Marcello, it means that film allows for "dualistic performances," in which vocal and visual components can either complement or contradict each other, whose extreme is found in animation.[71] Given these relationships between audio and visual, the cinematic bodyscape likewise incorporates vocal performances. These processes, and therefore the final product, are controlled and directed by the artists or filmmakers. They edit and manipulate the sound before synchronizing and suturing the two disparate parts. The result is collaborative as well as cyborg in nature. Even when the casting and recording processes prioritize naturalism, the final product is a marriage of mechanical and biological components, of technological and artistic mediation. As suggested by Marcello, all of these elements are exaggerated in animation.

Within animation, the voice can serve as a tether to the real world, grounding the medium's more fantastical elements. In this sense, the voice contains an element of indexicality absent from the visuals, with a body recorded in front of a microphone rather than in front of a camera. The nonindexical, iconic, and plasmatic animated bodyscape differs significantly from its live-action equivalent. By extension, so too does its relationship with cinematic sound. There is no profilmic body on the screen that may have been the physiological body whose voice is projected from the loudspeakers. The image is wholly constructed and incapable of producing a voice. Nevertheless, in an act of disavowal, the viewer believes that the figure moving its lips—or, more accurately, having its lips moved by animators—is the source of the voice that they hear. Even the nodding heads of the machinima *Red vs. Blue* (Rooster Teeth, 2003–present) are enough visual stimuli to justify such association.

On *Avatar* and *Korra*, following recording sessions, sound engineers selected the aural building blocks and arranged them into coherent dialogue tracks. First, certain takes were selected over others. Thus, five minutes of improvisation by Higgins would be reduced to four words.[72] Second, the products of various sessions were combined. Zach Tyler Eisen, the voice of

Aang, lived on the East Coast, and his lines were recorded separate from the other actors using an Integrated Services Digital Network (ISDN).[73] Both Kwan and Gabriel recorded some of their episodes remotely while they were out of town for other jobs.[74] In addition, Automated Dialogue Replacement (ADR) introduced components recorded after animation was completed, usually nonverbal grunts but sometimes entire lines of dialogue. Third, multiple actors may contribute to the vocal performance of one character, as was the case with Iroh after the death of his initial voice actor, Mako. While Baldwin officially took over the role in the third season of *Avatar*, he still contributed line readings for the character toward the end of the second season, credited under "additional voices." The resulting vocal performance was the product of two voice actors. Therefore, in the assemblage of aural building blocks, both the vocal performances and the rapport between characters are ultimately constructed. Finally, despite their indexicality, these recordings can be further manipulated. For example, during the third season of *Avatar*, a sound engineer pitched up Eisen's voice, as the actor had aged faster than the character.[75] The mechanical and the organic combine in the production of a coherent vocal performance. Credit for the result belongs to more than just the actors and voice director.

The resulting animated performances are the products of collaborations. As Konietzko describes the evolution of the character of Sokka:

> I see the animators in Korea [in the animated performances]. There's something that happens magically between Jack [DeSena]'s performance of Sokka and Yoo Jae-myung, one of the animation directors. When the two of them come together—the voice and the animation—it's just that's who Sokka is. That's him at his most pure state.[76]

This "pure state" is more than a sum of parts, and different voice actors had different reactions to hearing their voices attached to a different form. When asked by Konietzko whether she ever felt that her voice was detached from her "ego" while watching the animated performance of Korra, Varney replied:

> It's the first opportunity I've really had to be separate from my own performance. Because there's enough space between when we record and when I see the final product that I have a vague awareness that it's me, but the storytelling is so good and the animation is so gorgeous that it allows me to totally sort of remove myself. And that's such a gift because I can't stand watching myself on camera.[77]

Kwan has a similar reaction to seeing Suki for the first time. She told me:

> I didn't recognize myself in her, and that sounds weird because the way that I approached it is just, basically, if there were things I identified with Suki, then I would bring my own personal thoughts or my own personal experiences to her. And then, again, through the direction of the creators and director, we would meld her ... I've had acting coaches say, when you lose yourself in the character, it's such a great thing because you've let the character basically take over and come to life.[78]

However, these responses are not universal. Other voice actors viewed this synchronization of animated figure and vocal performance as a more disconcerting phenomenon. According to Basco:

> The wild thing about ... watching the cartoon now ... the animation ... is we've worked together so long, we've worked on these characters, and the characters are so whole and so well-rounded, three-dimensional characters that I actually see the actors in the cartoon characters. It's a very strange thing to see as an actor. We voice the characters, and then as I'm watching it now I see Mae [Whitman] in the performance. I see Jack [DeSena]. I see Jessie [Flower]. I see Grey [DeLisle]. And these are cartoon characters, so—it's like you said—it's very strange how the actor and the character kind of over the years melded into this one thing.[79]

Higgins had a more disquieted reaction, although he articulated his discomfort through humor:

> It's always shocking [*undecipherable*] voiceover jobs to actually see the character on screen. You know, I do the voice, you do it much earlier than you ever get to see the actual guy, and I see: "Is that my face? How odd. And he can lift his left eyebrow, and I can't."[80]

Some of the voice actors found these "pure states," these "fantasmatic animated bodies," to be "strange" and "shocking." Their voices had been severed from their physiological bodies, edited into dialogue tracks, and finally sutured to bundles of lines and colors. Although the actors do not discuss this process in terms of racial or ethnic identities, their voices became those of apparently

Asian and Indigenous animated characters. Yet, at the same time, for some, they remained recognizably their voices.

On one hand, the voice is completely severed from the physiological body in order to be sutured to the animated figure and incorporated into the animated bodyscape. On the other hand, some of these actors still recognize themselves and their colleagues in these characters because of their shared voices, indicating that the connection was not truly severed. In order to better understand this dynamic, we can examine the phenomenon of "celebrity voice actors." Within the US animation industry, casting personnel would traditionally hire anonymous actors, whose voices could be easily severed from their bodies and sutured to a range of animated figures. This conventional model changed in the 1990s and the early 2000s, with the rise and normalization of celebrity voice actors, who would voice characters clearly linked to preexisting "star personas" that had been established in live-action film and television.[81] Richard Dyer describes "stars" as the products of self-commodification, wherein the raw material of a real-life person is worked into a "star image" via the labor of multiple individuals across interviews, photo shoots, social media posts, and acting jobs.[82] To deepen characterization, animation filmmakers exploit those personas through three strategies. First, they hire celebrities whose voices are recognizable parts of their star persona. While most scholarship on star studies favors visual over vocal—the star *image* rather than the more inclusive star *persona*—there have been exceptions.[83] Second, they design characters to evoke the physical appearance of the celebrity, as seen with the caricatures of guest stars on *The Simpsons* or the protagonists in Robert Zemeckis's motion-capture films. Third, they implement marketing material and other paratexts to educate prospective audiences about the involvement of the celebrity in the central text. Colleen Montgomery and Rayna Denison have both written about this practice in relation to Pixar films and the English-language dubs of Studio Ghibli films, respectively.[84] Through these methods, audiences are encouraged to reforge the severed connections between physiological bodies and their voices, thus connecting the celebrity to the animated characters. Across this rebuilt bridge, elements of a star's persona may be transferred to an animated bodyscape.[85] For Tanine Allison, the celebrity's voice takes primacy over the animation as the chief signifier of identity, a cinematic hierarchy of which Altman would likely approve.[86] As a result, public discourse on "whitewashing" in animation has tended to focus on texts featuring hypervisible celebrity voice actors, as discussed in the introduction.[87] The advertised presence of these celebrities foregrounds the marginalization of actors of color in the casting process and thus their absence from recording sessions. As online fandoms help transform previously invisible voice actors into celebrities of their own right, as anyone can pause the end credits and memorize the listed names, audiences have been growing increasingly aware of the bodies behind the microphones. As a result, their identities and personas, often less massaged than those of more mainstream stars, are likewise incorporated into animated bodyscapes. In this respect, yes, the race of the voice actor does impact the construction and ascription of a racialized identity into the animated bodyscape.

Several voice actors in *Avatar* and *Korra* arrived with established star personas. However, neither series exploited their involvement that much. Within the main cast, the more famous actors often took steps to disguise their distinctive voices. Zhao's North American growl renders Jason Isaacs unrecognizable, especially to a mid-2000s audience most familiar with his work in *The Patriot* (2000), the *Harry Potter* film series (2001–11), and *Peter Pan* (2003). Tenzin's soft and breathy delivery is also a departure from J. K. Simmons's harsh bark from *Oz* (HBO, 1997–2003) and Sam Raimi's *Spider-Man* trilogy (2002–7). For some smaller roles, though, this franchise has alluded to established star personas within the narrative. In *Korra*, Aubrey Plaza and Jon Heder, both known for their bored monotones in *Parks and Recreation* (NBC, 2009–15) and *Napoleon Dynamite* (2004), respectively, portrayed similarly disaffected characters, Eska and Ryu, also respectively. Through the recognition of these voices, specific attributes were transferred to these animated bodyscapes, fleshing out characters in spite of their limited screen time. While the writing and vocal performances are aligned, the visuals still do not evoke the images of these stars. As stated in the previous chapter, while the character designs for both series emulated members of the crew, they were not modeled after their celebrity voice actors. For example, Ryu visually resembles producer Ki Hyun Ryu even though he was voiced by Heder. Furthermore, the celebrity members of the cast are almost entirely absent from promotional material and behind-the-scenes videos around the two series, which focused on the less-famous principal actors. Nevertheless, meaning is created through recognizable voices. For a metaexample, Dante Basco returned in *Korra* to voice General Iroh, the grandson of Prince Zuko. The new character's first appearance, part of a cliffhanger at the end of "Turning the Tides" (*Korra* S1E10), exploited audience familiarity with Basco's distinctive voice. However, instead of associating the voice with the actor, viewers were expected to associate it—and thus the new General Iroh—with the character of Zuko. The series attempted a similar trick in "Old Wounds," with Jessie Flower returning to voice young Suyin, the daughter of her character from *Avatar*, with less success.

CONCLUSION

Within animation, the voice functions as an element of indexicality within an otherwise nonindexical bodyscape. Like all sounds, it tethers the fantastical and the abstract to the real world. As an agent of mimesis, the voice signals the presence of a physiological body as well as of specific historical and cultural contexts. Through the evocation of a celebrity voice actor's star persona or through the performance of accents and dialects, the personnel who produce vocal performances can exploit that connection in the production of meaning, including the construction and ascription of racialized identities. These processes all involve collaboration and coordination between multiple personnel across multiple departments. A vocal performance is never the product of just the voice actor. Layers of artistic and technological mediation produce this cyborg voice. Decisions made during one stage echo throughout others. By tracking these decisions made in the production of a vocal performance, this chapter has observed how the issue of race is addressed or not addressed at the different stages. Casting decisions affect the line readings generated at recording sessions, and those aural building blocks impact the dialogue track and the final vocal performance assembled by sound editors.

Once sutured to an animated figure, completing an animated performance, these various significations are incorporated into the animated bodyscape. However, the animated bodyscape is more than the sum of these parts. It does not exist within a vacuum but in relation to an animated and fantastical diegesis. For a full accounting of the production of racialized identities within animation, one must also consider how these iconic and plasmatic bodyscapes absorb significations from their surroundings. Artists across departments construct additional visual, aural, and narrative components in the course of worldbuilding. These processes introduce new significations that can complement or complicate those already part of the animated bodyscape.

Chapter Three

THE NARRATIVE COMPONENTS OF THE ANIMATED BODYSCAPE

The animated bodyscape does not exist within a vacuum. Due to its iconic and plasmatic nature, it absorbs significations from its surroundings, and worldbuilding can complement or complicate identities within these complexes of signs. Just as race is derived more so from social and historical contexts rather than from biology, racialized identities are formed not only by emulating phenotypes but also by alluding to those contexts. In the case of *Avatar* and *Korra*, various departments and personnel contributed to the construction of an "Asian" fantasy world, building on and adapting each other's work as they passed through and between various production communities and departments. By incorporating signifiers of cultural Asianness, these artists supported and reinforced markers of racial Asianness. The following chapters consider how different types of components are incorporated into the animated bodyscape in this manner. First are the narrative components, produced chiefly through the writing process, followed by visual ones via art direction and storyboarding as well as by aural ones through music and sound editing. In order to discuss the impact of these elements on the identity of animated bodyscapes, we need to better understand their relationship to reality, specifically through the lenses of fantasy and cultural appropriation.

A nebulous term, "fantasy" has been described as a genre, a mode, and an impulse within literary studies.[1] W. R. Irwin defines fantasy as the impossible being rendered realistically, as realist conventions normalize the changes from reality for the benefit of reader immersion.[2] According to Rosemary Jackson, like a camera lens distorts the real world, so too does fantasy filter reality through "paraxial areas."[3] Kathryn Hume sees all literature as being comprised of the dual impulses of mimesis and fantasy, of the desire to imitate reality and the desire to alter it.[4] To paraphrase a statement from the first chapter, every work of fiction, regardless of how mimetic, is not reality; and every work of fiction, regardless of how fantastical, exists in relation to reality. Across all three scholars, fantasy and reality are not incompatible opposites but are instead intertwined. Their observations extend to other mediums. Film scholars traditionally see film and fantasy as intrinsically linked.[5] Animation, with its tendency toward abstraction, finds it even easier to break away from reality.[6] The *Avatar* television franchise is an example of "high fantasy." It is not set in some "lost age" or "distant future." It does not take place on an alien planet or in an alternate dimension. The *Avatar* world is wholly constructed, with no direct connection to our own. It is divided into wholly fictional nations, populated by practitioners of elemental magic as well as distinct flora and fauna. Yet, for these fantastical elements to be legible to an audience, they remain tenuously tethered to real-world contexts. The animals of *Avatar* may be wholly unique to that universe, but they are still largely hybrids of species recognizable from our reality. As animated television series, both *Avatar* and *Korra* filter real-world inspirations and referents through "paraxial areas," and the resulting diegesis is the product of those dual impulses of mimesis and fantasy. To better describe this transformative process, we can also examine it as an act of cultural appropriation.

In the simplest of terms, "cultural appropriation" refers to when an outsider takes an aspect of an insider's culture. This practice is typically viewed unfavorably, indicative of violent imperialism or neoimperialism. However, in the context of globalization, some scholars have attempted to expand this term, develop their own taxonomies, and offer greater precision for describing how different cultures interact. Art historian James O. Young is concerned with what specifically is being appropriated and offers the following classifications: (1) "object appropriation," referring to the transferring of tangible works; (2) "content appropriation," referring to the copying of intangible works; (3) "style appropriation" and (4) "motif appropriation," both referring to the reproduction of stylistic elements or motifs; and (5) "subject appropriation," referring to when an outsider represents and re-presents insider individuals or institutions.[7] Working in media and communications studies, Richard A. Rogers is interested primarily in power dynamics, identifying four categories: (1) "cultural exchange," in which the two parties are equivalent; (2) "cultural dominance," in which the insider is dominant; (3) "cultural exploitation," in which the outsider is dominant, the commonsensical definition of cultural appropriation; and (4) "transculturation," an alternative framework that focuses on how artifacts, concepts, and people organically flow between different cultures, themselves the accumulated results of such interactions.[8] Finally, sociologists Matthew Desmond and Mustafa Emirbayer emphasize the effects of cultural appropriation and therefore propose a stark binary. The practice is either (1) racist or (2) antiracist. The former refers to when the outsider whitewashes the history and context of what they are appropriating.[9] The latter refers to when the outsider neither deracializes nor dehistoricizes aspects of an insider culture as well as when that community receives compensation.[10] Over the course of the writing process—as well as other stages of production, as discussed in later chapters—*Avatar* and *Korra* lifted aspects of real-world cultures, removing them from their historical contexts, in order to produce these original texts.

THE FANTASIFICATION PROCESS

Because the world of *Avatar* and *Korra* is one of high fantasy, there is no in-universe connection to our world or to a version of it. The world of *Avatar* is not "Asia," even though it is still meant to be read as "Asian." Rather than creating a singular monoculture, these series constructed multiple fictional cultures and subcultures. So, while this fantasy world is meant to be read as Asian, that Asianness is not treated as a monolith. This was possible, in large part, because *Avatar* and *Korra* are both television series, and the writers and other personnel were able to take advantage of that format. These two shows are both comprised of multiple installments, with differing degrees of serialization. The inherent interplay of repetition and variation results in greater definition for main characters, primary settings, and series-long narrative arcs. In addition, it allows for greater scope to the worldbuilding, as writers and other personnel can convey the diversity within and between these fantasy cultures through guest characters, villages-of-the-week, and self-contained narratives. These episodic elements are simplified, subservient to the main characters and serialized narratives as well as with limited screen time. Therefore, while they do provide scope and diversity for this fantasy world, they individually lack depth and instead rely on various forms of shorthand in place of characterization. Over the course of the two series, for each and every episode, writers and other personnel transformed real-world referents into their fantastical counterparts into order to convey the desired meaning, preserving or massaging away details until they could be smoothly integrated into the existing diegesis.

Avatar head writer Aaron Ehasz spoke with me about this process, being careful to leave room for alternative and critical readings of his and the other writers' work:

> When you're being inspired by a culture that is not your own, you are being inspired by ideas that were not necessarily the ideas you were

brought up around. Right? Finding a way to do that that is respectful and authentic . . . can be tricky. Right? So, I think, we did our best when we saw something that was cool or interesting to interpret it and bring it into our world. I did want to say that we didn't want to appropriate something. Right? We didn't want to just take it. We wanted to make sure that there was a "lens of inspiration," which means instead of just saying, "Taking an idea from a culture," saying, "Well, if we see this idea that's interesting to us, does this idea make sense in our vision for Air Nomad culture or Earth Kingdom culture the way we view it, with elements and magic and the world we're creating? Can we interpret it through that lens in a way that feels inspired but also feels like it's a part of our world?" So, travel some distance, when it's going from inspiration to the actual part where it becomes fiction, you know? And you hope that, while it's traveling that distance, that's the difference between it being appropriated and it being something that is inspiration for something else . . . I can see in retrospect that it can be a fine line.[11]

Ehasz's language echoes Rosemary Jackson's concept of "paraxial areas." Like reality is refracted by a camera lens, so too are real-world referents refracted by the impulse toward fantasy, that "lens of inspiration." The referents "travel some distance" in order to become fantastical. Ehasz has specified that he and the other writers avoided positioning their fantasy cultures as direct representations of real ones, and *Avatar* and *Korra* writer Tim Hedrick has also stressed this point.[12] Nevertheless, these writers still appropriated aspects of other cultures. They sought a balance between the dual impulses of mimesis and fantasy, between tethering their creations to and distancing them from the real world. Fantasification may involve the removal of specific details or the incorporation of established elements to create the desired meaning. However, the appropriation and transformation of real-world referents can result in unintended significations. The following three examples examine the implications of this process.

Chakras

In "The Guru," Aang visits Guru Pathik at the Eastern Air Temple so that he can reach his full spiritual potential as the Avatar. The episode is then structured around the guru guiding Aang through unblocking his chakras while explaining their significance. In preparation for these scenes, episode writers Michael Dante DiMartino and Bryan Konietzko have referenced conducting research on this topic to ensure accuracy.¹³ Nevertheless, in their adaptation, they erased key details in order for Pathik and his teachings to be integrated into the established fantasy world. While the idea of *chakras* (चक्र) appears in various religious and philosophical traditions in India, Hinduism recognizes seven major "psychic centers"—six along the spine and one at the crown of the skull.¹⁴ Both practitioner Harish Johari and Sanskrit scholar John A. Grimes identify the seven *chakras* as the Mūlādhāra (मूलाधार) at the base of the spine, the Svādhiṣṭhāna (स्वाधिष्ठान) at the groin, the Maṇipūra (मणिपूर) at the navel, the Anāhata (अनाहत) at the heart, the Viśuddha (विशुद्ध) at the throat, the Ājñā (आज्ञा) at the forehead, and the Sahasrāra (सहस्रार) at the crown of the head.¹⁵ When adapting this religious concept to the *Avatar* world, the writers made creative decisions regarding how much of that specificity to retain in such a way that their chakras would signify Asianness but not explicitly Indianness or Hinduness.

In the show, Pathik takes Aang on a tour through the gardens of the Eastern Air Temple and explains:

> The water flows through this creek, much like the energy flows through your body. As you see, there are several pools where the water swirls around before flowing on. These pools are like our chakras... If nothing else were around, this creek would flow pure and clear. However, life is messy, and things tend to fall in the creek... Each pool of energy has a purpose and can be blocked by a specific kind of emotional muck.

In the subsequent scenes, each "pool of energy" is associated with a body part and an emotion. Their positions are preserved with the exception of the second one. Its location is unspecified presumably because its placement in the genitals would be inappropriate for a children's cartoon. Regardless of rationale, some of the specificity is erased. Furthermore, while the term "chakra" is preserved from the original Sanskrit, the names of the individual energy nexuses are not. The Mūlādhāra becomes the Earth Chakra, the Svādhiṣṭhāna the Water Chakra, the Maṇipūra the Fire Chakra, the Anāhata the Air Chakra, the Viśuddha the Sound Chakra, the Ājñā the Light Chakra, and the Sahasrāra the Thought Chakra. These new names tenuously remain linked with their referents. Both Johari's and Grimes's breakdowns of the first four chakras associate them with those elements.¹⁶ Although some specificity is retained, the writers still removed this Hindu concept from its original historical and cultural context by erasing language.

Furthermore, to "make sense" in the *Avatar* world, chakras needed to be compatible with established definitions and understandings of chi or *qi* (氣).¹⁷

Qi has its roots in Daoism and Confucianism within Chinese philosophy, religion, and medicine. Put simply, it broadly refers to the "energy" that flows through the body.[18] The concept also appears in connection to Chinese martial arts and their cinematic depictions.[19] Unlike many of its contemporaries within US television animation, *Avatar* treats it as a given that both characters and the audience are familiar with this concept. The lack of an explicit definition affords the writers some flexibility with their application of the idea. Firebenders can channel and redirect lightning through the chi flows in their body. Chi blockers can cause temporary paralysis or loss of bending by hitting an opponent's pressure points. In contrast, *Avatar* devotes a significant portion of this episode explaining chakras, signaling that neither the main character nor the presumed audience have prior knowledge. However, while chakras and chi are compatible in *Avatar*, the writing does not explicitly link the two. Pathik never uses the word "chi" in any of his appearances, only "energy." He also does not resort to the more appropriate Sanskrit equivalent *prāna* (प्राण), defined by Johari as "the energy that creates life, matter, and mind" and by Grimes as "life breath."[20] There appears to be a compromise. Both chakras and chi anchor the fantasy to real-world historical and cultural contexts, but their tethers do not intersect. These adaptations reveal two things. First, Sanskrit positions these chakras within a specific real-world context, that of India and Hinduism. Therefore, the concept needs further decontextualization to fit into the more overtly East Asian and Chinese signifiers found throughout the rest of the series. The concept of *prāna* is similarly translated as "energy." Second, the lack of linguistic specificity means that chakras as depicted in *Avatar* function as signifiers for a general spiritual Asianness rather than for a particular region or religion. While the Asianness of the signifiers is still projected onto the *Avatar* world and more specifically onto the character of Pathik, it has lost some specificity—an Indianness or Hinduness—associated with the original referent.

Acupuncture

In the third season of *Korra*, the character Lin Beifong visits Zaofu, which was founded and is ruled by her estranged sister, Suyin. The two had not seen each other for thirty years. In "Old Wounds," Lin is referred to an acupuncturist named Guo to help her deal with repressed feelings.[21] Episode writer Katie Mattila has talked about undergoing acupuncture treatment around the same time she was working on this script, but she was not clear whether she had intended it to be or viewed it as a research trip.[22] For these scenes, she was tasked with instilling the transformed referent with preexisting aspects from the *Avatar* world, allowing for better integration into the diegesis.

Writing on the subject of acupuncture, historian Roberta E. Bivins proposes that any medical practice and knowledge develops based on its culture's worldview. According to her, acupuncture is the direct product of a Chinese understanding of the human body as "a dynamically balanced whole."[23] From this worldview emerged the practice of inserting metal needles into mapped points as a means of removing blockages and correcting imbalances of qi.[24] Bivins has focused her research on Western understandings of this practice, with early adopters engaging in a condescending "medical orientalism," where they emphasized the physical over the metaphysical.[25] In *Korra*, acupuncture's spiritual background and connection with qi is foregrounded even when re-presented outside of its original historical and cultural context.

Healing through unblocking one's chi is commonplace in this fantasy world, as already demonstrated in the depiction of chakras. However, acupuncture is not specifically mentioned until the *Avatar* episode "Nightmares and Daydreams," where Toph humorously recommends the technique as a way to cure Aang's insomnia. Upon seeing her holding a baby boar-q-pine covered in bristling quills, the Avatar responds by running away. Acupuncture is reduced to a quick joke about how needles are scary. The writers place the emphasis on the mechanics of the medical practice, the needling, and ignore its metaphysical aspects. The sequel series depicts it with more respect. As Guo inserts needles into Lin's "acu-points," he tells her: "This process will correct the imbalances in your chi." As a final needle is inserted into her forehead, Lin has a series of flashbacks that eventually lead to familial resolution. While there are some obvious exaggerations—both the use of metalbending and the more visceral side effects—there is greater proximity than distance. The characters explicitly discuss chi, and the healing process is understood in those metaphysical terms. The practice is not reduced to the mechanics of needling as has historically been the case in Western adaptations. Such a depiction grounds the more fantastical embellishments of the scene, helping this re-presentation of acupuncture function as a cultural signifier of Asianness and Chineseness. These identities are then extended to those partaking in the practice, complementing the character designs and vocal performances.

The Dai Li

When Aang and his friends first arrive in Ba Sing Se in "City of Walls and Secrets," they encounter a dangerous organization known as the Dai Li. As the city's secret police, the Dai Li function as antagonists in both *Avatar* and *Korra*, serving as minions for Grand Secretariat Long Feng, Princess Azula, and Queen Hou-Ting at different points in the television franchise. At the behest of these villains, they imprison and brainwash dissidents, partake in a coup d'état, and kidnap airbenders to create an army. Episode writer Hedrick has proudly brought up the inspiration for their name as a sign of authenticity.[26] While preparing for the Ba Sing Se story arc, his research led him to the historical figure Dai Li, Chiang Kai-shek's head of secret policy in the Republic of China. As the founder of the Bureau of Investigation and Statistics or Juntong, Dai was likened to Heinrich Himmler in the Western press and has become synecdochic of Chiang's regime to Communist China.[27] Biographer Frederic E. Wakeman introduces him as "an extraordinary secret policeman," as "a sinister specter of the shadows," and as "the personification of Chiang's dictatorship."[28] Historian Wen-hsin Yeh's account focuses on how Dai positioned himself as absolutely loyal to Chiang.[29] In choosing to name the Ba Sing Se secret police "Dai Li" instead of "Juntong," Hedrick signaled that he was constructing a signifier not only for "Chinese Secret Police" but also for qualities that have been attributed to this historical figure.

In "City of Walls and Secrets," the heroes' guide and handler, Joo Dee, describes the organization thusly: "Those men are agents of the Dai Li, the cultural authority of Ba Sing Se. They are the guardians of our traditions." By the end of the episode, the Dai Li would threaten the protagonists, imprison a recurring character, and replace Joo Dee. Like their namesake, this fictional group and its members are known for their cruelty and shadowiness. They also serve a master rather than their own personal ambitions. However, these parallels remain tenuous and applicable to a number of real-world people and organizations. Why the name Dai Li and not some other referent from a different era of Chinese history? What does Dai Li specifically signify when removed from his original historical context? In our interview, Hedrick implied that he and the other writers did not have these considerations in mind when selecting and approving this name. Not recalling specifics, he suggested that he had probably Googled "Chinese Secret Police" and that Dai Li was the first name he saw. Without any objections from the Nickelodeon Clearance Department, it became the name for the fantasy organization.[30] If this account is accurate, then Dai Li was just meant to signify "Chinese Secret Police," and even that association would rely on historical knowledge of the Republic of China. Any other parallels between the two are coincidental. However, regardless of artistic intent, the name Dai Li carries greater significance, recalling a specific time in Chinese history, even when the surrounding text and production narratives do not support it. Both intended and unintended identities are equally projected onto the individual members of the Dai Li.

Throughout the above examples, a pattern emerges that will repeat throughout other production processes and that the following chapters revisit. In order to create and enrich the *Avatar* world, writers transformed real-world referents into their fantastical counterparts. They removed some details and incorporated new ones in order to depict concepts, practices, and groups that could be integrated into the established diegesis. Through this process, they sought to extract and construct meanings that could be absorbed into the *Avatar* world and projected onto certain characters, especially those with limited screen time. The chakras of *Avatar* and the acupuncture of *Korra* inform the characterization of Guru Pathik and Guo, respectively, highlighting and reinforcing the racialized Asian identities that were developed through character design and voice acting. Of course, these complexes of signs are not always under the full control of the artists. Unintended connotations can persist through the fantasification process, tethering these animated bodyscapes to specific real-world historical and cultural contexts. These creative decisions were made not only by individual writers but also as the result of the production culture of the writers' room.

THE WRITING PROCESS AND THE WRITERS' ROOM

Animated television series are created through the coordinated efforts of interlocking production communities, including the writers' room. By understanding the procedures and power dynamics at play within this process, by understanding the "production culture," we can better examine how individual artists within the writers' room create meaning. Both *Avatar* and *Korra* stand apart from their Nickelodeon contemporaries in their commitment to a serialized ongoing narrative. Observing this difference, cocreator and story editor DiMartino has noted that a freelance model would have been ineffective. The writers for both series had to work together closely to ensure continuity and consistency between and within episodes.[31] The writing of these long-form narratives can be broken down into two levels—the planning of a season and the writing of an episode. Each involved a degree of collaboration and delegation in the formation of a production community.

Season breakdowns were the first point at which the writers could affect the narratives of *Avatar* and *Korra*. Before each season, the writers and cocreators spent time brainstorming story arcs and proposing episode ideas—often as part of a writers' retreat. This step has been discussed by DiMartino, Ehasz, Hedrick, and Mattila across commentaries, interviews, and podcasts.[32] It is repeatedly characterized as a narrowing down or specifying of a season, with individual writers pitching characters, episodes, and themes. This environment persisted when they worked on individual episodes. Over the course of writing an episode of *Avatar* or *Korra*, three types of documents were produced: a premise, an outline, and finally a script. While usually only one or two individuals are credited per episode, accounts of the writing process by personnel from both series emphasize how the whole writers' room worked collectively in the creation and revision of these three documents.[33] Key to this collaboration was the implementation of a specific process, which Konietzko credited Ehasz for bringing to the production.[34] The two cocreators have confirmed that they continued using it on *Korra*.[35] During our interview, Ehasz described his process in detail. First, the writers' room determined the story so that the episode writer could write a two-page premise.[36] Mattila recalled how Ehasz encouraged the whole room, including assistants like herself, to contribute ideas.[37] With an acceptable premise, everyone would spend two to five days pitching the episode scene-by-scene as part of what Hedrick described as the "pitchout" until the assigned writer could go write a ten-to-twelve-page outline.[38] After getting feedback on this new document, they would then make their first draft, adding the action and dialogue.[39] This was, according to Konietzko, a "synthesis" of those story meetings.[40] Usually, Ehasz told me, the writer would receive initial feedback and turn in a second draft for the "note stage."[41] Konietzko admitted that most of his notes on these scripts were him being "pedantic" about the rules of bending.[42] Hedrick concurred about how martial arts heavy stories would "get a vigorous kung-fu pass."[43] For the note stage—or, as Mattila referred to it, the "room punch"—the draft was projected onto the wall, and everyone collectively went through line-by-line, tweaking the dialogue and story beats.[44] According to Konietzko, this process resulted in "a much more consistent voice" across episodes.[45] The life of the episode did not end here; other departments contributed to their construction and ascription of meaning as they adopted the script into character and BG designs, into storyboards and animation, and into vocal performances.

Under Ehasz and DiMartino, the writers' rooms for *Avatar* and *Korra* were designed to encourage a collaborative and collective writing process. Working within a shared space, they created something new, a synthesis of their individual contributions. However, while the writers' room may have been a self-contained production community, it and its products still relate to the other departments and processes, forming the central planet in our orbital model. In our interview, Ehasz told me:

> I think the best writing understands it's not the final product, that the writing's something that you're handing to someone else to breathe

life into, and you need to hopefully give them something that is inspiring and a launching point for them to add their creativity, their brilliance, to where you started.[46]

As he said, scripts are not the final product in animation; they need to be interpreted. The writers continued to be involved and make suggestions, as noted by Ehasz and Hedrick, but they were no longer in control of the content of a given episode.[47] Returning to the previous examples of fantastical adaptation, the unblocking chakras, Lin's acupuncture treatment, and the introduction of the Dai Li were ultimately rendered by storyboard artists and animators. In addition, writers have noted how episode directors and storyboard artists would insert visual jokes or embellish fight scenes.[48] While the Nickelodeon Animation Studio is a single, self-contained geographic space, the contained production culture is neither monolithic nor unified. Instead, it is composed of numerous production communities resembling a series of adjacent continents. They communicate and interact regularly but remain separate. Within this production culture, it is pertinent to analyze who is contributing and how that affects the construction and ascription of racialized identity, specifically of Asianness.

Across the two animated series, only one person of Asian descent had a writing credit: May Chan, staff writer on season 3 of *Avatar* and episode writer for "The Boiling Rock, Part 1." While no one in either writers' room sought to directly re-present a real-world Asian culture, everyone transformed aspects of multiple real-world Asian cultures in the course of fantasy worldbuilding. The majority of them did so as outsiders, engaging in a form of what Young has called "subject appropriation." Regardless of the accuracy of their work or of how much respect they have shown, an outsider can only re-present their own limited understanding of an insider culture.[49] Nevertheless, as Nancy Wang Yuen points out, the "write-what-you-know" mantra has long been used to justify the lack of characters of color in certain works. She argues that white writers should be perfectly capable of "doing their homework" and of accurately and authentically re-presenting other communities.[50] Of course, it should be stressed that Yuen is writing specifically about the lack of opportunities for actors of color in Hollywood as well as the "colorblind" excuses employed to justify their systemic exclusion. While the writers for *Avatar* and *Korra* were, by all accounts, capable of conducting research and possessing empathy for the "Asian" characters, their efforts did not result in expanded opportunities for Asian and Asian American actors. As the previous chapter states, aside from some guest spots in the first season of *Avatar*, the voice cast was predominantly non-Asian. Within a white-dominated industry, it requires special effort for casting personnel to scout and hire diverse talent. Similarly, it requires special effort to staff a writers' room with diverse talent.

The degree of collaboration attributed to the writers' room as well as between the different departments has the potential to mitigate these issues. In our interview, Ehasz boasted about how his coworkers were able to bring a broad range of perspectives:

> [T]he crew itself . . . was a pretty diverse crew and there were people not only from the US but from all different cultures including some of the cultures that may have influenced or inspired the show. So, we were able to talk about things with people whose parents were born in those countries and things like that.[51]

According to this formulation, the writers' room and, more broadly, the Nickelodeon Animation Studio functioned as a "contact zone," which Mary Louise Pratt defines as "social spaces where disparate cultures meet, clash, and grapple with each other, often in highly asymmetrical relations of domination and subordination."[52] The concept allows for the recognition of transculturation outside of traditional colonial frontiers. Thus, Kim Soyoung adopts the term when analyzing the formation of action genres, and John T. Caldwell uses it to refer to interactions between industry insiders and outsiders.[53] For this project, we can look at the interlocking production communities of *Avatar* and *Korra* not as sites of cultural appropriation but instead as sites of transculturation. Referents, inspirations, and even people flowed across traditional borders in the creation of something new.

To activate this transcultural potential, production narratives for *Avatar* have described two different strategies. First, Ehasz had credited an informal approach to incorporating a range of cultural perspectives. Returning to his previous quote on the "pretty diverse crew," he described casual conversations between people from different cultural backgrounds. They are the sort of interactions that could only take place within a self-contained creative space, such as a writers' room or an animation studio. His formulation thus treats transculturation as something that occurs naturally within the parameters of a contact zone. It also shifts much of the burden of authenticity to individuals who are expected to act as representatives of their respective out-groups. While their contributions can mitigate the pitfalls of subject appropriation, each individual can still only re-present their experiences of a culture, even if it is their own. In contrast to Ehasz's approach, Nickelodeon addressed the issues around cultural representation in a more deliberate and regimented way.

As a part of the writing process, Nickelodeon executives regularly gave notes on premises, outlines, and scripts, acting as satellites within the planetary model.[54] For the first two seasons of *Avatar*, that feedback included reports from cultural consultant Edwin Zane. Rather than rely on the sort of organic flow described by Ehasz, the network contacted and hired someone to ensure that the show's use of Asian referents and signifiers was respectful. A former vice president of the Media Action Network for Asian Americans (MANAA), Zane claimed that his name "came up a lot" when executives were contacting Asian American media organizations.[55] As the show's cultural consultant, he recalled providing feedback on scripts, storyboards, animatics, and rough cuts.[56] Still, his contributions have been positively framed by other parties. In a CNN article, Ehasz is quoted describing Zane's as "read[ing] the scripts and essentially mak[ing] sure they were culturally sensitive."[57] In *Diversity in U.S. Mass Media*, the authors include a formal complaint from MANAA president Guy Aoki regarding the live-action film adaptation of *Avatar*. In his letter, Aoki credits the positive reception of the original show in part to the participation of his organization's former vice president.[58] Notably, Zane was never physically present at Nickelodeon studios outside of annual meetings. Instead, he worked remotely, sending his notes to Nickelodeon executive Jenna Luttrell, who then relayed them to the relevant departments.[59] Neither Ehasz nor Hedrick recalled any significant interactions with him or his feedback.[60] Furthermore, as far as I can tell, neither of the cocreators have mentioned him in interviews or studio-produced paratexts—in contrast to the spotlighting of the other consultants with whom they had more regular interactions. Like the executives, Zane operated like a satellite orbiting around the contact zone of the Nickelodeon Animation Studio, contributing to and affecting the construction and ascription of Asianness without becoming immersed in the production communities.

Even within the context of fantasy worldbuilding, the writers' rooms of *Avatar* and *Korra* sought to avoid the pitfalls of subject appropriation through the incorporation of a range of artistic perspectives. Their strategies included hiring personnel from different backgrounds, within limits, and an outside consultant to operate as representatives of their cultures. In this regard, the Nickelodeon Animation Studio operated as a contact zone, where individuals and ideas from different cultures collaborated and combined to form something new and transcultural. Instead of a singular self-contained space, the production narratives of *Avatar* and *Korra* reveal that the Nickelodeon Animation Studio is composed of a series of separate but still interlocking production cultures with various remote satellites orbiting around them and beaming down data. Within and in response to this complex web of collaboration and delegation, individual artists operated and made choices that affected both the development of a fantasy diegesis and the construction of racialized identities. Again, this pattern recurs across production processes, as the following chapters observe.

NORTH AMERICAN ENGLISH

Before concluding this chapter, there remains an often-unspoken aspect of the writing process that has a major impact on the construction of meaning and identity. In *Avatar* and *Korra*, language operates as a cultural signifier, affecting the construction and ascription of Asianness to animated bodyscapes. While the previous chapter touches on the development and pronunciations of proper names, this section focuses on the ramifications of having the characters speak English. On one hand, given that these are mainstream US television series, there was never really a viable alternative to using the country's *de facto* official language. However, while there is a trope within fantasy of positioning character dialogue as having been translated for the benefit of the audience or reader, that is not the case for *Avatar*.[61] The characters are written to speak English in a way that is specific to that language, a practice that clashes with the non-English linguistic elements of the franchise.

This Anglophonic centering is most apparent in the proliferation of puns. In "The Earth King" (*Avatar* S2E18), Sokka gloats about an antagonist's arrest: "Looks like Long Feng is long gone." The wordplay emphasizes this homonym between a common English word and an Asian-derived name, crafting an Anglocentric pun at the expense of the latter. In "Rebel Spirit," Mako practices one-liners: "Looks like you guys should put more 'try' in Triad." The word "try" is aurally identical to the first syllable of the criminal organization. These are two English words that need to correspond in order for the pun—even an intentionally bad one—to work. Bolin engages in a similar type of wordplay in "The Stakeout" (*Korra* S3E09). While preparing to play the fictional board game Pai Sho, he declares to his opponent: "Well, looks like we have ourselves a Pai Sho-down." Naturally, the practice of dubbing—translating, rewriting, and rerecording the dialogue for other national markets—complicates this dynamic. However, this book focuses on the original versions of the texts. Dubs and other localizations were made outside of the initial production processes and by different crews, and they should be viewed as different texts.

The franchise does feature one prominent example of a non-English pun. In "The Drill" (*Avatar* S2E13), General Sung boasts about his city's defenses:

"Nevertheless, that is why the city is named 'Ba Sing Se.' It's the 'impenetrable city.' They don't call it 'Na Sing Se.' [*laughs*] That means 'penetrable city.'" The structure and delivery of line—the initial pun, pause, and subsequent explanation—communicates that, while the speaker understands his joke, the other characters and the audience do not and therefore require a translation. English is positioned as the default and knowledge of other languages as the outlier, something that can be mined for humor. After all, the joke in this scene is not the pun but the awkward pause. In contrast, the protagonists are able to read Chinese calligraphy—even the most archaic of scripts—without difficulty. Consider a scene from "The Serpent's Pass" where the heroes find some graffiti on a wooden post. The carvings depicted in a close-up read 絕望, but instead of reciting "jué wàng," Katara says "abandon hope." She reads those words aloud specifically for the benefit of the blind Toph. However, in doing so—especially during a close-up of the logograms—she also translates the phrase for a presumed Chinese-illiterate audience. This practice continues in *Korra*, as people read Chinese aloud in English tenuously for other characters but primarily for the audience. For example, in "The Terror Within" (*Korra* S3E08), Mako finds a note with the logograms 隊伍齊集待命行事, and—with the calligraphy once again framed in a close-up—he reads the message to the rest of the room. He says: "Team assembled. Ready to rendezvous" instead of "Duìwǔ qí jí. Dàimìng xíngshì." Even while the visuals signify Asianness and Chineseness, the dialogue centers English as the default. The following chapter explores the creation and incorporation of Chinese calligraphy in both shows in greater detail.

Across these instances, the writers of *Avatar* and *Korra* treat English as a neutral element that neither contributes to nor detracts from other cultural identities. However, regardless of artistic intent, spoken language operates as a signifier just as much as written language. What, then, does English signify in the *Avatar* world? What identities does it project into the animated bodyscape? In the real world, English has come to mean many things in different contexts, as numerous scholars have explored.[62] It would be a mistake to position the language exclusively as a signifier of a particular nation, such as the United States or the United Kingdom, because versions and variations exist in other cultures. The language is spoken on such an international and intercultural level that linguist Braj B. Kachru can observe there are now more non-native speakers than native ones.[63] Of this "universalization," he notes two impacts. First, there is an "Englishization" of native languages, which ties in with connotations of imperialism, colonialism, and neocolonialism. Second, there is a "nativization" of English, with the "dominant" language undergoing hybridization with local ones.[64] What happens when English is removed from these real-world contexts and transplanted into a fantasy setting? There are two primary options. First, the language carries some mixture of the multiple connotations described above. After all—with few exceptions, such as substituting "movie" with "mover" in season 2 of *Korra*—there is little fantastical distancing between North American English and *Avatar* English. Instead of archaisms suggesting a distant past, plain language normalizes fantastical elements.[65] If the calligraphy conveys Chineseness, then by extension the dialogue should convey an Americanness. Alternatively, English is truly a default placeholder with no greater significance. The dubbing of these shows for international distribution would support this stance since the practice positions both spoken language and vocal performances as incidental and interchangeable. However, this second option still ties into and reinforces English's real-world status as a "universal" language, with all of the imperial and neocolonial implications that come with that designation. Fantasy conventions could have papered this over, but the disparity between spoken and written languages in the series highlights the use of English and its incongruity within the diegesis. Even though English is spoken in various Asian countries, and even though there are native English speakers who are Asian, the application of this language in *Avatar* and *Korra* incorporates an Americanness into the animated bodyscapes of the characters.

CONCLUSION

Through fantasy worldbuilding, personnel from various departments are able to construct additional significations that are then incorporated into associated animated bodyscape, complementing or complicating animated performances. With both Guru Pathik and Guo, their dialogue and scripted behavior support and are supported by their character designs and vocal performances. As with the other processes, writers are able to mediate connections between the real world and their creations, controlling the meaning of the narrative components. For *Avatar* and *Korra*, they sought to balance the dual drives of mimesis and fantasy, of extracting the desired meanings from their referents as well as integrating their work into the established diegesis. For these transformations, they erased, altered, and added details, as seen with the amended names for the chakras and with the use of metalbending for acupuncture. At the same time, because the writers forged connections to real-world cultural and historical contexts, they risked introducing unintentional significations. By naming Ba Sing Se's secret police "the Dai Li," the writers of *Avatar* evoked a specific era of Chinese history. By using English as the vernacular, they allude to a long and complicated history of imperialism and globalization. Even if audiences do not recognize these meanings, they remain dormant within the animated bodyscape.

These narrative components were produced not only by individual artists but also within the confines of a production culture. How are production communities formed? How do they operate? What are their relationships to other departments? The answers to these questions inform what they produce. In the case of the writers' rooms for *Avatar* and *Korra*, the system of collaboration and delegation impacted episode premises, outlines, and scripts. In turn, it affected the transformation of real-world referents into their fantastical counterparts as well as how those narrative components constructed and ascribed identity to animated bodyscapes. Aaron Ehasz's approach, which treated these production communities as contact zones, with individuals organically sharing cultural knowledge, placed the burden of representation on certain artists within those spaces. In contrast, Nickelodeon's formal and official relationship with Edwin Zane kept the cultural consultant distant from the writing process and the writers' room, limiting his influence on daily proceedings.

The remaining chapters observe how these patterns repeat across other production processes and communities. Real-world referents are transformed into their fantastical counterparts through the retention and elision of details, projecting new sets of signs into associated animated bodyscapes. The nature of the various production communities and their relationships with each other informed this process. In addition to determining how animated productions like *Avatar* and *Korra* contribute to worldbuilding visually and aurally, these next two chapters also delve deeper into the reasoning, framing, and ramifications of these creative decisions.

Chapter Four

VISUAL WORLDBUILDING AND THE ANIMATED BODYSCAPE

As established in the previous chapter, the animated bodyscape absorbs meaning from the surrounding diegesis. I have already covered how the writing process contributed to worldbuilding and thus to the construction and ascription of Asianness, reinforcing visual and aural signifiers of that racialized identity. Other production processes serve a similar function, adapting real-world referents into their fantastical counterparts for the creation of meaning. This chapter looks at visual worldbuilding. While the earlier observations about the writing process could be applied to live-action productions, the same cannot be said about the visual components of *Avatar* and *Korra*. Here, the animatedness of these shows is foregrounded. Animation, as a filmmaking practice, is inherently fantastical, just as it is inherently abstracted. There is an overlay between Kathryn Hume's dual impulses of mimesis and fantasy as well as Maureen Furniss's continuum between mimesis and abstraction. In other words, this animated fantasy world was built to be both tethered to and distanced from the real world. How, then, were these referents selected? How were they adapted for integration into the established diegesis? What meanings do they actually project into animated bodyscapes?

If this process is meant to incorporate or otherwise reinforce a racialized Asian identity—something derived from real-world historical, social, and cultural contexts—then the question of "authenticity" arises. Across production narratives for *Avatar* and *Korra*, authenticity is something prized and celebrated. Concerning the writing process, Aaron Ehasz said that their work must be "careful, sensitive, respectful, and authentic."[1] A similar framing can be found regarding other production processes. However, this drive for authenticity requires unpacking. Matthew Desmond and Mustafa Emirbayer trace this preoccupation back to colonialism, when there was an obsession with seeking out "uncontaminated" and "primitive" cultures untouched by Western influences.[2] Nicholas Mirzoeff also addresses this tendency in his analysis of Herbert Lang's colonial photography, which intentionally elided indicators of Western intervention in their framing.[3] Similarly, art scholar Jean Fischer writes about how North American art exhibitions favor "authentic" Native American artwork, meaning ones that non-Natives have deemed appropriately "tribal."[4] She positions this practice within a longer history of Euro-American forces defining and limiting "Indianicity," privileging their own white perspectives.[5] This conceptualization relates to how Edward W. Said describes Western writers and thinkers as trying to control and establish authority over "the Orient" by defining and thus limiting it.[6] Achieving cultural authenticity within a work of art, as an outsider to that culture, is an impossible task fraught with colonial weight, risking fetishization and misrepresentation.

Therefore, *Avatar* and *Korra*, by their nature, cannot be culturally authentic, and it is not an especially helpful rubric by which to judge either series. After all, the *Avatar* world is not our own, nor is it meant to be. However, due to the emphasis on authenticity within production narratives, we are prompted to examine how individual personnel negotiated the relationship between their work and the real world, to understand what authenticity meant for them throughout those processes, as well as to determine what intentional and unintentional meanings were produced and incorporated into these animated bodyscapes. This chapter has narrowed its scope to three main production processes, each of which unveils the different ways that these series have striven for authenticity as well as the ramifications of their efforts. First is background design and painting, wherein artists sought to convey the "feeling" or "essence" of real-world places, exploiting those connections without accurately recreating them. Second is fight choreography, wherein consultants and storyboard artists strove for "archival authenticity" and "corporeal authenticity." Finally, there is the integration of Chinese calligraphy as an in-universe writing system, which reveals the drawbacks of specificity within fantasy worldbuilding.

BACKGROUND DESIGN AND PAINTING

According to Maureen Furniss, there are two main categories of animated images: characters and backgrounds.[7] The latter layer, henceforth abbreviated to BG or BGs, is commonly rendered first as black-and-white line drawings and later as relatively detailed paintings or computer-animated models. In addition to being the literal context in which the animated characters exist, BGs are frequently the most stable visual element within an otherwise fluid world. Their consistency across frames can help communicate an equally immutable identity that can then be incorporated into plasmatic animated bodyscapes. As with the writing process, the production of BGs involves the transformation of real-world referents into something that can be integrated into an established fantasy world. I have previously written on this particular topic and will summarize and adapt some of my observations and conclusions throughout this section.[8]

Once again, the first step involves the location and selection of real-world referents, which was accomplished through Internet searches, an in-house reference library, and personal research trips. *Avatar* BG supervisor Elsa Garagarza recounted:

> We would gather as much photographic reference as possible to immerse ourselves truthfully in the environments we were creating. Every reference was presented to Bryan Konietzko ... Every location was meticulously studied to create [an] authentic look and feel.[9]

She also recalled composing "a small booklet of references" for the *Avatar* BG painters.[10] *Korra* BG painter Emily Tetri reiterated the importance of such research. She told me, "We built large libraries of reference material from real world places, from pictures online, in books, and from our own travels."[11] Only a few books from the apparently vast collection have been named. Bryan Konietzko has written and spoken about a behind-the-scenes book on *Atanarjuat: The Fast Runner* (2001)—presumably the one credited to Paul Apak Angilirq—and *Natural Architecture* by Alessandro Rocca.[12] In our interview, *Korra* BG designer Angela Sung mentioned using the reference library but did not recall any specific titles.[13]

Across production narratives, the cocreators were more likely to spotlight their international travels as ways to accumulate reference photography. They have most frequently spoken and written about how their trip to Beijing influenced the architecture of the Earth Kingdom city of Ba Sing Se, how Bryan Konietzko's journey to Iceland inspired the landscape of the Fire Nation, and how Michael Dante DiMartino's trek to Buddhist sites in Bhutan impacted the designs of the Air Nomad temples.[14] In our interview, Sung also stressed that travel was arguably the most important type of research for a BG designer. Being somewhere was always different from seeing photographs. For her, just the experience of hiking through California's national parks made her designs feel more like real places.[15] In an episode of the *Imaginary Worlds* podcast, Tetri repeated the sentiment of how "it's really important to have been in a place."[16] She expanded in our interview: "The importance of being in a place was the actual feel and sense of the real materials that things are made of, the texture, the colors that your eyes see rather than what a camera captures."[17] Tetri was clear that such references were for lighting and atmosphere conditions rather than for specific spaces. They were not meant to explicitly signify Asianness but instead to convey a real-world specificity in the service of hyperrealism. In another example, Konietzko recounted instructing the BG painters to reference photos from their sound designer's trip to Antarctica. He said: "You do get a lot of these beautiful warm tones because the sun is often very low."[18]

Across these testimonies, there is a repeated interest in fidelity to the real world, or at least to some aspect of it. It is a drive toward mimesis that counterbalances the inherently fantastical and abstract nature of these two animated series. However, not all sources are treated equally. By tethering fantasy to reality, the BG designers and painters are also tethering their work to specific historical and cultural contexts. In order to convey different identities—including a racialized Asian identity—that could be absorbed by the characters, they privileged some cultural sources over others. Garagarza has spoken about how the designs were primarily modeled off of Chinese, Japanese, Tibetan, Thai, and Indian referents. She mentioned non-Asian influences as well, notably Inuit aesthetics for Water Tribe architecture and Icelandic topography for Fire Nation landscapes.[19] In our interview, Garagarza repeated much of the same list as well as adding Mesopotamian and Vietnamese referents.[20] *Avatar* BG designer Tom Dankiewicz also described this step of the process: "I would get on [the] computer and look up images online from any and all Asian nations, not limited to just Chinese stuff. It could be from Bhutan or Tibet, as long as there was something to grab onto."[21] By naming specific countries and cultures that they had researched, rather than gesturing toward a generic "Asia" from their shared cultural memory, these artists are making a claim of authenticity.

With the referents selected, BG designers transformed them into black-and-white line drawings, which were, in turn, rendered as color paintings or as computer-animated models by BG painters. There were a couple of concerns in the minds of the artists as they adapted their real-world referents in a way that—as Garagarza put it earlier—conveyed an "authentic look or feel" of a place, an approximation rather than exact fidelity. Even though BGs are the most stable visual elements in shows like *Avatar* and *Korra*, there were still concerns about the amount and type of detail. For scenes with more complex staging, the BG painter would create a key BG with overseas studios reproducing the setting from different angles and distances. *Korra* BG painter

Frederic William Stewart emphasized this need to "streamline things in a way that is repeatable and consistent."[22] He needed to be conscious of how his overseas counterparts would interpret his work. Too much atmospheric fog in an establishing shot would translate to washed-out color in the close-ups.[23]

These BGs crossed borders into South Korea, where they were adapted from different angles and distances by people like JM Animation BG director Jeong Sang Woong. He spoke at length about a particular difficulty:

> The hardest part was the trees. The reason drawing trees was difficult was that we don't see many conifer trees in Korea. *Avatar* trees were like Scandinavian conifer forests. In *Avatar*, there were always conifer trees. It would have been easier if it was something I grew up with.[24]

The above quote illustrates a dissonance between the American and South Korean crews, between primary and secondary sites of production. This dynamic favors the creative input of the stateside staff, keeping the production of the show and its identity centralized in the Nickelodeon Animation Studio. However, that does not diminish the impact of decisions made at JM Animation. The trees—at least during the wintery first season of *Avatar*—were based on what Jeong identified as Western conifers as opposed to the Korean flora with which he and his team would have been more familiar. That said, pine trees are hardly alien to the Asian continent; therefore, they do not inherently connote Westernness. More importantly, the final images that appear in the show are Jeong's and others' interpretations of key BG paintings. They are Korean renderings of Western referents, products of transculturation.

Additional changes had to be made for integration into the established diegesis, resulting in alterations in color and iconography. Dankiewicz spoke with me about being tasked with designing the exterior of the Fire Sage's temple, first seen in "The Winter Solstice, Part 1: The Spirit World" (*Avatar* S1E07). He had found inspiration in the Yellow Crane Tower located in Wuhan, China, and recalled Konietzko's enthusiasm upon first seeing it.[25] On this location, DiMartino and Konietzko wrote, "We thought that the curling, flame-like rooftop corners were a perfect motif for Fire Nation architecture."[26] However, as Dankiewicz pointed out in our interview, the "flames" that the cocreators had described as so perfect for the Fire Nation were actually fish.[27] The Yellow Crane Tower—or, at least, the current iteration of it—sits along the Yangtze River, hence the aquatic motif. Granted, the fish with their upturned tails do somewhat resemble tongues of flame. A streamlined recreation might not capture the distinction from a distance. Nevertheless, stylistic elements of a real-world referent were intentionally altered to suit the needs of the show. Similarly, when Will Weston painted the final BG, he used the Fire Nation's established color scheme of red, gold, and gray instead of the orange, yellow, and white of the Yellow Crane Tower. On *Korra*, BG painter Lauren Zurcher faced a similar task, where she transformed a Buddhist temple into an Air Nomad temple in "Venom of the Red Lotus" (*Korra* S3E13). On this painting, Konietzko wrote:

> Nearly every one of our reference photos of Buddhist temple interiors were predominantly red. So Lauren [Zurcher] had the challenge of converting the color scheme to one that would fit the Air Nomad aesthetic while still conveying the same feeling as those real-life temples.[28]

Even when fidelity gives way to fantasy and internal consistency, there remains a continued emphasis on conveying the "feeling" of a place, that its "spirit" is the source of a purported authenticity. According to these formulations, stylistic elements and motifs remain representative of their original cultures, communicating their essence even when altered or hybridized.

The Fire Sage's temple. Still from "The Winter Solstice, Part 1: The Spirit World" (*Avatar* S1E07). Blu-ray release of *Avatar: The Last Airbender—The Complete Series* (2018).

Air Temple Island. Still from "Venom of the Red Lotus" (*Korra* S3E13). Blu-ray release of *The Legend of Korra—Book Three: Change* (2014).

Across this process, as art director, Bryan Konietzko would approve the selection of referents and their transformation into animated BGs. According to Garagarza:

> Normally Bryan Konietzko had a vision for each location. He would point us to what civilization he was visualizing for each location. We would research on it and present the rough concepts for his approval, or for more finessing. Sometimes, he would not have a set vision in mind for a specific village and he would be open for our input, whether it was my background (BG) design team or me, or the episode Directors.[29]

When asked about the same subject, Dankiewicz recounted:

> A script would come out, a list of BG Designs would be drawn up, and I would often discuss with [Konietzko] what he wanted to see. Often he himself would draw up a quick sketch ("something like this") and I could pursue that line of visualization and he'd leave the sweetening and detail to me. Other times it was left to me to come up with a design from scratch.[30]

Finally, for *Korra*, Sung recalled that Konietzko would provide feedback or draw-overs when a design was not working. Otherwise, she described him as trusting his BG designers' instincts.[31] For example, Garagarza detailed the production of the Sun Warrior ruins in "The Firebending Masters" (*Avatar* S3E13), where Konietzko's original prompt was ultimately supplanted by the creative decisions of the other personnel. She said:

> In the original start up meeting, Bryan [Konietzko] expressed his vision of a civilization with visual influences of ancient Mesopotamia, particularly the tiered pyramids (called Ziggurats). The city was to have a ziggurat in the vary [*sic*] center and then continue to tier down outwards. In that meeting, [Seung Hyun] Oh, the supervising director sketched a possible shot down looking [at] the valley where this city would be. I took the direction and the shot and made a rough city design (this shot basically) with its tiers and avenues and clusters of temples engulfed in foliage, which subsequently Bryan approved to hand to Giancarlo Volpe, the director of the episode, for boarding. Normally because of scheduling, each designer is in charge of his or her own section. But here I took the opportunity to give the same location to my team of designers, Jevon Bue and Enzo Baldi, so that they could separately add their ideas. After a week, I took these drawings to my weekly design meeting and all visions were incorporated into

The Sun Warrior ruins. Still from "The Firebending Masters" (*Avatar* S2E13). Blu-ray release of *Avatar: The Last Airbender—The Complete Series* (2018).

the city. For example, Jevon added interesting motifs like the inverted cones on some rooftops, and some building placement around the ziggurat is Enzo's. Then I could finish the master shot that you see here.³²

This production narrative suggests a collaborative environment in which individual artists could incorporate their unique perspectives in the creation of something new. However, it should be noted, collaborative does not mean communal. Konietzko still needed to sign off on these designs, and his many responsibilities—especially in the first season of *Avatar*—made scheduling meetings difficult. During our interview, Dankiewicz wrote about his frustrations at trying to acquire timely feedback or approval for his designs. An attempt to alleviate this workload by hiring an intermediary apparently backfired and worsened the situation so much that Dankiewicz left before the end of the first season.³³ Garagarza took a supervisory position for the second and third season with seemingly greater success.

The production of BG paintings was not always as straightforward as the above accounts about the Fire Sage's temple or the Air Nomad temple. Instead, in order to build multilayered fantasy cultures, these artists would mix cultural referents from various sources, as seen in the above account about the Sun Warrior ruins. One can observe this pattern by tracking the evolution of Fire Nation architecture, starting with Dankiewicz's original designs, with additional artists incorporating other sources in order to convey specific meanings. For her first assignment as a BG designer, Garagarza was tasked with designing the Fire Lord's throne room in "The Storm." DiMartino and Konietzko wrote about giving Garagarza three instructions: "Egyptian, Chinese, scary."³⁴ When asked, she cited the Great Hypostyle Hall in Karnak, Egypt, and its long rows of large and ornate columns as inspiration.³⁵ The Yellow Crane Tower and the Great Hypostyle Hall were melded together in order to construct and convey Chineseness, Egyptianness, and scariness, qualities then ascribed to the unseen Fire Lord Ozai.

Ahead of the second season, Garagarza was promoted to BG supervisor, a position she held for the remainder of *Avatar*. Henceforth, she started receiving primary credit from the cocreators for the BG designs. The third and final season, set almost entirely in the Fire Nation, gave Garagarza and her team an opportunity to further expand that culture's aesthetic. For the struggling town in "The Painted Lady" (*Avatar* S3E03), Garagarza cited the floating fishing villages in Halong Bay, Vietnam as influences.³⁶ For the luxurious resorts on Ember Island in "The Beach" (*Avatar* S3E05), Konietzko credited the BG supervisor for incorporating various Thai elements.³⁷ Finally, her team's designs for the aforementioned Sun Warrior ruins envisioned the precursors of the Fire Nation as more reminiscent of the Mayans than of the Chinese.[38] Across these examples, BG designers under Garagarza combined referents from a range of non-Western sources in the creation of a complex fantasy culture. In doing so, those real-world cultures were reduced to signifiers of region, class, and time as opposed to of their own specific and nuanced cultural identities. Vietnam is flattened in order to be associated with poverty. Thailand becomes a signifier for wealth and tropical vacations. The Mayans convey a lost civilization. Overlaying these signifiers, Chinese cultural markers are used as synecdoches for Asianness. At no point does the show directly re-present these cultures; they were always hybridized, de-contextualized, and fantasicized. While internal consistency is preserved—the aforementioned locations are unquestionably Fire Nation—the use of different sources allowed the BG designers to depict aesthetic variations based on diegetic factors.

In the above examples, *Avatar* BG designers and painters selected Asian—or, in the case of the Sun Warrior ruins, at least non-Western—referents. However, for the sequel series, there was a notable shift to spotlighting non-Asian inspirations. *Korra* is set primarily in the industrialized Republic City, with recognizable fantasy versions of major US landmarks, such as Central Park and the Statue of Liberty from New York City. By privileging Asian and non-Western referents in earlier production narratives, there is a claim of authenticity, that this fantasy world captures and conveys the "essence" of real Asian cultures. By highlighting these newer influences, the production narratives for *Korra* appear to undermine that. However, it would be a mistake to read industrialized and modern as inherently and quintessentially Western. After all, various cities did not cease being Asian because they adapted and responded to Western influences. While the New York City visual parallels stand out, especially to US viewers, Republic City and other settings in *Korra* continued to find inspiration from the Asian continent. The BG designers and artists also combined the Harmandir Sahib from Amritsar, India, and the original Saltair Pavilion from Utah into the pro-bending arena in Republic City.[39] Hong Kong and Shanghai alongside New York City and Chicago have been cited as referents for various other locations.[40] For the previous series, these artists also adapted Western referents. The Venetian canals inspired the layout for the Northern Water Tribe capitol, and the Parisian catacombs inspired the tunnels under Lake Laogai.[41] The integration of Western referents does not erase the meanings produced by Asian and non-Western ones.

An independent part of the Earth Kingdom, the Metal Clan city of Zaofu was introduced and prominently featured in the third and fourth seasons of *Korra*. When discussing this location's architecture, Konietzko has repeatedly referenced the art deco movement as opposed to the Asian and non-Western influences he would usually cite.[42] In the art book, he wrote:

> Zaofu was an inspiring location for me to art direct. I gathered Art Deco photo reference of architecture, interior design, furniture, sculpture, lighting fixtures, clothing, jewelry, etc. When it came time for the designers to start generating concepts for this episode, I went through the reference folder with each of them, pointing out the design elements I liked best, and how I wanted them to think about streamlining the complex aesthetics down to its essentials so it could be reproduced repeatedly for animation.[43]

With a streamlined version of art deco as a key part of his personal vision, Konietzko wanted to convey certain characteristics of the fantasy subculture. Therefore, this choice of referent warrants further consideration. Art deco is an art style or movement developed and popularized in Europe and the United States in the 1920s and 1930s.[44] It was defined initially by geometric patterns and zigzags and then later by streamlined curves.[45] A modern style, art deco looked toward the future through an optimistic or utopian lens.[46] In the words of Michael Windover, it was what modernity "should look like" even when at odds with the economic reality of the time.[47] In application, art deco came to represent the ideals of social mobility and individual pleasure, becoming associated with places of middle-class luxury and leisure.[48] The elegant and streamlined aesthetics signified wealth and sophistication in the machine age.[49] Therefore, this art style situates this fantasy within an age of mechanization and modernity. It conveys that Zaofu is the "city of the future"—to quote Konietzko—where its citizens lead fulfilling and easygoing lives.[50] Even reformed criminals can leave their past behind and become the best versions of themselves. Before she is even introduced, these qualities are projected onto Suyin Beifong, the leader of the Metal Clan.

Given how North American constructions—especially New York skyscrapers—have become such dominant representatives of art deco, it is tempting to read the style exclusively as a cultural signifier for Americanness or more broadly for a pan-Europeanness. However, that would be a limiting conceptualization. Not only is art deco a production of transculturation, drawing on a range of inspirations, but it was also adopted and adapted for numerous local contexts.[51] In addition to specific European art movements, scholars have identified the appropriation of stylistic elements and motifs from non-Western and Indigenous cultures. The most commonly cited ones are ancient Egypt; Native Americans, from both North and South America;

The Beifong Estate. Still from "The Metal Clan" (*Korra* S3E05). Blu-ray release of *The Legend of Korra—Book Three: Change* (2014).

and African tribes, typically listed without greater specification.⁵² Bevis Hillier and Bridget Elliot even position the development and popularization of art deco in the context of "Egyptomania" following the unearthing of Tutankhamen's tomb in 1922.⁵³ How art deco manifests as a signifier of modernization and urbanization varies across nations.⁵⁴ Even within the United States, scholars note difference between regions.⁵⁵ Accounts on the history and meaning of the art style in Bombay, Mexico City, and Shanghai further illustrate its mutability.⁵⁶ In choosing to emulate art deco, Konietzko may have had certain stated intentions in mind. However, that does not mean that the resulting images do not carry additional meanings beyond his and his crew's control. The aesthetics of the Metal Clan recall not only the modernism of New York but also that of Bombay, Mexico City, and Shanghai. Art deco is not only a signifier of Americanness or pan-Europeanness but also of Indianness, Mexicanness, and Shanghainess.

In my interview with her, Sung further complicated this reading. While she did confirm art deco as an inspiration after being prompted, she primarily recalled being instructed to utilize Asian referents for Zaofu and for the Beifong Estate in particular. She specifically recounted Konietzko directing her to emulate "Chinese terraces" for the BG design as well as to think through how the Metal Clan would have built them using metalbending.⁵⁷ This testimony demonstrates the importance of looking deeper than the official production narratives, revealing a continued line of Asian referents that was not being publicized. If so, then why focus on art deco and not on other referents? As previously discussed, art deco carries with it certain connotations that help differentiate this fantasy subculture. Zaofu is a modern utopia where the heroes can feel safe. Communicating that message was more important than highlighting the persistent and consistent use of Chinese referents.

With BG design and painting, a familiar pattern has recurred. Visual elements are removed from their real-world contexts for artists to extract certain meanings. While Asianness remains core to the identity of the fantasy cultures and subcultures of *Avatar* and *Korra*, a range of referents from a broad spectrum of sources differentiates them and ascribes specific attributes. These qualities are then absorbed by associated animated bodyscapes, reinforcing established or incorporating new facets of their identities. This phenomenon can be most plainly seen with characters who are "introduced" through their settings, such as Ozai with his throne room and Suyin with Zaofu. The stated goal of authenticity can be understood as capturing and conveying a core "essence" or "spirit" of a place or people, rather than accurately re-presenting them wholesale. Too much specificity would risk introducing unintentional significations, with tethers to the real world growing too strong, as seen in the following two production processes.

FIGHT CHOREOGRAPHY

Through fight choreography, *Avatar* and *Korra* sought to ascribe certain qualities to their characters, including reinforcing their racialized Asian identities. The re-presentation of *wushu*, or Chinese martial arts, is a fundamental part of this franchise. Every episode opens with silhouetted figures demonstrating different disciplines as they manipulate or "bend" the four elements—water, earth, fire, and air. According to cocreators Michael Dante DiMartino and Bryan Konietzko, this aspect set the first series apart from the then-dominant "magic wand" fantasy franchises—*The Lord of the Rings* and *Harry Potter*—as well as contemporaneous superhero cartoons.[58] Paratexts for both shows have emphasized the authenticity of these fight sequences.[59] The first behind-the-scenes extra on a home video release of *Avatar* features martial arts consultant Sifu Kisu discussing and demonstrating the four "Chinese martial arts" that inspired the different types of bending, educating audiences of their real-world connections while his movements are juxtaposed with animation from the show; this featurette was assembled from videos that Nickelodeon would air during commercial breaks for the first season of *Avatar*.[60] These production narratives highlight the fidelity of the choreography, placing it within a wushu lineage. At the same time, these re-presentations deviate from and hybridize established norms for the sake of internal consistency and character development. Through the selection and blending of referents, this franchise ascribed identity in both intended and unintended ways via their development of fantastical martial arts.

Siu Leung Li and Leon Hunt have both noted how the discourse on the mimesis of cinematic re-presentations of wushu converges around two points. First is "archival authenticity," meaning fidelity to a cultural tradition.[61] Due to the fantasy setting, the choreography inevitably entailed a degree of decontextualization. Despite *Avatar* and *Korra*'s fantastical distancing, the production narratives around these shows have emphasized their accuracy. Second, for Li and Hunt, "corporeal authenticity," the assurance that the actions on screen were performed by physiological human bodies without the aid of special effects, is of greater importance.[62] While seemingly less relevant for animation due to technological mediation, this concern also factored into the choreography of *Avatar* and *Korra*, as seen in the employment of martial arts consultants and the filming of original reference footage. The imitation of these disciplines and movements grounded these animated bodyscapes in reality, meaning both the historical and cultural contexts of wushu as well as the physiological specificity of the human body.

Historical Referents and Archival Authenticity

Historians Brian Kennedy and Elizabeth Guo write about the many ways in which wushu have been imprecisely categorized. The first distinction is between hard (*waijia*) and soft (*neijia*), based on whether the system is designed to foster external and physical strength or internal power through the cultivation of qi.[63] They and other scholars have noted that this division is largely arbitrary as all systems contain "hard" and "soft" elements.[64] Nevertheless, they remain indicative of another set of classifications, that of Shaolin and Wudang, of Buddhism and Taoism, respectively.[65] Kennedy and Guo find this classification to be the least helpful, as it reveals more of myth than history. They note that the three primary Wudang systems—Tai Chi, Bagua, and Xingyi—were not founded or developed in the predominantly Taoist Wudang Mountains.[66] In his region-based list of wushu "families," martial arts scholar Wang Guangxi places these three systems in their own separate categories distinct from Wudang.[67] Despite this reality, these two branches of Shaolin and Wudang still correspond with issues of national and cultural identity. Another dichotomy is between northern and southern systems, with the former defined by kicks and higher stances, while the latter is defined by hand techniques and low stances, prompting the expression "Northern Leg, Southern Fist."[68] While both still utilize kicks and punches, they are framed as signifiers of regional specificity, of a tension between mainland China and Hong Kong, especially in their cinematic re-presentations.[69] Through the referencing of one group of systems over another, *Avatar* and *Korra* choreographers navigate and negotiate these distinctions in their construction of waterbending, earthbending, firebending, and airbending, even when they do not recognize or acknowledge doing so.

Even though *Avatar* paratexts have stressed practical applications of wushu, the creators and producers have also cited Chinese martial arts films—especially *Shaolin Soccer* (2001)—as inspirations.[70] Therefore, it would be beneficial to situate these shows in relation to the corpus of that cinematic genre. While not an absolute distinction, wushu films are often divided into two categories—*wuxia* and kung fu. The former embraces the fantastical and the stylistic, with characters using their qi to fly and exercise "Palm Power."[71] Scholars have noted that this cinematic genre—commonplace on the mainland—is more evocative of Chinese culture and history, that it holds greater nationalist potential.[72] Kung fu, on the other hand, is more emulative of Hong Kong sensibilities, "a cultural hybrid" with greater international appeal.[73] Instead of the specificity of *wuxia*, these films are more grounded in reality and modernity, with hard and muscular bodies exhibiting *waijia* with minimal interference from special effects.[74] The choreography of *Avatar* and *Korra* combine aspects of both types of wushu films. Benders use chi to fight and fly in fantastical and acrobatic displays, but these acts are still tenuously grounded in reality. Benders manipulate their respective element to shoot projectiles, heal, or propel themselves through the air rather than directly evoking chi. Like with kung fu cinema, the *Avatar* franchise emphasizes hard and muscular bodies, although children and the elderly are depicted as able to compete with or even surpass able-bodied and middle-aged benders. Through both choreography and character design, *Avatar* and *Korra* sought to emulate the more fantastical tendencies of *wuxia* as well as the relatively mimetic instincts of kung fu in their construction and ascription of Asianness. However, these strictly categorical approaches to discussing wushu risk ignoring how these different styles have influenced each other. As many scholars have argued, wushu in both their practical and cinematic iterations are informed by national, transnational, and transcultural factors in their production, content, and reception.[75] Even the overtly national significations are formed in response to outside influences.[76] Writing primarily about Korean cinema, Kim Soyoung adopts Mary Louise Pratt's concept of the "contact zone" to describe the meeting and mixing of international ideas and conventions in the formation of action genres, including Hong Kong kung fu cinema.[77] Through the appropriation and adaptation of traditional and cinematic wushu, *Avatar* and *Korra* position their fantasy cultures and their characters in relation to these real-world identities.

According to Konietzko, the original plan for *Avatar* was for everyone to practice Northern Shaolin, citing how the discipline's "balletic" and "dynamic" qualities would translate well to animation.[78] However, their consultant, Kisu, recommended an alternative approach, using multiple types of wushu to differentiate and ascribe characteristics to the four fantasy cultures—the Water Tribe, Earth Kingdom, Fire Nation, and Air Nomads.[79] On one hand, their consultant's proposal averts one type of cultural flattening, where a single discipline would have become representative of all wushu. On the other hand, through this approach, Chinese martial arts become representative of all of Asia. Nevertheless, even within this limited scope, the pool of referents is deep and diverse, with each system subdivided into multiple styles.

In a brief promotional interview for *Nickelodeon Magazine*, Kisu emphasizes the importance of making waterbending feel "fluid and smooth."[80] In other paratexts, he discusses choosing Yang-style Tai Chi[81] as the primary referent for this fantastical martial art, highlighting how its softness can be indicative to water.[82] In addition to this aesthetic quality, martial artist Lu Shengli defines Tai Chi as a constantly changing balance of *yin* and *yang*.[83] In the episode "Bitter Work" (*Avatar* S2E09), Iroh describes the four types of bending to Zuko: "Water is the element of change. The people of the Water Tribe are capable of adapting to many things. They have a deep sense of community and love that holds them together through anything." Without overtly citing Taoism or *yin* and *yang*, the dialogue highlights the qualities of change and adaptation present in Tai Chi and indicative of the element of water. The development of waterbending provides a model for the analysis of the other bending disciplines. The use of a specific referent positions a fantastical martial art in relation to real-world historical and cultural contexts. For the creators and crew of *Avatar*, that entails the signification of Asianness as well as of Chineseness, but it can be more specific. Some fantastical distancing is inevitable. After all, there is no China or Taoism in the *Avatar* world, and real-world practitioners of Tai Chi cannot bend water. Furthermore, the emphasis of the aesthetics of a wushu over its background is another form of decontextualization, an attempt to sever and hide the factors that led to the development of these systems and styles as well as what that context signifies.

The development of earthbending and its function as a cultural signifier are more complex. Across paratexts, Kisu has described the people of the

Earth Kingdom as formidable, strong, and grounded.[84] In Iroh's aforementioned speech in "Bitter Work," the character recites many of these traits: "Earth is the element of substance. The people of the Earth Kingdom are diverse and strong. They are persistent and enduring." The emphasis is on how this bending discipline is representative of its practitioners. In order to convey these attributes, Kisu selected Hung Gar[85] as the primary referent. He emphasized that, as a southern system, it has low and strong stances, which indicate a close connection to the earth.[86] This creative decision also places earthbending within a specific historical and cultural framework. In her analysis of Hong Kong kung fu cinema, Gina Marchetti defines contemporary Hung Gar as an entwinement of both a traditional wushu system and its re-presentation in popular entertainment.[87] Specifically, the modern iteration of Hung Gar is largely derived from the output of director, choreographer, and actor Lau Kar-leung. Because of his work for the Shaw Brothers in the 1970s, Lau has been credited for creating a distinct, authentic, and "specifically southern" cinematic kung fu style.[88] Like with waterbending and Tai Chi, earthbending's association with Hung Gar is based primarily on aesthetics. A low stance conveys literal and figurative proximity to earth. However, Hung Gar also connotes a southern and Hong Kong identity, in opposition to a northern and mainland one. In this regard, there is a possible parallel between fantasy and reality, as the Earth Kingdom is also in tension with the cultural and military imperialism of the Fire Nation.

This identity is further complicated in the second season of *Avatar*, with the addition of a new main character in "The Blind Bandit." Unlike other earthbenders, Toph is blind and self-taught, emulating the movements of badgermoles. Later in the series, she uses her personalized techniques to become the first metalbender. To create this unusual style, Kisu brought in Sifu Manuel Rodriguez to shoot reference footage for Chu Gar-style Southern Praying Mantis,[89] his specialization.[90] While Chu Gar is not as widespread or as chronicled a style as Chow Gar, all variations of Southern Praying Mantis have a shared myth of their founder developing the discipline by studying the movements of a praying mantis. Even Northern Praying Mantis, a separate system with a different set of moves, reports a similar origin myth.[91] This referent was selected primarily because it could signify Toph's uniqueness. Although they are both examples of southern wushu, Southern Praying Mantis is its own distinct system and not a subset of Hung Gar. Still, a shared regional specificity connects them even as it breaks from the commitment to archival authenticity. The development of earthbending and its variations demonstrate how the selection of a referent can construct unintended cultural signifiers. In addition to ascribing identity to whole fantasy cultures, the choreography of *Avatar* can also distinguish individual characters. A similar process occurs with other bending disciplines.

For firebending, Kisu wanted to convey aggressiveness with quick and sharp moves.[92] He therefore chose to model this fantastical martial art after his specialization, Northern Shaolin.[93] In interviews, Kisu has highlighted the strong and dynamic kicks, punches, and stances associated with Northern Shaolin.[94] Such visuals are emblematic of how Iroh describes the fantastical martial art in "Bitter Work." He tells his nephew: "Fire is the element of power. The people of the Fire Nation have desire and will and the energy and drive to achieve what they want." Northern Shaolin allowed the choreographers to visualize those attributes through strong and aggressive moves. However, once again, Kisu also positioned firebending in relation to reality. As previously addressed, Northern Shaolin falls into two categories of wushu. First, it is northern, with its emphasis on "high flying kicks." While more emblematic of the mainland, this visually stimulating wushu also became commonplace in Hong Kong kung fu films.[95] Regional specificity is not a primary signification. Second, the referent is Shaolin, which—as historian Peter Allan Lorge writes—is emulative of a specific historical context. During the Ming and Qing dynasties, as it was being mythologized, Shaolin became shorthand for foreigners. It was an external and Buddhist martial art framed as inferior to internal and Taoist systems, such as the aforementioned Tai Chi.[96] While the background of Hung Gar can be seen as in parallel with that of earthbending, the narrative of *Avatar* precludes an equivalent interpretation of Northern Shaolin and firebending. The Fire Nation are imperialist invaders imposing their rule on others, not a religious minority group targeted by reactionary nationalists. The show and the choreographers are seemingly uninterested in fostering such a reading, instead just using the dynamic movements of Northern Shaolin to convey aggressiveness.

Like with earthbending, the second season of *Avatar* introduced a new character who further complicated the significations of this fantastical martial art. Making her first proper appearance in the season two premiere, Azula exercises a variant of firebending defined by her "effortless" movement.[97] To create this style, Kisu has discussed incorporating elements of Chaquan,[98] which he described as "a northern Islamic style which is associated with Northern Shaolin" and that was utilized by Genghis Khan.[99] The namedrop is a deliberate call for archival authenticity, forging a lineage between a famous historical figure and a fictional character. Kennedy and Guo also identify this system as an "ethnic martial art" practiced by the Hui people.[100] Like with Toph, a real-world wushu ascribes an identity to a specific character. Azula is a prodigy to whom firebending comes naturally. The association with a fellow northern system was enough for Kisu to justify choosing Chaquan as inspiration for a personalized subset of firebending. Otherwise, the referent was completely decontextualized, with its background only brought up in passing in interviews and not alluded to within the narrative of the show. Nevertheless, through the selection of both Northern Shaolin and Chaquan, the choreographers of *Avatar* equated ethnic and religious minorities in China with the Fire Nation and one of the primary antagonists. As Edwin Zane warned in the first chapter, there is always a danger to equating villains with real-life communities. Fantastical distancing can dissuade direct comparisons, but the signification persists and is incorporated into these complexes of signs.

For airbending, Kisu primarily emulated Bagua,[101] with its wind-like circular hand movements and footwork.[102] His description of the system echoes that of Kennedy and Guo; the principle of both the fantastical and real-world martial art is to move around one's opponent and prevent them from landing an effective hit.[103] Once again, Kisu does not mention the broader historical context for the development and popularization of the wushu system. Like Tai Chi, Bagua was a response to Shaolin during the Qing Dynasty, emphasizing soft and internal power over hard and external strength.[104] Kisu does however allude to how the Taoist text *I Ching* forms the philosophy behind this system but offers little elaboration within the paratexts.[105] According to Iroh in "Bitter Work," "Air is the element of freedom. The Air Nomads detached themselves from worldly concerns and found peace and freedom." This description offers only a general association between air and the principle of "freedom," emblematic more so of the monastic lifestyles of Air Nomads than the specifics of airbending. Less publicized was the incorporation of elements of Xingyi[106] for the more linear movements of this fantastical martial art.[107] This wushu was also part of the anti-Shaolin backlash during the Qing Dynasty.[108] Given this historical context, there is an incongruity in the construction of Air Nomad culture. Their architecture, names, and additional aspects were derived from primarily Buddhist referents. Yet, Shaolin martial arts are associated not with the Air Nomads but with the Fire Nation. Instead, in order to suggest the movement of air, the choreographers appropriated and combined elements of Taoist wushu. Nevertheless, as these signs are mixed together in the construction of a coherent and cohesive fantasy culture and set of animated bodyscapes, signifiers for Buddhism and Taoism were flattened together, and the tension between the two were elided. The resulting signification was of Asianness and Chineseness rather than of a more specific Taoistness or Buddhistness.

The development of airbending is the first major example of hybridization in the choreography of *Avatar*, with Bagua and Xingyi transformed into a single discipline. As previously stated, the mixing of different martial arts systems and styles is not a new phenomenon, either in reality or in fiction. According to Lu Shengli, these two airbending referents are often practiced concomitantly and "are said to be one family."[109] While there have been and continue to be a number of wushu "purists" or "traditionalists" who emphasize the authenticity and lineage of their chosen disciplines, there have also always been an equal number of "eclectic types" who borrow from multiple sources.[110] Kennedy, Guo, Lu Shengli, William Acevedo, Mei Cheung, and Lorge have all traced how the histories of the formation and development of wushu systems and styles are defined by hybridization.[111] The transregional, transnational, and transcultural cross-pollination continued in cinematic re-presentations, as Hunt and Kim Soyoung have noted the influence of Korean Taekwondo on Hong Kong kung fu films.[112] The ability to adopt, adapt, and mix different disciplines is also treated as a strength within the narrative of *Avatar*. The theme is most explicitly conveyed in "Bitter Work," when Iroh tells Zuko:

> It is important to draw wisdom from many different places. If we take it from only one place, it becomes rigid and stale. Understanding others—the other elements and the other nations—will help you become whole . . . It is the combination of the four elements in one person that makes the Avatar so powerful, but it can make you more powerful too.

He then proceeds to demonstrate how to redirect lightning by emulating waterbending. In the series finale, Zuko uses stances and moves from the other bending disciplines in his climatic firebending duel with Azula. Both these characters and the show's choreographers appropriate and transform different martial arts systems and styles.

Korra choreographers continued to hybridize real-world martial arts disciplines in the process of worldbuilding and characterization. Ahead of the sequel series' premiere, DiMartino told *The A.V. Club*: "Republic City represents that big melting-pot aspect of the *Avatar* universe, so it's the blending of all these cultures, and that affects the martial arts as well."[113] *Korra* producer Joaquim Dos Santos elaborated: "Mike [DiMartino] and Bryan [Konietzko] were setting [*The Legend of Korra*] seventy years later and the world has evolved and so had the martial arts. So we got to incorporate a lot of different styles."[114] In our interview, *Korra* martial arts consultant Jake

Huang added: "They wanted to evolve [the bending] into something new where Korra didn't have a specific style from [*Avatar*]."[115] He continued: "I had to go back and watch all of the original *Airbender* series so I could get familiar with their motions, their powers, of all the elements and whatnot, to see kind of how to evolve it."[116] While the legacy of the disciplines developed by Kisu and the other *Avatar* choreographers persisted, traditional wushu was hybridized with a new pool of referents. Their Asianness and Chineseness endured but were now accompanied by other significations. Rather than pursue archival authenticity, *Korra* choreographers incorporated non-Chinese martial arts, contributing to the construction of a cosmopolitan "melting pot."

After moving to Republic City, Korra witnesses her world's ultimate example of martial arts transculturation: pro-bending. This professional sport is a major part of the first season, as the title character joins a team with Mako and Bolin. Even though each side is composed of a waterbender, an earthbender, and a firebender, their stances and moves are indistinguishable, all defined by quick hooks and jabs. The evolution and blending of martial arts and its benefits are addressed within the series. Although Tenzin describes the sport as "a mockery of the noble tradition of bending" in "A Leaf in the Wind" (*Korra* S1E02), his student Korra only progresses in her airbending training not through his traditional methods but through her involvement in pro-bending. To create this new and modern fighting style, the choreographers referenced mixed martial arts (MMA), albeit omitting the grappling component.[117] To ensure authenticity, the show hired two MMA fighters, Mac Danzig and Jeremy Umphries, to choreograph the pro-bending matches, visually distinguishing those sequences from the rest of the series. Further emphasizing this connection, the title character was partially modeled after former MMA fighter Gina Carano.[118] Like pro-bending, contemporary MMA is also a transcultural blending of styles, especially of Asian and Western disciplines after the two had been developing separately for so long.[119] Regardless, there persists an attempt to legitimize the sport by positioning Bruce Lee and his Jeet Kune Do[120] system as a precursor.[121] Dana White, president of the MMA organization Ultimate Fighting Championship (UFC), was once quoted saying:

> Actually, the father of mixed martial arts, if you will, was Bruce Lee. If you look at the way Bruce Lee trained, the way he fought, and many of the things he wrote, he said the perfect style was no style. You take a little something from everything. You take the good things from every different discipline, use what works, and you throw the rest away.[122]

Despite the hybridization and flattening inherent in contemporary MMA, White and others have still pursued a form of archival authenticity by framing the sport as the successor to a specific Asian martial art as well as to a specific Asian martial artist. An MMA fighter is an explicit example of the "eclectic type" of which Kennedy and Guo wrote, taking elements from different sources until they have formed a repertoire that best suits their needs or brand. Likewise, Korra and other characters do the same, unwittingly following Iroh's advice from the previous series. They adopt and adapt a range of real-world and fantastical martial arts in order to become more powerful benders. While doing so does complicate the construction and ascription of Asianness, it does not completely erase it. Like with MMA, pro-bending remains linked to the original Asian inspirations. However, finding and transforming these referents is just the first step to the fight choreography; they still needed to be rendered in storyboards and animation.

Reference Footage and Corporeal Authenticity

The components of the animated bodyscape flow between production cultures, acquiring new significations. The development of martial arts choreography is part of that process, also undergoing a journey through different departments as individuals made their contributions. The first step was an initial meeting with some combination of the creators, producers, directing teams, and consultants to read through the finished script for an episode. While in the same room, they interpreted and embellished the writers' descriptions by pitching ideas and sometimes shooting improvised reference footage.[123] According to Huang, it was an environment where everyone was encouraged to contribute.[124] In this regard, the initial meeting operated as a contact zone in the same way as the writers' room. Representatives from different production cultures as well as from the orbiting consulting satellites collaborated and synthesized ideas from their distinct perspectives. Following this stage, the directing teams started storyboarding.

The first drafts, alternatively called "roughs" or "thumbnails," established the major action beats for a fight scene. As a result, *Avatar* and *Korra* crew members have described the storyboard artists as the primary choreographers for the franchise.[125] In addition to discussion and footage from the initial meeting, episode directors and storyboard artists utilized preexisting reference material for these sequences. *Avatar* storyboard artist Juan Meza-Leon specifically cited *Samurai Champloo* and Jackie Chan films as common referents.[126] *Korra* co-director Olga Ulanova recalled finding relevant videos either on YouTube or on the shared production server. She specifically discussed referring to a folder of Bagua clips for the airbending sequences as well as Dos Santos's well-curated collection of barrel rolls.[127] By the time these two had joined their respective series, the different bending disciplines and their primary referents had been well established. Their contributions to the choreography were not in the selection of inspirations but in establishing the major beats and movements of the scene. For guidance on first drafts, both have emphasized the use of Asian referents, either real-world demonstrations of martial arts or their artistic re-presentations. As Ulanova elaborated: "It was understood . . . don't look at traditional Western styles of fighting, look at Asian martial arts . . . It was very specific in that regard."[128] In following this directive, the directing team reinforced the connection between the choreography and Asianness. Upon completion of the roughs, the choreography underwent another pass with the consultants, the most foregrounded part of this process in the production narratives.

With the general blocking and beats established, a martial arts consultant was brought in to help refine the choreography ahead of revisions. Their job was to perform the blocking from specific camera angles.[129] For Zaheer's introductory fight scene in "A Breath of Fresh Air" (*Korra* S3E01), episode director Melchior Zwyer recalled: "We'd show up with boards, the rough boards. [Huang would] take a look at it and just go, 'No, that's impossible. How about we do this instead.' And he'd show us a move, and it's even way better than what we boarded out."[130] While Konietzko framed the directing teams as the principal choreographers, he credited the consultants for adding "specificity" and "that extra fine-tuning."[131] *Avatar* director Giancarlo Volpe, Dos Santos, Meza-Leon, *Korra* co-director Owen Sullivan, and Ulanova have all praised the consultants for inserting realism and accuracy into the fight sequences.[132] The mimesis provided by Kisu, Huang, and others was not merely archival authenticity from their demonstrations of traditional disciplines. It was also corporeal authenticity through the real-life performances of the choreography. The connection between the physiological bodies of the consultants and the animated bodyscapes of the characters is reflected in the language used to describe this step in the process. For Konietzko, they are taking moves "from [Kisu's] body into the animation."[133] According to Huang, the storyboard artists would "capture" his performance and "draw [his] motions over the characters."[134] There was a greater degree of technological and artistic mediation than these quotes suggest. Hence, Hunt's third category of "cinematic authenticity" is not especially applicable.[135] Meza-Leon recalled how the *Avatar* storyboard artists would play the new footage of Kisu on QuickTime, going through frame-by-frame, tracing poses on post-it notes before translating them onto cleaned-up storyboards.[136] The practice was not quite rotoscoping, with ample room left for embellishment. As Meza-Leon noted, Kisu was not as acrobatic as many of the characters.[137] These practices persisted once the storyboards and the reference footage were sent overseas. Seung Hyun Oh spoke about how he and other animators adapted the recordings of these martial arts sessions: "Of course, it's not that I copy things directly. I maximize its effect by turning it into animation so I can get a better kung-fu move, or find a better angle in the shot and the right proportions, and also a nuance of the kung-fu movements."[138] Furthermore, as Ulanova recalled, the consultants were not required to perform every action in a sequence, just the more complicated ones or those framed from a difficult angle.[139] In addition, a single martial arts session might have entailed moves from various sequences from multiple episodes. At the same time, a particular move may have been repeatedly performed and refined across numerous sessions over the course of several months. Because of this disjointed process, Huang had difficulty differentiating the bending sequences from *Korra* without the final animation in front of him.[140] A consultant's performance of the choreography only became coherent and cohesive through the technological and artistic mediation of storyboarding. With these observations in mind, how much corporeal authenticity persists in these martial arts sequences? How much of a role does it play in the construction and ascription of Asianness to these animated bodyscapes?

The first chapter addresses how storyboard artists would sometimes use both preexisting and original reference footage to construct performances in *Avatar* and *Korra*. Rather than transfer specific cultural, national, or racial attributes—although they inadvertently did—this practice was intended to use the specificity of the human body to ground the fantastical and abstracted animated bodyscape. The production of original martial arts reference footage also aimed to tether these animated bodyscapes to reality rather than exploit their plasmatic potential. Despite technological and artistic mediation, the choreography has been framed as the actual movements of trained martial artists. That specificity, "that extra fine-tuning," was still transferred to the animated bodyscapes. However, the question remains: How much of the performer's body is still present in the final animation? Film scholar Tanine Allison touches on this question when she writes about the use of motion capture in the computer-animated film *Happy Feet* (2006), specifically the transposing of the moves of Black dancer Savion Glover onto one of the character models. According to her, the film not only appropriated the movements of a Black body; those movements were explicitly and culturally encoded as Black.[141] Do the fight sequences of *Avatar* and *Korra* function similarly? There were physiological bodies with their own racial identities performing traditionally but not exclusively Asian martial arts. However, the conversion of the movements of consultants into those of animated figures was not as direct. Without rotoscoping or motion capture, there was greater artistic mediation on the part of the directing teams. Despite claims made in paratexts, the movements of the animated bodyscapes are not identical to those of the consultants. Furthermore, whereas the nonhuman protagonist of *Happy Feet* is otherwise coded as white, the characters from *Avatar* and *Korra* are primarily signified as Asian, as the preceding chapters detail. Nevertheless, like the acting references, the performances of the martial arts consultants contributed to the complexes of signs that comprise these animated bodyscapes. The resulting animatics—the products of collaboration between production cultures within the Nickelodeon Animation Studio as well as orbiting satellites—were subsequently sent overseas for final animation.

By examining how *Avatar* and *Korra* transformed real-world martial arts into fantastical bending, this section has demonstrated how the drive toward authenticity can manifest in different ways. By striving for archival authenticity, the choreographers sought to legitimize their work by situating it within a lineage of martial arts systems and styles, anchoring it within certain historical and cultural contexts. By striving for corporeal authenticity, they sought to ground their work by evoking the presence of physiological bodies, regardless of degrees of artistic and technological mediation. In both cases, production narratives helped to educate audiences about these connections between fantasy and reality. The above accounts also demonstrate how, through their choice of referents, these artists produced unintentional significations, recalling specific real-world histories. Among other creative decisions, they chose wushu as representative of all Asian martial arts, in turn positioning China as representative of all Asia. A similar pattern emerges in the production of calligraphy.

CALLIGRAPHY AND TRANSLATION

No matter how distinct they are in architecture, topography, or fighting style, every nation in *Avatar* and *Korra* uses the same Chinese calligraphy. Fully fantastical names like Katara are written as 卡塔拉 (Kǎ tǎ lā), hybrid names like Korra as 寇拉 (Kòu lā), and real-world names like Mako as 馬高 (Mǎ gāo). This translated calligraphy communicates authenticity but also erases the differences between real-world and fantasy cultures. After all, these names are not written in "Asian" but in Chinese. Even the Japanese name Mako becomes Chinese.[142] This rendering of the world and characters of *Avatar* and *Korra* as Chinese was accomplished through the hiring of Siu-Leung Lee as translator and calligrapher. In our interview, he told me of the impact of his work on the franchise's identity: "If . . . the sound track was in Chinese, it would be just like a Chinese production."¹⁴³ To him, the use of accurate Chinese calligraphy, even for names not directly of Chinese origin, extended a Chinese identity to this fantasy world and to the shows.

Lee's responsibilities were threefold. He would translate text provided to him by Konietzko, compose the calligraphy, and provide layouts for the art department. Of the first one, he said: "They rely totally on my translation. The most time we spent was on the title logo. For the rest, it is almost always just one-shot—my final is their final."¹⁴⁴ When asked whether he recalled any particularly troublesome translations, he replied: "There is no difficulty in the translation or calligraphy."¹⁴⁵ Konietzko recalled tasking Lee with what he considered to be a tough assignment for "The Drill": "I asked him to translate 'slurry.' That was one where I thought he would kick back and be, like, 'There is no Chinese character for slurry.' And, no complaints, like one hour later, got the Chinese translation."¹⁴⁶ The final episode features the logograms 泥漿管道 (níjiāng guǎndào) as the translation for "slurry pipeline." When asked about how he translated and wrote proper names, Lee responded:

> The same sound in English can be transliterated into different words, the combination of which may take different meanings. I do carefully consider different words for each name to present the character/place appropriately. I try to avoid dialects so that most of the Chinese audience would sound them out the same way as the English audience does. That is another reason the Asian audience love[s] the TV series, because I speak their language, literally.¹⁴⁷

Lee highlights the appeal to Asian—meaning, to him, Chinese-literate—audiences. Only once did the franchise translate his work via English subtitles. The ending for the *Avatar* series finale featured 劇終 (jù zhōng) alongside "The End." The final shot of *Korra* used the same two logograms sans English accompaniment, leaving Chinese-illiterate viewers to surmise its meaning through context. Again, there is a flattening. If regarded as a signifier of Asianness, then the calligraphy positions China as representative of all of Asia, eliding cultural differences in both real-world and fantastical contexts.

In the art book for *Avatar*, Konietzko expanded on his admiration for their translator and calligrapher:

When I would send Dr. Lee a request for a poster or a decree, he would quiz me about what unseen fictional character had done the calligraphy in the show. If it were a highly cultured royal attendant, he would use a refined, elegant style, but if it were a low-level clerk, he would use a more pedestrian handwriting style.[148]

The cocreator also wrote on how Lee would use a more archaic writing style when depicting "ancient texts about the spirits or elements."[149] The calligrapher corroborated: "They [the emails] include instructions on the time period and style they expect (e.g., the degree of literacy of the writer) so I can design the script and style accordingly."[150] Therefore, the calligraphy of the shows is not entirely reductive, leaving room for class-based and temporal differences. Konietzko praised Lee's level of expertise: "His vast knowledge and command of various styles of calligraphy throughout China's history added a culturally grounding component to the show."[151] Such language positions Lee and his authority as signifiers of cultural authenticity.

In addition to producing direct translations, Lee served as calligrapher and provided layouts for the art department. He specifically mentioned his work on the various wanted posters featured throughout the series; the *Avatar* art book highlights several examples, and one was featured in a special *Avatar* issue of *Nickelodeon Magazine*.[152] His creative input extended into developing the inscriptions on the calendar seen in "The Library" (*Avatar* S2E10), with the art book crediting him for including "historically based names for sixteen eras."[153] However, the development of written language in *Avatar* and *Korra* did not end with Lee. His work still needed to be interpreted by the art department. Both Garagarza and Sung recalled leaving blank spaces in their BG designs for the logograms to be added digitally by someone else.[154] Only Konietzko regularly communicated with Lee.[155] The art director spoke of the journey taken by the aforementioned piece of graffiti in the episode "The Serpent's Pass." He recalled:

I got the calligraphy from S. L. Lee, our calligraphy expert, but then I had to make it look all scratchy, like graffiti. But then I needed to show it to someone who could read Chinese and make sure it was still legible or didn't say something bad.[156]

The result was 絕望 (jué wàng) or "abandon hope" as read by the characters. This anecdote demonstrates the transformation that the calligraphy would undergo when incorporated into animation as well as the dangers involved.

For *Korra*—set in an era where the world had developed printing—Lee's input was diminished. Indeed, whereas the *Avatar* art book gave the calligraphy a four-page spread, it is barely mentioned in any of the four for *Korra*. When asked about the differences between the two series, the translator recalled: "I [had] much less involvement in *Korra* because it is a modern set[ting] that required modern print fonts rather than calligraphy."[157] This marginalization led to instances like the title card for the "mover" *Nuktuk, Hero of the South* or 努篤 南方英雄 (Nǔ dǔ nán fāng yīng xióng), where a decidedly modern 3D font supplants Lee's original work. In the art book for the second season, Konietzko took credit for this stylization; he wanted it "to have that action/adventure *Indiana Jones* feeling."[158] Lee's wording and Konietzko's choice of referent suggest that the loss of the original calligraphy is also a loss of authenticity with the move from accurate calligraphy to Western stylization. However, like with the use of art deco to design the Metal Clan or the hybridization of martial arts styles, this melding of sources does not invalidate the Asianness of the final product. The translations and calligraphy still operate as cultural signifiers, and the printing press was hardly exclusive to Europe. Regardless, the written language's uncontaminated nature—so prized in the preceding series—is not preserved in the construction of a more modern identity.

Lee has taken great pride in his impact on this franchise. During our correspondence, he shared links to webpages discussing and celebrating his calligraphy and boasted about the emails he received from fans complimenting his work. He credited the incorporation of his calligraphy for the success that the franchise has had, especially with Asian viewers.[159] As signifiers of Asianness, the use of Lee's Chinese calligraphy plays an important role. Indeed, his involvement was highlighted in a *New York Times* article promoting the *Avatar* series premiere, where he is mentioned alongside the martial arts consultant.[160] In perhaps the biggest indication of Lee's contribution, the logo for first series prominently features his translation for "Avatar," 降古神通 (jiàng shì shéntōng). Such iconography demonstrates how Chinese calligraphy extends an Asian identity to the show and thus to its characters.

CONCLUSION

At the intersection between Maureen Furniss's continuum and Kathryn Hume's dual impulses, the animated and fantastical world of *Avatar* and *Korra* was built to be both tethered to and distanced from reality. Through this tenuous connection, the artists behind these shows transferred significations from real-world cultures to their fantastical creations. True authenticity may have been an impossibility for these shows, yet the drive persisted and should be interrogated. What was the relationship between fantasy and reality in the *Avatar* franchise? How did the various artists exploit that relationship for their visual worldbuilding? The section of BG designs and paintings demonstrates how authenticity can manifest as a desire to capture and retain the "essence" of a place, something that can survive the various modifications and hybridizations that a referent would undergo during fantasification. The section on fight choreography illustrates how artists can strive for archival or corporeal authenticity. They can seek to legitimize their creations by evoking particular historical and cultural contexts. They can ground their work by gesturing to the presence of a physiological body. For calligraphy, *Avatar* and *Korra* transplanted a real-world writing system into their diegesis.

In this and previous chapters, production narratives have revealed a preference for Chinese referents to signify that this fantasy world is culturally Asian in support of the ascription of racialized Asian identities to animated bodyscapes. They have cited Chinese architecture as inspiration for their BG designs and paintings, adapted wushu or Chinese martial arts into their fight choreography, and used Chinese calligraphy for their in-universe writing system. Such preferences in the construction of an "Asian" identity position the real-world China as representative of all of Asia. Now, China is far from a monolith, as demonstrated by the breadth of referents that these artists were able to find while constructing various distinct fantasy cultures and subcultures. What we now recognize as China is composed of various regions, ethnicities, religions, and languages, all preventing it from being reduced or summarized as a single identity. In *Avatar* and *Korra*, this diversity can be seen in how Chinese buildings could inform the architecture of fictional cultures as disparate as the Earth Kingdom and the Fire Nation, in how wushu could be adapted into distinctive fantastical martial arts, and in how Chinese calligraphy could be written with degrees of formality and antiquity.

However, the *Avatar* world is not a fantastical version of China, where such a reliance on Chinese cultural referents for worldbuilding would be understandable. While China is often treated as a stand-in for Asia, other Asian cultures are instead flattened into single adjectives to be applied to particular characters or groups. This tendency appears in the BG designs and paintings for various Fire Nation towns in the third season of *Avatar*. It can also be seen in the use of "ethnic" martial arts for certain characters. There is a feedback loop, then, where these adjectives are then applied to the real-world cultures that served as the original referent. Within this framework,

Western referents are implemented to evoke modernity and industrialization, especially in *Korra*, as seen in the architecture of Republic City and Zaofu, the pro-bending fighting style, and the preference for printing over calligraphy. However, once again, it would be a mistake to conclude that Western and modern are synonymous with each other. Non-Western cultures are not invalid for incorporating or responding to outside influences, and Western cultures have responded to and incorporated influences from outside sources as well. The real-world sources for these referents have more complex and complicated histories than can be perceived from how they are adapted for a fantasy show, which can result in a range of unintended significations.

These various and sometimes contradictory meanings are then projected and incorporated into the animated bodyscape as the new sets of visual components intersect with existing visual, aural, and narrative ones. Thus, the products of BG design and painting, fight choreography, and calligraphy inform the characterization of individuals and groups within the diegesis of *Avatar* and *Korra*. Through the highlighted use of Asian cultural referents, these various processes and artists supported the ascription of a racialized Asian identity to these animated bodyscapes. The following chapter explores how the soundscape functions similarly, looking at how the development of music and sound effects contributes to worldbuilding and the production of identity within the animated bodyscape. The chapter also addresses how production narratives frame these acts of fantasification.

Chapter Five

AURAL WORLDBUILDING AND THE ANIMATED BODYSCAPE

Just as vocal performances contribute to the construction and ascription of identity for an animated character, so too do other types of sound contribute to fantasy worldbuilding. Both music and sound effects have the power to anchor a diegesis to reality, either through a general mimesis or through the direct evocation of real-world historical and cultural contexts. Claudia Gorbman refers to film music as a "suturing" device that "lowers thresholds of belief."[1] Similarly, Gianluca Sergi describes sound effects as "something that is used in works of fiction to add realism."[2] Janet K. Halfyard expands upon Gorbman's claims: "If music is felt to be needed in realist cinema, it is clearly even more essential in fantasy cinema."[3] Paul Taberham extends this framework to animation: "Sound sells the reality of animation to its audience, encouraging viewers to invest in the onscreen event."[4] Through these effects, a soundtrack can solidify and validate the significations of visual and narrative components, rendering the more fantastical elements of an animated text more believable. In addition, music itself can introduce specific racialized meanings. James Buhler writes about how certain musical topics in film can become associated with particular racial and ethnic groups, often in dehumanizing ways.[4] Throughout their edited collection, musicologists Ronald Radano and Philip V. Bohlman also regard music to be a major, if largely ignored, signifier of racial identity and difference.[5] Through repetition, these musical cues associate on-screen characters, settings, and events with real-world people, places, and histories, regardless of accuracy or authenticity.[6] These connotations and significations are then absorbed into the animated bodyscape, interacting with the other visual, aural, and narrative components.

The music and sound effects of *Avatar* and *Korra* impact the balance of mimesis and fantasy within their worldbuilding. As the aforementioned scholars have argued, these aural components tether their more fantastical or abstracted elements to reality. However, these parallel processes can have more complicated and nuanced effects. In addition to abetting an audience's suspension of disbelief, nondiegetic music also functions as a series of cultural signifiers through the selection of instruments, instrumentations, and performers. By tethering these shows to the real world, the music also tethers them to specific historical and cultural contexts, having an impact on the racialized identities of associated animated bodyscapes. Production narratives for *Avatar* and *Korra* highlight and seek to exploit these connections by educating perspective and established audiences. Sound effects are comparatively straightforward agents of mimesis. While they can evoke specific forms of animation production, they generally serve to ground the more fantastical elements of a text, in turn validating more specific cultural and racial signifiers. Nevertheless, individual personnel still contended with factors of authenticity, technological mediation, internal consistency, and production limitations. The resulting soundscapes constructed, ascribed, and grounded Asianness within this television franchise.

COMPOSING MUSIC

When writing about how musical scores can be used to denote specific places, Mark Brownrigg identified several key strategies of film composers.[7] Among them are approaches taken by Jeremy Zuckerman for *Avatar* and *Korra*. In order to build what he has described as a "fictional and ancient" musical score, Zuckerman gathered "ethnic instruments" to create "world music."[8] In order words, he used instruments associated with certain regions or places in order to evoke those regions or places.[9] His use of the term "world music" also requires further unpacking. In her analysis of Disney's *Brother Bear* (2003), Janice Esther Tulk critiques that film's reliance on "world music"—where typical instrumentation was accompanied by "hybrid 'flavours' of non-western instruments"—as signifiers for exoticism and Otherness at the expense of cultural specificity and accuracy.[10] Through composing "world music," then, Zuckerman was attempting to affect a form of exoticism within the scores of *Avatar* and *Korra*, was attempting to mark his musical topics as Other and different from "white culture." It is, as Buhler notes, an explicitly racialized goal.[11] Brownrigg also observes how filmmakers regularly conflate place and ethnicity as well as nation and race through film music.[12] Of course, while *Brother Bear* attempted to re-present a real—albeit nonspecific—Indigenous North American tribe, *Avatar* and *Korra* take place in a wholly original fantasy world. Even with this leeway, Zuckerman still made creative decisions that impacted the construction and ascription of an Asian identity.

One of the goals of this section is to determine how Zuckerman navigated and negotiated the racial and cultural significations of his instruments, instrumentation, and performers while creating a "fictional and ancient" soundscape. From its inception, the music of *Avatar* was envisioned to be non-Western, nontraditional, and nonspecific. Zuckerman strove for these goals through the balancing of mimesis and fantasy in his compositions. In production narratives for the first series, he has emphasized the instruments over the instrumentation as the primary cultural signifiers. As a result, he has spoken about purposefully avoiding Western instruments and large orchestras, although both appear in the series.[13] He has also stated: "It's really important to us to try to understand these instruments as much as we can and to treat them with respect."[14] Because he considered them to be signs of an authentic cultural identity, Zuckerman has regularly listed the instruments utilized for the show, being sure to acknowledge their national and cultural backgrounds.

For example, he has mentioned using the plucked chordophones *guzheng* and *pipa*, identifying them as ancient and Chinese, and has discussed how he studied them under "a master musician named Celia Liu."[15] The former is a kind of zither, one of the oldest of its type, that was played by both nobles and peasants.[16] The latter is a lute that originated in India before becoming "indispensable" to traditional Chinese music, a reminder that these instruments are not beholden to a single national or regional identity.[17] Both are noted for their versatility and range.[18] By naming these chordophones, Zuckerman established a link between his work and the historical and cultural contexts in which these instruments were first developed and popularized. Their ancient and Chinese identities were therefore transferrable to Zuckerman's compositions. He further strengthened that connection by mentioning his teacher, thus positioning himself within and a part of a musical lineage. In doing so, he indicated an impulse toward the type of archival authenticity discussed in the previous chapter, carrying on a tradition. In an interview, Zuckerman went into greater detail about what attributes these types of instruments signified in addition to ancientness and Chineseness. He recounted: "The xun is an especially powerful instrument. It is one of the oldest Chinese instruments with about 8,000 years of history and is believed by some to have been invented to imitate the crying of the villagers in a war torn village. It really does sound sad."[19] Author Li Xiaoxiang confirms that this particular aerophone produces a "deep and sorrowful tone" but dates it at 7,000 years old.[20] When naming the *guzheng*, the *pipa*, and the *xun*, Zuckerman emphasized their being Chinese as well as their being ancient or traditional. When he did go into greater detail, he focused on the emotional function of the instruments. In the case of the *xun*, rather than being divorced from its historical and cultural context, that connotation was highlighted and reinforced.

In addition to these primarily Chinese instruments, Zuckerman has also discussed using non-Asian instruments for *Avatar*. Two of the most common examples are the *duduk* or *tsiranapogh* and the *kalimba* or *mbira*. He has identified the former as an Armenian woodwind and the latter as an African chordophone.[21] Their being traditional and non-Western "ethnic instruments" was seemingly enough justification to be part of the *Avatar* soundscape. When he did elaborate, Zuckerman focused on the tones of the instruments rather than their backgrounds. In one interview, he referred to the *duduk* as "very melancholy . . . and extremely expressive."[22] Musicologist Andy Nercessian has also noted the "velvety and deeply evocative sound" of this double-reed aerophone, his book on the subject emphasizing the strong link between the *duduk* and Armenian national identity.[23] Similarly, the *mbira* has been positioned as emblematic of the Shona people, an ethnic group currently centered in Zimbabwe.[24] However, when discussing that chordophone, Zuckerman reduced its identity to simply "African." The elision of these national and ethnic specificities is understandable given that they risk diluting or counteracting the Asianness and Chineseness of the more dominant instruments and thus of the aural worldbuilding. Instead, Zuckerman has prioritized their being traditional and non-Western, flattening or erasing any greater specificity. Furthermore, the emphasis remains on emotional impact. He has adopted the same approach in his rare mentions of Western instruments. When talking about the use of the cello, for example, he does not elaborate on the historical and cultural background of the chordophone, instead only describing it as being good for "scary sounds," function divorced from context.[25] The discrepancy between the framing of different types instruments can be plainly seen in Zuckerman's account of an alternative version of the Fire Nation theme:

> Azula's theme is a variation of the main Fire Nation theme that is used throughout the series. That theme is mostly comprised of drums, bass trombones and French horns in very low registers. It's pretty masculine. We wanted to portray her femininity and power and so used the gamelan (Indonesian orchestra comprised of pitched percussion) to achieve this. We combined the gamelan's eerie bell like quality with a choir to highlight her deeply rooted and very controlled evil.[26]

For most of the series, the Fire Nation is represented with a theme that consists of predominantly Western instruments. The choice would be appropriate for an industrialized, imperialist superpower. However, Zuckerman did not feel the compulsion to expand about the backgrounds of the drums, bass trombones, and French horns utilized for the theme. For him, they signified masculinity rather than any real-world national or ethnic specificity. In contrast, when discussing Azula's pitched variation, he identified the instrumentation as Indonesian in addition to as signifiers of femininity and precision. For the former, the historical and cultural contexts of the instruments are treated as incidental. For the latter, those identities are highlighted as transferable to the final compositions. Of course, significations occur regardless of an individual's intentions. The *duduk*, *mbira*, cello, and other instruments are bearers of national and ethnic identities beyond the emotional impact of the sounds that they produce. The artist is never in complete control of these complexes of signs, as can also be further seen in the production narratives on how these instruments were performed.

In an interview for the Racebending.com, Zuckerman defined the underlying philosophy behind the instrumentation of the music of *Avatar*. He told the now defunct website: "We didn't want to portray any negative characteristics . . . to any specific culture."[27] Elsewhere, he elaborated: "I didn't want a certain culture to be ascribed to the bad guys and another culture to be ascribed to the good guys. And that was also part of the advantage of not being super traditional musically."[28] This central concern has reappeared throughout the production processes of both series. Fantastical distancing and hybridization had allowed them to appropriate and incorporate stylistic elements and motifs from a range of cultures without directly re-presenting or representing them. Sometimes, the adaptation was relatively straightforward, as seen with the Bei Fong theme introduced in "The Blind Bandit." Written to be performed on the *guzheng*, this track was adapted from the Chinese folk song "Jasmine Flower."[29] Zuckerman told Racebending.com, "They [the Bei Fong family] were upscale, and I imagined they were very traditional, and the song is very traditional. The only traditional song I really knew. Slightly modified."[30] The use of songs from a specific place to connote real-world nations or regions is another of the strategies identified by Brownrigg.[31] Musicologist Jin Jie identifies "Jasmine Flower" both as "the first Chinese folk song to become popular and well known outside China" and as a song of great cultural importance within China.[32] Once again, the qualities of being traditional and being Chinese are the ones Zuckerman stressed. He did not discuss the possible parallels between the narrative of the song—a girl wants to pick a beautiful flower but fears repercussions—and that of the episode—Toph is stifled by her rich family. Instead, its traditional nature became a signifier of the Bei Fong family's conservative values. Through all of this, Zuckerman remained adamant that—while the interviewer recognized the connection between the two—the Bei Fong theme is an adaptation of "Jasmine Flower," that it is not a direct reproduction. This composition is a rarity within the *Avatar* soundscape. For most of the music, the composer engaged in more obvious hybridizations.

According to Zuckerman, he avoided making fantasy cultures synonymous with real-world ones by playing traditional instruments in nontraditional ways.[33] It is an inverse of the second technique described by Brownrigg; instead of using traditional Western instruments to imitation non-Western instrumentations, Zuckerman used non-Western instruments to imitate Western instrumentations.[34] He elaborated: "We wound up making this kind of compromise between the ethnic instrumentation and the Western stuff. And out of that naturally, the styles merged."[35] According to the composer, this sort of transculturation was a positive for the series because—in his words—"the mixing of instruments from completely different cultures has had some really interesting results."[36] One example was the Foggy Swamp Tribe theme featured in "The Swamp." In this episode, the main characters meet a group of waterbenders coded as American "hillbillies." In addition to the aforementioned vocal performances, part of that signification comes from nondiegetic music, a *pipa* being played like a banjo, adding a bluegrass twang absent in more traditional compositions.[37] While both chordophones, these two instruments are otherwise distinct. Emblematically American, the banjo was adapted from tribal equivalents by enslaved Africans as an alternative to forbidden drums. Because of this background, Joanna R. Smolko interprets the banjo music featured in some *Looney Tunes* cartoons as signifiers of Blackness.[38] The instrument later became associated with white backwoodsmen and mountainfolk in Appalachia, as exemplified in the "dueling banjos" scene from *Deliverance* (1972).[39] The latter connotation is the one exploited in this episode of *Avatar*. Through his method, Zuckerman aimed to signify Asianness through the instrument and backwoodsness through the instrumentation. These identities were therefore combined and projected onto the associated animated bodyscapes of the members of the Foggy Swamp Tribe, complementing their character designs, animation, and vocal performances. He adopted a similar approach to conveying different identities in *Korra*. With this and other examples, Zuckerman sought to balance mimesis and fantasy. He located authenticity in the instruments rather than in how they were played. He also displayed an impulse toward mimesis in the performance of his compositions.

A second way that this composer displayed an impulse toward mimesis was through the privileging of live recordings over digital synthesis. By having physiological bodies play these membranophones or percussion instruments, aerophones or wind instruments, and chordophones or stringed instruments rather than a computer simulate those sounds, the human imperfections and texture were supposedly retained. Thus, Zuckerman sought to tether the music of *Avatar* and *Korra* to reality, to position it in relation to real historical and cultural contexts as well as the physiological bodies of the musicians. Indeed, the production narratives surrounding *Avatar* have framed live recordings as the ideal even if they were not always feasible. This emphasis can be plainly seen in discourses around the series finale, where Zuckerman indulged by hiring a sixteen-piece orchestra.[40] He recalled: "We couldn't resist the orchestra."[41] This preference is visible elsewhere in the production of the series. Tellingly, Zuckerman has been insistent that "all the ethnic instruments are performed" rather than fabricated on a computer.[42] Akin to the martial arts choreography, the physiological body of the musician is highlighted to indicate a sort of corporeal authenticity. There was a real person holding a real instrument, generating those sounds with minimal technological mediation. Otherwise, Zuckerman relied heavily on sound editing, on digitally manipulating musical notes from original or library recordings. For example, he has spoken about recording a live *taiko* performance in order to create a reference library that he could sample for new compositions.[43] Still, when following this process, he has emphasized the need for the instruments "to sound physical and acoustic."[44] He discussed the difficulty of accomplishing this task in regards to the sequel series as well: "When you use computer music elements, you don't want them to sound tech-y. It still had to sound very natural and organic and very physical and real."[45] Rather than exploit the abstract potential of synthetic music, his goal was to hide the technological mediation by aping the aural qualities of a live recording. As a result, the music helps ground the more fantastical elements of worldbuilding. The archival authenticity of the instruments and the corporeal authenticity of the performances complement and compound each other in the shared drive toward mimesis.

The blending between the natural and technological—as well as between the non-Western and the Western—is on display in the tsungi horn, a fantastical instrument heard both diegetically and nondiegetically in *Avatar*. Both Zuckerman and sound designer Benjamin Wynn have discussed the creation of this aerophone across various interviews and podcasts. They described the music as the result of "convolution," of digitally combining characteristics of the *duduk* and the trombone.[46] For Zuckerman, the goal was to make the result "sound real" and to not "sound modern and computerized."[47] If the tsungi horn did exist, then this is how a live recording would sound, so he claims. A culmination of the music of *Avatar*, this synthetic aerophone demonstrates the value placed on traditional and non-Western instruments, how they were hybridized with Western instruments and instrumentations, as well as the imitation of live recordings to disguise technological mediation. Even with the selection of a specifically Armenian woodwind, Zuckerman has emphasized its emotional function—the ability to convey melancholia—over its historical and cultural background. Regardless, those connotations remain embedded in the final sound. The blending of instruments and instrumentations result in a mixing of significations, both intentional and unintentional. The artist is never in full control of these complexes of signs. Finally, computers created fantastical sounds that did not or could exist in the real world—such as a combination of reed and brass—while still trying to sound organic. Realist conventions belie a false mimesis for something that never existed in the real world yet still tethers the fantasy to reality, a key aspect of sound design explored in a later section. These considerations persist in the production narratives surrounding the music of *Korra*.

As with *Avatar*, Zuckerman still stressed the use of traditional and identifiably Asian instruments and instrumentation for the sequel series, especially for the two-part flashback "Beginnings" (*Korra* S2E07–08). In the commentaries for these episodes, the composer identified the *guqin* as Chinese and the *shamisen* as Japanese. He also talked about researching *tanggu* and *paigu* "rhythms" as well as reusing *gamelon* orchestration.[48] However, the music for these episodes is atypical for the series, which is defined by what cocreator Bryan Konietzko described as "Chinese instruments . . . playing sort of American-style jazz."[49] This designation and its ramifications on the franchise require deeper analysis as they position the music in relation both to ancient China and to the early twentieth-century United States.

Musicologist Daniel Goldmark has written about how early US animators used jazz to signify Blackness, which for them was synonymous with primitiveness.[50] Similarly, Buhler has noted jazz's racialized function in live-action film.[51] These were not Zuckerman's stated goals with *Korra*. Instead, like the imitation of art deco and MMA, jazz signified that the world introduced in *Avatar* has evolved into a more modern and cosmopolitan one. While jazz can and has been understood primarily as American and as Black, its production and consumption have often adopted elements of hybridity, multiculturalism, and transculturation since inception. For example, E. Taylor Atkins, Alyn Shipton, Peter Keppy, and Eugene Marlow all write about how jazz spread through Asia since the 1920s.[52] Even within the United States, it would be a mistake to identify jazz as exclusively Black music just as it would be a mistake to erase the significance of Black American culture to its formation and development. Musicologist Loren Kajikawa writes at length about how Asian American musicians of the 1980s and 1990s had sought to define their racial and cultural identities through the appropriation of jazz. He specifically references how Japanese American Glenn Horiuchi and Chinese American Francis Wong navigated their heritages by performing jazz music on the *shamisen* and the *erhu*, respectively.[53] So, Zuckerman was not the first to play traditional Asian instruments in such a manner. Much like Horiuchi and Wong, Zuckerman sought to convey a hybridized identity. Whereas the first two were expressing an Asian American "essence"—to borrow Kajikawa's term—the latter sought to convey both Asianness through the instruments and a turn-of-the-century cosmopolitanism through the instrumentation. Like when he played a *pipa* as though it were a banjo, Zuckerman centered national and ethnic specificities in the instruments rather than in how he and others used them. As a result, music played on Chinese instruments would always be in some way Chinese. However, through nontraditional instrumentation, he could instill other qualities. In other words, the instrument is the noun, and the instrumentation is the adjective.

When discussing the music of *Korra*, Zuckerman frequently talked about studying early jazz or "the roots of jazz" in preparation. He specified emulating ragtime and Dixieland, going so far as to hire a professional Dixieland band to perform some incidental music that he would insert throughout the show, akin to the *taiko* drums for *Avatar*.[54] Both of these styles of music carry with them specific meanings. Ragtime has been described as an early precursor to jazz, offering similar syncopations or irregular rhythms, with its origins in the Black American music of the 1890s.[55] Dixieland refers to both the Original Dixieland Jazz Band—an all-white group from 1910s New Orleans—as well as their imitators in the 1930s and 1940s.[56] Both music styles were developed and popularized within specific historical and cultural contexts that result in particular regional as well as racial connotations. However, for Zuckerman, the most important qualities that these types of jazz offered was temporal. They complemented the visual and narrative elements that situated *Korra* in that world's equivalent of the 1920s. Anything else was incidental. To further stress this emphasis on jazz as a temporal signifier, Zuckerman described his music for the final season of *Korra*—set three years after the previous one—as emulative of the evolution from Dixieland to the "straight-ahead jazz" of the 1930s.[57] To him, the regional and racial specificity of these subsets was less relevant than how they could position the series within and in relation to the early twentieth century. This desire for hybridization in the construction of Asianness was also reflected in how these compositions were performed and recorded.

While on the *Nick Animation Podcast*, Zuckerman spoke about wanting to duplicate his experience on the *Avatar* series finale for the entirety of *Korra*: "After having the live strings, I just couldn't go back."[58] Retaining a sixteen-piece orchestra would not have been financially feasible for the new series, resulting in a string sextet. Rather than a hindrance, the composer has described the small size of his team as an advantage because it resulted in more "intimate" and more "human" sounds where one could hear the "details" and the "discrepancies."[59] Once again, the language he has used in regards to live recordings highlight the physiological bodies of the musicians, fetishizing their imperfections as indicators of a corporeal authenticity. According to Zuckerman, a key figure in realizing the vision of Chinese jazz was Hong Wang, a multi-instrumentalist with a background in both Chinese folk styles and jazz.[60] In a piece spotlighting this musician, the *Las Vegas Sun* credited Zuckerman as saying that "Wang will add little, stylistic embellishments to the music that a Western composer cannot write . . . It is these articulations that bring the music to life and add extra depth."[61] While not framed as a direct quote from Zuckerman, this sentiment suggests that, despite the emulation of American jazz, the music of *Korra* was still observably non-Western. Not only was that identity derived from the instruments being performed, Wang also contributed an irreproducibly Chinese embellishment. There is a parallel between how Zuckerman credited Wang for the music of *Korra* and his previous reference to studying Chinese instruments under Liu before *Avatar*. In both cases, their involvements signified an Asianness that Zuckerman's compositions alone could not. Across interviews and commentaries, he was not only explicitly referring to them as experts in their field, he was also implicitly identifying them as *Asian* experts in their field. That racial and cultural identity was transferred to the music that they either helped inspire or performed.

The music of *Avatar* and *Korra* are the results of transculturation, of ideas and inspirations crossing borders from a variety of sources to form new compositions. Unlike the other contact zones discussed in previous chapters, here Zuckerman is the primary contributor and the sole credited musician across both series. In his production narratives, he has emphasized the traditional and non-Western backgrounds of his selection of "ethnic instruments" as signifiers of Asianness. Nontraditional instrumentation helped distance this music from being synecdochic of specific real-world cultures as well as contributed supplemental connotations. Simultaneously, he pursued mimesis through the privileging or the aping of live recordings, emphasizing the physiological bodies and physical instruments that produced these sounds in ways that recall discussions of corporeal authenticity in the fight choreography. The result for Zuckerman and for the cocreators was a fictional and ancient soundscape, one that contributed to and reinforced the construction and ascription of Asianness. Many of these factors also impacted the production of the other aural components.

CREATING SOUND EFFECTS

On both *Avatar* and *Korra*, the sound effects were produced concurrently with the music. For each episode, Zuckerman and Wynn attended a spotting session along with the Foley team and the cocreators to go over finished animation and make initial creative decisions.[62] While music could signify Asianness through choice of instrument, instrumentation, and performance, sound effects were more restricted. Their sources generally lack equivalent explicit historical and cultural contexts that could be exploited as signifiers of Asianness. They could imitate aural conventions found in Asian media—such as anime, as *Korra* sound designer Steve Tushar noted in our interview—but such instances were exceptions within this franchise.[63] Instead, these shows primarily aped the realist conventions of live-action filmmaking practices, albeit with some room for exaggeration, akin to Taberham's "poetic authentication mode" of sound design or Paul Well's definition of hyperrealism.[64] As the primary sound designer on *Avatar* and *Korra*, Wynn drew a distinction between what he called the "realistic" or "detailed" and the "magical" or "abstract," expressing preference for the former.[65] Therefore, the mission statement for the sound effects of *Avatar* and *Korra* was to tether the fantastical elements of the franchise to reality, in turn helping ground the significations produced by visual, narrative, and other aural components. Personnel for both series strove for this goal through Foley, the live recording of original sounds, and sound design, the synthesis and editing of original sounds. Once again, in keeping with the previous section's analysis of live recordings, such mimesis also compounds signifiers of racial and cultural Asianness even when not directly contributing such connotations.

Film scholar and practitioner Vanessa Theme Ament offers a definition for Foley as "the sonic performance of the character."[66] She describes the process as supporting, enhancing, or replacing reality through the sounds of character movement.[67] These functions are exaggerated in animation, which tasks Foley artists with creating new realities.[68] *Avatar* and *Korra* Foley supervisor/mixer Aran Tanchum concurred, defining Foley as "the types of sound that are recorded . . . in sync to picture. So, that's generally the sounds of movement."[69] *Avatar* Foley engineer/mixer Jeff Kettle also described it as "anything we can record in a studio."[70] On social media, Tanchum expanded and listed three categories of Foley sound: cloth, footsteps, and props.[71] According to these personnel, there was something inherently organic and authentic to the noises that they recorded because they came from real-world sources as opposed to from technological synthesis. As Tanchum wrote: "You can think of [Foley] as the natural, organic sounds of movement."[72] Such language emphasizes a connection between the physiological bodies of the Foley artists and the animated bodyscapes of the characters. Their actions—or, more precisely, the aural recordings of their actions—are sutured to these figures, signifying mimesis and grounding them to reality by giving them weight and texture. Those sounds, therefore, become another element of indexicality within these complexes of signs. As such, they help bring this animated bodyscapes into the lived realities of the viewers, authenticating the meanings conveyed by the other components.

This process is not straightforward, as the crews of *Avatar* and *Korra* have noted. The object used to generate the sound is rarely identical to the one on screen. In a discussion with Wynn and Tanchum, Konietzko cited the use of cornstarch for snow in an episode of *Korra*.[73] Foley artist Vincent Guisetti stepped on this prop to imitate the sound of walking through snow. That specific recording was then synchronized with the animation. For such a sequence, the process would have to be invisible so as to not draw attention to itself. An audience must not think of the true source of that sound effect. While this instance allowed the Foley team to subtly and unobtrusively connect animated bodyscapes to reality, sound effects could also be either exaggerated or diminished for narrative or stylistic needs. On the commentary track for "The Terror Within," while Tanchum and Wynn discussed the accuracy and realism of the soundscape, Konietzko chimed in to point out how they would enhance certain sounds, such as cloth movement, for dramatic effect.[74] To illustrate, in a video Tanchum uploaded onto social media, Guisetti flaps a leather coat in sync with Tenzin's decidedly nonleather cape; the recorded noise is noticeably more pronounced than if he had used a more accurate material.[75] For the inverse, Konietzko also recalled that Foley for the metalbender cops' metal boots had to be removed because it was distractingly loud.[76] The primary goal of Foley on *Avatar* and *Korra* may have been to produce realistic sound effects to be sutured to these animated bodyscapes, but fantastical distancing still occurred. The props were not always identical to their on-screen counterparts, and the resulting sound effects were sometimes exaggerated or diminished. Furthermore, despite the emphasis on physiological bodies wielding physical props, technological mediation still occurred. The sounds heard by human ears are different from those recorded by a microphone, which is why Foley artists are paired with Foley engineers or supervisors in a sound booth.[77] Discourse around Foley indicates that—despite technological mediation—that connection with a physiological human body and thus with reality was preserved. Therefore, these animated bodyscapes acquired new sets of signs that grounded their more fantastical elements. By extension, connections between signifiers of Asianness and the real world were likewise reinforced.

Whereas Foley is the live recording of natural noises with minimal technological mediation, sound design entails manipulating sounds—either from a library or an original recording—to suit the needs of a given scene. While working on *Avatar*, Wynn explained how as a sound designer he would modify the envelope or shape of an existing sound effect.[78] He later expanded:

> For this show, a lot of the sounds start as some sort of natural recording but then get modified to form the movement. Again, a lot of it is about movement, and a lot of it is about intensity and filling the whole audio spectrum. So, a lot of making something impactful and powerful was about giving it bass and giving it some treble and really filling out the range so that it sounds huge.[79]

There is an incongruity between the desire for organic sound effects and the processes by which the sound designers constructed them. In this quote, Wynn emphasized the naturalness of the originals, but they nevertheless underwent technological manipulation and synthesis in order to be synchronized with final animation. The internal consistency of the show superseded the desire for real-world fidelity. Sequences featuring bending, comedy, and the Spirit World illustrate how the sound designers sought to balance mimesis and fantasy through the construction of hard sound effects—featured sounds that draw attention to themselves and to what they are sutured to—as well as of ambiences—environmental sounds without an identifiable on-screen source.

As discussed in the preceding chapter, some characters in *Avatar* and *Korra* possess the ability to manipulate or bend the elements. While water, earth, fire, and air do exist in the real world and can produce or be used to produce sounds, they do not naturally move or act in the same way as depicted in these shows. Because an unadulterated recording of reality could not be adequately synchronized to animation of bending, technological mediation was required. Wynn went into detail about how he approached creating these types of hard sound effects:

> Bryan [Konietzko] and Mike [DiMartino] always wanted the show to sound completely natural, as if the events were happening in reality. This ruled out synthesis and processing that was too obvious. So that steered me to try to find the best recordings of water, air, earth/rocks, and fire I could find. I then combined and processed these sounds to create the various different elements. We also came up with a [variety] of semi-transparent processes that I do to the sound design. Certain tricks to make it more impactful, deeper, more intense, etc. And lots of the natural sounds are augmented by highly designed ones.[80]

Like with the tsungi horn, the goal for the bending sound effects was a false mimesis. This was what bending would sound like if it existed in the real world, so he claims. Once again, the goal was to ground the more fantastical elements of the animation. Namely, it made the impossible act of someone bending water, earth, fire, or air appear believable, in turn helping make all other aspects of the show appear believable. As Tushar said, "We got to sell what they draw with the sound."[81] This task was only accomplishable through the digital manipulation of either original or preexisting audio recordings. For a waterbending subset called "bloodbending," Wynn and Tanchum removed the higher frequencies from Foley of twisting vegetables in order to "suggest muscles stressing."[82] For the earthbending in *Avatar*, Wynn processed excerpts from a sound library of crushing rocks and falling boulders.[83] On the sequel series, Tushar created the earthbending sound effects in part from work that he did for the videogame *Harry Potter and the Deathly Hallows: Part 1* (2010).[84] Wynn also pitched recordings of his own voice in order to create sound effects for firebending and airbending.[85] In regards to the former fantasy martial art, Tushar recalled editing or "tweaking" preexisting kits, specifically Wynn's work on the original series as well as his own on *Ghost Rider: Spirit of Vengeance* (2012), although those only comprised one layer out of many.[86] Whether derived from original, archival, or previously constructed sources, the sound effects used to create bending are emphasized as being mimetic, even when they were not produced by real water, earth, fire, or air. Regardless, they were digitally manipulated to create the desired effect and to synchronize with the animation. Even with this technological mediation, the resulting sound effects are identified as natural and organic, their synthetic background hidden.

For some of the more comedic moments, on the other hand, Wynn broke away from this impulse toward mimesis, although he still did not fully engage in what Taberham describes as the "flamboyant and incongruous" "zip-crash mode" of sound design from US cartoon shorts of the 1940s and 1950s.[87] For example, toward the beginning of the "The Storm," Aang jolts awake after having a nightmare, waking up Katara and Sokka. As the two boys try to go back to sleep, Katara attempts to coax Aang into talking about what is bothering him. When Sokka then offers to tell the group about his dream, his sitting up and lying down are accompanied by a rising and falling whistle. The sounds not only call attention to the character entering and exiting the frame but also mark his presence as a comedic interjection into an otherwise somber scene. A similar sound is heard in "The Cave of Two Lovers" (*Avatar* S2E02), when Sokka incredulously raises and lowers one of his eyebrows in response to a group of singing nomads. This facial movement is accentuated once again by a rising and falling whistle. This sound is indeed unrealistic, as no eyebrow is capable of producing such a noise, but it accentuates the comedy of Sokka's expression. Returning to the examples of *manpu* from the first chapter, such nonmimetic sound effects can enhance the humor of these moments as well as sometimes ground their inherently fantastical nature. When Aang gets so angry that steam shoots out from behind his head in "Lake Laogai," we hear the sped-up sound of that nondiegetic steam. In "The Beach," when Chan goes from being attracted to Azula to being intimidated by her, we hear an object whistling past, reminiscent to the Doppler effect of Wile E. Coyote falling off a cliff, synchronized with an oversized drop of sweat forming and falling down his face. Moving on to *Korra*, these comedic sound effects become more subtle. To convey Ikki's primal aggravation at being left out in "When Extremes Meet," she emits a series of animalistic snarls, nonmimetic but still associated with a diegetic element from the show, the character herself. In "Darkness Falls," after being startled by his sister, Tenzin tenses up, and we hear a faint wet flapping sound, as though the shock is reverberating throughout his body. Such aural elements, even when overtly cartoonish or exaggerated, introduce a corporality into these animated bodyscapes, grounding them in reality and therefore authenticating other sets of significations.

Wynn discussed the intentions and inspirations behind the comedic sound effects of the first series:

> The cartoonish sounds are always interesting because we've wanted to be true to the silliness of the moment but at the same time try to give them a unique sound. We didn't want to get fully [Hanna-Barbera] as

that would sound too distant from the tone of the rest of the show. The approach that we developed somewhere in the middle of the second season was using my Cwejman analog synthesizer. There's something about the color of the analog that attaches itself really easily to the world, and at times it sounds almost organic, amazingly. This style is more a nod to *FLCL* than [Hanna-Barbera].[88]

While the results were more abstracted than mimetic, Wynn's explanation still attempted to tether his sounds to the real world in two ways. First, he emphasized his desire to convey an "organic" feeling for these moments. Even though these sound effects went against realist conventions, he still tried to camouflage their synthetic nature, hence the expressed preference for analog over digital. This practice was exaggerated in *Korra*, with the sound designer recalling that the new comedic beats were more realistic and less synthetic.[89] Second, by citing the original video animation *FLCL* (2000–1) as a chief inspiration in explicit opposition to US cartoons, Wynn situated his work in relation to Japanese animation. Even if the sound effects are not mimetic, they could still be signifiers of Asianness, could still support the production of a racialized Asian identity. There is a parallel between these moments and the exaggerated facial expressions from the first chapter. When *Avatar* breaks from its hyperrealist tendencies, it often incorporates anime convention as an alternative way to connect with the real world, meaning with a specific national animation industry rather than everyday reality. These aural exaggerations are diminished in the sequel series. Tushar observed: "It's not like with *The Powerpuff Girls*, when they were just imitating Japanimation."[90] Instead, even the more fantastical and abstracted moments of comedy were anchored by relatively realistic sound effects.

Both the bending and comedic sequences in *Avatar* and *Korra* prioritized hard effects as ways to establish a link between the visuals and the real world. In addition to such moments, the sound designers also created naturalistic ambiences to construct a believable fantasy world. The negotiation of fantasy and mimesis is exemplified in sequences set in the Spirit World. Generally, everything related to the Spirits are without real-world aural referents, yet they had to be integrated in the established diegesis of *Avatar* and *Korra*. Therefore, as Wynn recalled: "That's another huge challenge with the show, portraying these things that aren't natural in our world in a sort of naturalistic way that isn't sci-fi."[91] He wanted to hide the technological mediation even when the sounds are purely synthetic. For sequences set in the Spirit Wilds in the "Beginnings" two-part episode, the sound designer recalled: "So the ambiences are . . . jungles but pitched down so they're different but sort of familiar."[92] Tushar concurred:

> There's a lot of ambiences going on that we didn't have in the first season that we had to create. Stuff that had to sound otherworldly, so we couldn't just use birds and crickets and the normal stuff. Sometimes, we would use the birds and crickets, but they'd be heavily pitched down and processed to give that otherworld kind of sound.[93]

He also recalled recycling some of the appropriately "surreal" ambiences that he had previously made for *Oz the Great and Powerful* (2013).[94] Like with the bending sequences, Wynn and Tushar filtered sounds through technological mediation in the service of internal consistency and synchronization. Furthermore, they took steps to hide the Spirit Wilds ambience's synthetic nature. Like with the comedy sequences, even though they apparently broke from mimesis through fantastical sound design, they still emphasized the organic nature of the initial audio. The nonsynthetic origins of the sounds are positioned as anchors to reality. The resulting ambience was designed to be both fantastical and grounded, to keep audiences invested in the constructed diegesis and narrative as well as to validate accompanying signifiers of Asianness.

CONCLUSION

With the rare exception, sound functions as an agent of mimesis, as an element of indexicality within the otherwise nonindexical animated diegesis. As with the visual components of worldbuilding, the production of music and sound effects reveals how the personnel of *Avatar* and *Korra* strove for authenticity, for a close association between their creations and the real world. The concepts of archival and corporeal authenticity, as described in the previous chapter, remain relevant. By naming the various musical instruments and providing a brief overview of their histories and identities, productions narratives evoke specific historical and cultural contexts. They intentionally educate audiences about the selection of referents, signaling the authenticity of the score. Even when played in a nontraditional manner, emulating banjo music or jazz, there is an expressed desire to extract and retain the "essence" of the original instrument, like with the BG designs and painting discussed in chapter 4. Non-Asian and Western instruments generally receive less attention, as they can complicate or contradict the "Asian" identity for which these shows strived. Regardless, due to their own rich and complex histories, they too introduce a range of connotations, even those that the artists do not wish to exploit. Furthermore, through the citation of live recordings, either of musical performances or of Foley sessions, there is a gesture toward corporeal authenticity. Not unlike the voice captured during a recording session, these sounds indicate the existence of a source, something real and tangible, which grounds the more fantastical and abstract elements of this animated diegesis. In turn, such aural elements help to validate or authenticate other sets of significations. Such mimesis persists, even though the recordings are highly manipulated by a sound editor, even when they are sutured to impossible objects.

Within the animated bodyscape, music and sound effects play a supporting role, enhancing and supporting existing characterization and significations provided by the animated performance, narrative components, and visual worldbuilding. In the case of *Avatar* and *Korra*, these aural components contribute to the construction of a racialized identity, an "Asianness" that audiences recognize through the evocation of real-world historical and cultural contexts as well as through the grounded sound design. Thus, a new set of components are integrated into these complexes of signs.

CONCLUSION

The animated bodyscape is a complex of signs, composed of visual, aural, and narrative components, created via distinct production processes, assembled to create the impression of a unified whole. Furthermore, animation and thus the animated bodyscape are nonindexical, iconic, and plasmatic, qualities that impact how identities form within the animated bodyscape. Over the course of five chapters, this book has tracked each type of component through various production stages, in their development of animated figures, vocal performances, and the surrounding diegesis. At each stage, individual artists made creative decisions that incorporated meaning into these components and thus into the resulting animated bodyscape. At different steps in the process, they adapted and built upon each other's work, within a complex web of delegation and collaboration. The products of their labor intersected and interacted with each other, creating new sets of meaning. By viewing production narratives through the lens of the animated bodyscape, we can better understand how and by what means animation produces and ascribes such significations, including racialized identities. While this book has limited its focus to *Avatar* and *Korra* and to the development of racialized Asian identities, the concept of the animated bodyscape remains widely applicable. Not only can it be used to study the production of other racialized identities within this television franchise, such as how it conveys Indigeneity with the Water Tribe, it can also be utilized for analyzing how visual signifiers, cultural markers, and agents of mimesis combine to create racialized identities within other animated texts.

ASSEMBLING THE ANIMATED BODYSCAPE

In the construction of the animated bodyscape, visual components combine to form the animated figure, a collection of lines and colors that resemble physiological bodies. Even when inspired by or based on a specific real-world body, these figures are wholly constructed or nonindexical. Within animated productions, the visual components originate with the character design and local color on a model sheet. It is also here where an artist first forges a connection between the animated bodyscape and the real world. They select some inspiration, including the use of models or intertextual referents, and adapt it into a character design. Through this connection, character designers and colorists transfer meanings from reality to their design, even if those connotations are not instinctively apparent to the outside viewer. In order to understand the signification of modeling Piandao after Sifu Kisu, a viewer would have to be aware of the martial arts consultant and of what he looks like. On the other hand, audiences may already have been familiar with former MMA fighter Gina Carano and have been able to recognize aspects of her appearance in Korra's design. Character designers mediate these connections by choosing which details to retrain, erase, or exaggerate. Within animation, especially mainstream US television animation, a design must be reproducible by various other personnel. In other words, it must be iconic. Through the removal of some design elements, others are amplified, in turn intensifying their significations as well as leaving room to incorporate new ones.

Next, episode directors and storyboard artists adapt these character designs into new poses, forming storyboards and eventually animatics. By exploiting the inherent plasmaticity of animation, these personnel are able to introduce additional meaning to these visual components. Their efforts are, again, aided by forging connections between their art and the real world. They can use original or preexisting reference footage, such as for acting or fight choreography, to create more realistic movements and expressions. The resulting poses are, thus, closer to an audience's understanding of how a physiological body would move, grounding other significations. In addition, the storyboard artist can add intertextual references, evoking memories of certain films, television series, or other pieces of media. For example, the ending of the fight between Katara and Pakku in "The Waterbending Master" references the *wuxia* film *House of Flying Daggers*. The image of Katara holding Aang's lifeless body in "The Crossroads of Destiny" resembles Michelangelo's *Pietà*. The use of *manpu* and exaggerated expressions across the franchise places these characters and series in relation to Japanese animation. However, the animated figure is more than a collection of line drawings. They must be animated through the production of key and in-between frames as well as digital inking and coloring. Once again, artists at this stage can introduce new meanings to these visual components. Once again, the use of reference footage can tether their work to the real world. After animation, there is a period of correction and retakes, especially for adjusting the colors. The result is the animated figure.

Now, the specifics of this extensive process can differ depending on what kind of animation is used for a particular text. Given their nature, *Avatar* and *Korra* exemplify the nonindexicality, iconicity, and plasmaticity of the animated bodyscape. However, the prevalence of these qualities can be mitigated by alternative types of animation. As addressed in the first chapter, rotoscoping and motion-capture both introduce a stronger element of indexicality into an animated bodyscape, recording the movement of physiological bodies if not their form. Still, layers of artistic and technological mediation can introduce additional meaning. In addition, depending on the type of material used for the puppet, stop-motion can affect iconicity or plasmaticity. In general, without the need for key or in-between animators to reproduce an image across multiple stills, a character's design can possess greater detail and specificity in stop-motion animation. Furthermore, by working with a limited number of puppets per character, there is less room for animators to radically alter their visual appearances without damaging or substituting the puppets between frames. Finally, for computer animation, we run into a similar scenario, just with a digital puppet rather than a material one. However, this type of animation does grant animators a greater ability to exploit the animated figure's plasmaticity. When analyzing the animated bodyscapes produced by these additional animation methods, one should take into account how these processes impact the creation and assemblage of visual components. That said, the resulting animated figure still serves the same function within the animated bodyscape, introducing sets of visual signifiers that can ascribe racialized identities. Regardless of the method of its production, upon competition, the animated figure is ready to be sutured with a vocal performance and form an animated performance.

The vocal performance is composed of aural components, developed across another extensive series of production processes. While sound offers an element of indexicality, they are ultimately defined by layers of technological and artistic mediation. Recording sessions generate line readings or aural building blocks, which are recorded via microphones, the first layer of technological mediation. This stage is informed by the casting process, by the decision of who to invite into this room for these sessions. The actor's creative instincts and how they pronounce certain words inform the nature of these aural building blocks, the first layer of artistic mediation. These line readings are also affected by feedback from the voice director and other personnel, a second layer. Through these collaborations, line readings suggesting age, gender, nationality, and other dimensions of identity may be introduced and incorporated into an animated bodyscape. The aural building blocks are then assembled into a dialogue track. Sound editors select which line readings to incorporate as well as digitally manipulate the sound as needed. For example, for the third season of *Avatar*, Zach Tyler Eisen's voice was artificially pitched to match Aang's age. Mako's and Greg Baldwin's line readings as Iroh were combined to create a single vocal performance for some episodes toward the end of the second season. These additional layers of artistic and technological mediation result in a cyborg voice, neither fully organic nor fully mechanical. Depending on when they were produced, the dialogue track can inform the development of storyboards and of animation or vice versa. Once animation has been completed and after a round of corrections and retakes, these vocal performances are synchronized with animated figures, producing animated performances. The voice is thus severed from a physiological body and sutured to an animated figure. Now, the practice of dubbing does cast doubts on the importance of vocal performances within the animated bodyscape. After all, if they can be replaced for international releases without fundamentally altering the core text, then how significant can they be to the production of identity? The best solution, in my mind, is to view the dubbed versions of a text as wholly separate from the original, with their own sets of distinct animated bodyscapes.

Finally, an animated performance is not the same as an animated bodyscape. These figures do not exist within a vacuum but within and in relation to a fantastical diegesis that was also wholly constructed. This world-building occurs when artists select a real-world referent and adapt it into visual, aural, or narrative components, which accumulate to form the diegesis of a text. Narrative components are produced via the writing process. To create an episode, a premise is developed into an outline and then into a script, which in turn is adapted into storyboards, with studio executives interjecting with their notes along the way. When creating a setting, BG artists adapt real-world referents into BG designs, which BG painters adapt into BG key paintings, which overseas BG painters adapt into additional BG paintings depicting the setting from other angles and distances. For fight choreography, storyboard artists adapt the scripts, notes from consultants, and reference footage into storyboards, which are then adapted into animation. For both music and sound effects, original and preexisting recordings are edited into the soundscape. These and various other processes synthesize to produce a fantastical world or diegesis, one connected to but distinct from a viewer's lived reality. As examples of high fantasy, *Avatar* and *Korra* illustrate an extreme version of this fantasification. However, the process occurs even within animated works that hew closer to our lived reality, that are set in more explicit versions of our world. Regardless of where a text falls on the spectrum between mimesis and fantasy, the adaptation and transformation of real-world referents creates meaning not only for the constructed world but also for the characters who live in it. These sundry visual, aural, and narrative components form the context for the animated performance, projecting new layers of signification that are incorporated into the animated bodyscape, complementing or contradicting preexisting significations.

Thus, the animated figure, vocal performance, and diegesis unite to form the animated bodyscape, a complex of signs produced by a series of artists across various processes. While the animated bodyscape is defined by its nonindexicality, its constructedness, it is also defined by its highly mediated relationship with reality. Through the process of fantasification, meanings from our world have been transferred to animated ones. These connections must exist, otherwise the content of an animated text would literally mean nothing to either the artists producing it or to the audience consuming it. The viewer must relate what they see and hear in a show to their own lived experiences or to their understanding of the real world in order for these visual, aural, and narrative components to actually mean anything. Thus, real-world understandings of race are adapted into racialized identities.

CREATING MEANING IN ANIMATION

Artists can and do manipulate the connections between fantasy and reality to create meaning. They remove, add, and modify certain details to both extract desired significations and integrate their work into an established diegesis. When the real-world connection is blatant, then there is a risk of introducing unintentional significations. As *Avatar* cultural consultant Edwin Zane warned, there are consequences to creating a villainous culture within a fantasy world. The connotations can go both ways, especially within a media environment with limited representation for certain communities. By modeling early drafts of Fire Nation armor after Japanese samurai, character designers marked both the Fire Nation as Japanese and the Japanese as the bad guys. By naming the Ba Sing Se secret police after Dai Li, the writers evoked that real person's long and complicated history as well as reduced him to a villain. This is a common pattern within the *Avatar* television franchises. While there are some deep dives into the significance and significations of real-world concepts, places, and histories, various personnel also evoked rich historical and cultural contexts when they were only seeking superficial connotations. Thus, fight choreographers transformed the quick and dynamic kicks of Northern Shaolin into firebending, irrespective of the style's actual history. Thus, BG designers reduced entire Southeast Asian nations into signifiers of wealth or poverty for different Fire Nation villages. These practices are not inherently bad. Those artists were tasked with creating visual, aural, and narrative components that would signal to a viewer what to think about certain characters, settings, and objects. However, those meanings were derived from real-world contexts with their own rich and complex histories. A work of narrative fiction, especially one otherwise so divorced from our own reality, cannot fully unpack them. The real-world sources for these referents are infinitely more nuanced and complicated than how they could possibly be rendered.

The adaptation and incorporation of Western referents in this television franchise introduces additional issues, from the centering of North American English to the fantasification of European and US landmarks. Within the age of globalization and neocolonialism, determining what is truly Western or non-Western is a fraught and perhaps even self-defeating task. There is a fallacy of authenticity, which privileges premodern and preindustrial versions of certain cultures, ignoring or erasing how they have evolved in recent centuries. Still, it should be noted that the artists behind *Avatar* and especially *Korra* were unable or perhaps unwilling to imagine a version of this fantasy world that undergoes modernization and industrialization without taking on the attributes of specific real-world Western cultures. This is, in no small part, due to how "modernization" and "industrialization" are so synonymous with "Westernization." Thus, an alternative path of technological development was inconceivable, at least in a way that both the artists and their presumed audience could recognize. Remember, for any of these components to have meaning, both producers and consumers must be able to relate them to what they have experienced, to what they have been taught, or to other pieces of media. At the same time, a non-Western culture that adopts, adapts, or otherwise responds to Western influences is not invalidated, is not inauthentic. For example, Asian countries and artists have transformed art deco architecture and jazz music to suit their purposes, which *Korra* duplicates in its rendering of a modern world. Both can and do evoke modernity without erasing Asianness.

There are also some components that, at first, do not seem to have explicit racial or cultural significance, but they are nevertheless part of the animated bodyscape, intersecting and colliding with other elements within those complexes of signs. Such components do not evoke specific communities or contexts so much as they convey a general mimesis, grounding and validating the more fantastical elements of a text. They thus reinforce the meanings and identities produced by other visual, aural, and narrative components. For example, a hyperrealist animation aesthetic seeks to render animated worlds and characters as though they were recorded by a camera. Doing so strengthens the tethers between the designs of these settings or figures and the real world, helping viewers recognize them from and relate them to their own lived experiences. Similarly, naturalistic vocal performances suggest how these characters would talk if they were real, in turn grounding both the speakers and the content of their dialogue, regardless of how fantastical either of them is. In addition, realistic sound design conveys what certain actions—especially character movement—or environments would sound like if they were recorded by a microphone. In *Avatar* and *Korra*, sound helps authenticate the acts of bending and therefore the martial arts associated with them. Thus, the archival and corporeal authenticity of the choreography are abetted through sound. These agents of mimesis are important parts of the animated bodyscape as they play a supporting role in selling the meanings that the other production processes generate. Attempts to analyze the production and ascription of racialized identities in animation should therefore also give attention to how such components are produced as well as how they function within the animated bodyscape. However, while *Avatar* and *Korra* usually aim for hyperrealism and naturalism, there are moments when they lean closer to abstract than mimetic. For this franchise, such instances typically gesture toward conventions within Japanese animation, forging connections to specific national industries rather than expressing a general mimesis. Nevertheless, such agents of abstraction within these and other animated texts can distance the animated bodyscape from the real world and the viewer's lived experiences. The production and function of both types of components—those that ground and those that distance—should be considered when discussing racialized identities and the animated bodyscape.

The meanings of a text are produced not only by the artists who made it but also by the audience who consumed it. Thus, while the animated bodyscape relies on connections that artists forged between its various components and the real world, the efficacy of those signifiers is dependent on audience knowledge. Sometimes, a viewer may interpret things differently than the artist had intended. As discussed in the first chapter, Zane read Zuko's scar as emulative of a port-wine stain, which in turn he read as indicative of an Asian identity. One can also consider the tendency for ORP among white anime fans. For the most part, though, artists rely on what they assume to be common knowledge among a prospective viewership. Celebrities are cast because of their recognizable voices, which infuse their line readings with aspects of their star personas. *Korra* utilized this method to flesh out characters with limited screen time, casting Aubrey Plaza as Eska and Jon Heder as Ryu. In such instances, the voice was never fully severed from the physiological body that generated it; the two remained tethered for the transference of meaning. This phenomenon is even starting to apply to more traditional voice actors, as online fandoms transform them into celebrities in their own right. Actors are also directed to perform certain types of accents and dialects, exploiting stereotypes for characterization. Across the *Avatar* television franchise, elderly characters deliver sage advice in Asian accents. The concepts of "yellow voice" and "brown voice" literally describe how such performances are not reflective of real-world accents or dialects but instead of the expectations of white Euro-American audiences when they see an Asian character on screen. Playing on this theme, artists can exploit often distorted views of real-world communities, which can be derived from other forms of popular entertainment. How much of the "Asia" that informed the worldbuilding of the *Avatar* television franchise was based on exported wushu films and anime rather than on actual cultures and histories?

Alternatively, in order for the desired meaning of a text to be perceived, artists take steps to educate prospective and established audiences about the connections between their work and the real world. For larger projects, studios produce sundry paratexts that surround the core text. For *Avatar*, behind-the-scenes videos were aired during commercial breaks, informing viewers about the real-world wushu that inspired the different types of bending. Such paratexts also appeared on home video releases, providing curated insights into the various production processes and introducing key personnel. Official art books, published by Dark Horse, listed the real-world referents for character, BG, and prop designs. Outside of the direct control of the studio, third-party publications aided in the education process. Across interviews and podcasts, individual personnel from *Avatar* and *Korra* filled in the gaps of the studio-affiliated paratexts, often providing greater detail on their selection of real-world referents. Such sources tend to fall into two categories: text-focused ones, which were often promoting a new season of a show, and artist-focused ones, which emphasized the role of one person within the production process. In addition, these individual artists, in the course of developing and maintaining their own personal brands, would utilize social media platforms, highlighting how they informed the construction and assemblage of the animated bodyscape. Armed with information from these sources, audiences are able to better recognize how certain components of an animated bodyscape are tethered to specific historical and cultural contexts as well as when a character design is modeled after a real person. Such knowledge impacts how the racialized identities ascribed to these animated bodyscapes pertain to the viewer's real-world understanding of race.

This book has focused on production narratives for *Avatar* and *Korra*, on how individual components were created and assembled into seemingly unified wholes. However, it could also have been about how viewers recognize and interpret those visual, aural, and narrative elements. The animated bodyscape, as a concept, can be utilized in a variety of ways, not just as outlined in this volume. Similar to Amy Shirong Lu's study of ORP in connection to anime, one could examine of how different viewers react to the animated figures, vocal performances, and surrounding diegesis of *Avatar* and *Korra*, taking into account their own racial backgrounds, their prior knowledge of these series, and their exposure to behind-the-scenes paratexts. How would these subjects read these individual components as indicative of a racialized identity? Such a project would greatly complement my own. This approach could also be utilized for the study of other animated texts.

USING THE PLANETARY PRODUCTION MODEL

While individual artists can make creative decisions regarding the production and ascription of racialized identity to the animated bodyscape, they do so within the confines of specific production cultures. The choices and actions of individuals are informed by a complex web of collaboration and delegation. By understanding their place within such work environments, we can better understand the role of individuals within the production of meaning. By adopting the concept of the animated bodyscape, this book has been able to illustrate the intricate network of communities that transmit visual, aural, and narrative components between each other in the production of an animated text. This system can be best conceptualized in the form of a planetary model, depicting a series of interlocking production communities that adapt and modify each other's work. As the components of the animated bodyscape progress through the different processes, layers of artistic and technological mediation emphasize the nonindexicality, iconicity, and plasmaticity of animation. Everything is constructed. Even recordings of reality, such as the voice, music, and other sounds, undergo intense digital manipulation for synchronization with animation. Everything is streamlined. Designs must be reproducible by various artists across departments and across national borders. Everything is fluid. Across various reproductions and adaptations, space opens up for artists to introduce new meanings, even within a hyperrealist aesthetic.

At the center of this model is the main planetary body or primary site of production. While part of the same whole, this sphere is divided into several distinct continents, each representing a different department or process. The art department oversees character design, coloring, BG designs and paintings, and prop designs. The various directing teams are composed of storyboard artists. The writers' room contains the writing staff. Due to their physical proximity, the residents of these different continents remain in regular and informal communication with each other. Thus, head writer Aaron Ehasz can discuss how the writing process was informed by his casual interactions with BG supervisor Elsa Garagarza. This attribute helps to transform these production communities into contact zones, where representatives of different cultures—both within and outside of this planetary model—exchange ideas.

These relationships are noticeably different from those between the main planetary body and its orbiting satellites. Surrounding the primary site of production are various freelancers, remote workers, consultants, and executives who beam down formal communication without being fully integrated into any of the production communities. As sound designer on *Korra*, Steve Tushar worked from home. As the voice of Aang, Eisen conducted his recording sessions remotely, as did Jennie Kwan and Seychelle Gabriel for select episodes. As the translator and calligrapher, Siu-Leung Lee only corresponded with Bryan Konietzko via email. Even the ultimate decision makers, the executives, communicated their wishes through formal notes to the respective departments. Casual conversations during lunch or while passing each other in the halls could not be a regular occurrence. Nevertheless, all of these artists still impacted the production and ascription of meaning to animated bodyscape.

Farther beyond these orbiting satellites are lunar bodies or secondary sites of production. These production communities are geographically distinct from the central planetary body and are often divided into their own sets of continents, representing their own distinct departments and processes. In addition to domestic companies that provided postproduction services, the most visible type of lunar body for *Avatar* and *Korra* has been the overseas animation studios. These secondary sites receive some of the visual, aural, and narrative components from the central planet and transform them into the final animation, with only retakes, corrections, and the postproduction work remaining for when they send their work back stateside. Given how much of their efforts remain visible in the final product, one could argue that shows like *Avatar* and *Korra* are ultimately more Korean than American. At the very least, it certainly adds credence to Yoo Jae-myung's claim of ownership over these productions. Nevertheless, these overseas studios are only one of the many stops that these visual, aural, and narrative components make before they are finally assembled into the animated bodyscape.

The concept of the animated bodyscape encourages the examination not only of the individual components that make up animated figures, vocal performances, and the surrounding diegesis but also how those elements were made. Specifics may vary between texts, but largescale productions like *Avatar* and *Korra* are universally the result of interlocking communities as outlined above. Therefore, the planetary model can be easily adapted to suit the needs of a given case study. When applied to an animated film or television series, it illuminates the choices and actions of individual artists, how they operated within a production culture, as well as how they all responded to, adapted, and built on each other other's work. The planetary model thus highlights that the final product, the animated bodyscape—a seemingly unified whole with a seemingly unified racialized identity—is in fact a complex of complementary and contradictory signs.

CLOSING THOUGHTS

The concept of the animated bodyscape has applications beyond this one case study. While the *Avatar* television franchise is an illustrative example of the strengths of this approach to analyzing race and animation, the purpose of this book has always been to provide a blueprint for future research. As demonstrated across the past five chapters, the animated bodyscape emphasizes how constructed identities are formed through the production and assemblage of distinct components across different processes. By understanding these individual steps, the creative choices made by individuals, and the relationships within and between production communities, we have a better understanding of how and by what means racialized identities are produced and ascribed in animation. Animated texts construct meaning by forging, mediating, and exploiting connections to the real world, which audiences are then either expected or instructed to recognize. Race may not exist in animation, but real-world understandings of race inform the production of racialized identities within animation. The animated bodyscape also has applications beyond the study of racialized identities, as any type of constructed identity derived from the real world and depicted in an animated text can be analyzed using this concept. Looking at *Avatar* and *Korra* alone, one could utilize this concept to explore how these series construct gender and sexuality, especially with the character of Korra, or ability, especially with the character of Toph. In general, though, race, gender, sexuality, age, ability, nationality, and infinite other systems of categorization and types of communities are all conveyed through the animated bodyscape.

NOTES

INTRODUCTION

1. Irene Kotlarz, "The Birth of a Notion," *Screen* 24.2 (1982): 21–29. Kotlarz makes a passing reference to Japanese caricatures, but her focus remains on Blackness.

2. Ibid.: 21–22.

3. For articles, see Karl Cohen, "Racism and Resistance: Black Stereotypes in Animation," *Animation Journal* 4.2 (1996): 43–68; Richard Neupert, "Trouble in Watermelon Land: George Pal and the Little Jasper Cartoons," *Film Quarterly* 55.1 (2001): 14–26; Xavier Fuster Burguera, "Muffled Voices in Animation. Gender Roles and Black Stereotypes in Warner Bros. Cartoons: From Honey to Babs Bunny," *Bulletin of the Transilvania University of Brașov* 4.2 (2011): 65–76. For book-length studies, see Christopher P. Lehman, *The Colored Cartoon: Black Presentation in American Animated Short Films, 1907–1954* (Amherst, MA: University of Massachusetts Press, 2007); Nicholas Sammond, *Birth of an Industry: Blackface Minstrelsy and the Rise of American Animation* (Durham, NC: Duke University Press, 2015).

4. For some exceptions, see Daniel Goldmark, *Tunes for 'Toons: Music and the Hollywood Cartoon* (Berkeley, CA: University of California Press, 2005), 77–106; Joanna R. Smolko, "Southern Fried Foster: Representing Race and Place through Music in Looney Tunes Cartoons" *American Music* 30.3 (2012): 344–72. In his book on music in classic cartoons, Goldmark devotes a chapter to the racial components of jazz. Smolko similarly explores the racial components of Stephen Foster songs in *Looney Tunes* and *Merrie Melodies* cartoons.

5. Sarah Banet-Weiser, *Kids Rule!: Nickelodeon and Consumer Citizenship* (Durham, NC: Duke University Press, 2007), 154, 171. For more articles on Blackness in relatively more recent US animation, see Sianne Ngai, "'A Foul Lump Started Making Promises in My Voice': Race, Affect, and the Animated Subject," *American Literature* 74.3 (2002): 571–601; C. Richard King, Mary K. Bloodsworth-Lugo, and Carmen R. Lugo-Lugo, eds., Animated Representations of Blackness [Special Issue], *Journal of African American Studies* 14.4 (2010); Michael Boyce Gillespie, *Film Blackness: American Cinema and the Idea of Black Film* (Durham, NC: Duke University Press, 2016). On a related subject, for a study of how some early 2000s cartoons appropriate cultural forms and practices from Black culture in order to reify whiteness, see Michael A. Chaney, "Coloring Whiteness and

Blackvoice Minstrelsy: Representations of Race and Place in *Static Shock*, *King of the Hill*, and *South Park*," *Journal of Popular Film and Television* 31.4 (2004): 167–84.

6. Hugh Klein and Kenneth S. Shiffman, "Race-Related Content of Animated Cartoons," *Howard Journal of Communication* 17 (2006): 163–82.

7. Ibid.: 174.

8. C. Richard King, Mary K. Bloodsworth-Lugo, and Carmen R. Lugo-Lugo, "Animated Representations of Blackness," *Journal of African American Studies* 14.4 (2010): 395; Lehman, 1; Sammond, 5–7, 29–30.

9. Shilpa Davé, "Apu's Brown Voice: Cultural Inflection and South Asian Accents," *East Main Street: Asian Popular Culture*, eds. Shilpa Davé, LeiLani Nishime, and Tasha G. Oren (New York: New York University Press, 2005): 313–36; Shilpa Davé, *Indian Accents: Brown Voice and Racial Performance in American Television and Film* (Champaign: University of Illinois Press, 2013); Alison [Reiko] Loader, "We're Asian, More Expected of Us: Representation, The Model Minority & Whiteness on *King of the Hill*," *Animation Studies* 5 (2010); Hye Seung Chung, "From 'Me So Horny' to 'I'm So Ronery': Asian Images and Yellow Voices in American Cinema," *Film Dialogue*, ed. Jeff Jaeckle (New York: Wallflower Press, 2013): 172–91.

10. Abid Rahman, "The Simpsons' Addresses Apu Stereotype Controversy," *Hollywood Reporter* (8 Apr. 2018); Yohana Desta, "*The Simpsons* Still Doesn't Understand the Problem with Apu," *Vanity Fair* (9 Apr. 2018); Bill Keveney, "'The Simpsons' exclusive: Matt Groening (mostly) Remembers the Show's record 636 episodes," *USA Today* (27 Apr. 2018); Pilot Viruet, "The Creator of 'BoJack Horseman' Doesn't Want to Ignore Animation's Diversity Problem Anymore," *UPROXX* (30 Jan. 2018); Inkoo Kang, "*BoJack Horseman*'s Raphael Bob-Waksberg Talks About Coming to Terms with the 'Original Sin' of the Show's All-White Cast," *Slate* (12 Sep. 2018); E. Alex Jung, "Raphael Bob-Waksberg, In Good Faith the *BoJack Horseman* creator on Times Up, Bad Men, and His Apology Tour," *Vulture* (20 Sep. 2018); Erik Pedersen, "Watchdog Group Chides Laika for 'White-Washing' 'Kubo and the Two Strings,'" *Deadline* (23 Aug. 2016); Mikelle Street, "The 'Kubo and the Two Strings' Controversy Proves Whitewashing Is More Complicated Than You Think," *Complex* (23 Aug. 2016); Steve Rose, "Wes Anderson's Isle of Dogs: Loving Homage to Japan or Cultural Appropriation?," *The Guardian* (26 Mar. 2018).

11. Rick Porter, "'Big Mouth,' 'Central Park' to Recast Jenny Slate, Kristen Bell with Black Actors for Biracial Characters," *Hollywood Reporter* (24 Jun. 2020); Rick Porter, "'The Simpsons' to Recast Characters of Color, 'Family Guy' Actor Stops Voicing Black Role," *Hollywood Reporter* (26 Jun. 2020); Sonia Rao, "'The Simpsons' and 'Big Mouth' Are Recasting Nonwhite Roles. But It's About More Than Finding the Right Voices," *Washington Post* (2 Jul. 2020).

12. Denise Petski, "'Central Park': Emmy Raver-Lampman Joins Apple Series in Recasting for Mixed-Race Character Originally Voiced by Kristen Bell," *Deadline Hollywood* (24 Jul. 2020); Danielle Turchiano, "'Big Mouth': Ayo Edebiri to Replace Jenny Slate as Missy (EXCLUSIVE)," *Variety* (28 Aug. 2020); Denise Petski, "'The Simpsons': The New Voice of Hank Azaria's Carl Is Revealed," *Deadline Hollywood* (24 Sep. 2020); Nellie Andreeva, "'Family Guy': Arif Zahir Replaces Mike Henry as Cleveland Brown on Fox Animated Series," *Deadline Hollywood* (25 Sep. 2020).

13. Samantha Blackmon, "Pickanninnies and Pixels: On Race, Racism and Cuphead at E3," *NYMG* (17 Jun. 2015); Yussef Cole, "Cuphead and the Racist Spectre of Fleischer Animation," *Unwinnable* (10 Nov. 2017).

14. Matthew Desmond and Mustafa Emirbayer, "What Is Racial Domination?" *Du Bois Review: Social Science Research on Race* 6.2 (2009): 336; Matthew Desmond and Mustafa Emirbayer, *Race in America* (New York: Norton, 2016), 32.

15. Robin O. Andreasen regularly acknowledges this discrepancy in his own work. For more, see Robin O. Andreasen, "A New Perspective on the Race Debate," *British Journal for the Philosophy of Science* 49 (1998): 199–225; Robin O. Andreasen, "Race: Biological Reality or Social Construct?" *Philosophy of Science* 67 (2000): S653–S666; Robin O. Andreasen, "The Cladistic Race Concept: A Defense," *Biology and Philosophy* 19 (2004): 425–42; Robin O. Andreasen, "The Meaning of 'Race': Folk Conceptions and the New Biology of Race," *Journal of Philosophy* 102.2 (Feb. 2005): 94–106.

16. Carl Linneaus, *Systema Naturae*, 10th ed., vol. 1 (1758), 20–22.

17. For more on this history, please see the following work, which I have very briefly summarized above, Edward W. Said, *Orientalism*, 25th anniv. ed. (New York: Vintage Books, 1994); Elazar Barkan, *The Retreat of Scientific Racism: Changing Concepts of Race in Britain and the United States between the World Wars* (Cambridge: Cambridge University Press, 1992); Audrey Smedley and Brian D. Smedley, *Race in North American: Origin and Evolution of a Worldview* (Boulder: Westview Press, 1993); Stephen Jay Gould, *The Mismeasure of Man* (New York: Norton, 1996); C. Loring Brace, *"Race" is a Four-Letter Word: The Genesis of the Concept* (Oxford: Oxford University Press, 2005).

18. Walter Lippmann, *Public Opinion* (New York: Harcourt, Brace and Company, 1922), 79–94.

19. While they were not the first writings on social attitudes toward race, the following studies on the development and impact of racial and ethnic stereotypes reveal a shift in attitudes toward race as a scientific concept in the 1930s and 1940s: Daniel Katz and Kenneth Braly, "Racial Stereotypes of One Hundred College Studies," *Journal of Abnormal and Social Psychology* 28.3 (1933): 280–90; Richard T. LaPiere, "Types-Rationalizations of Group Antipathy," *Special Forces* 15.2 (1936): 232–54; Daniel J. Levinson and R. Nevitt Sanford, "A Scale for the Measurement of Anti-Semitism," *Journal of Psychology* 17.2 (1944): 339–70.

20. Gayatri Chakravorty Spivak, "Can the Subaltern Speak?" *Marxism and the Interpretation of Culture*, eds. Cary Nelson and Lawrence Grossberg (Urbana: University of Illinois Press, 1988), 276.

21. Donald Bogle, *Toms, Coons, Mulattoes, Mammies, and Bucks: An Interpretive History of Blacks in American Films* (New York: Continuum, 2000), 4.

22. Anne Anlin Cheng, *Ornamentalism* (Oxford University Press, 2019).

23. For more on the "perpetual foreigner" myth and its impact on Asian American individuals, communities, and identity, see Frank H. Wu, *Yellow: Race in American beyond Black and White* (New York: Basic Books, 2003), 79–129; Nancy Wang Yuen, "Performing Race, Negotiating Identity: Asian American Professional Actors in Hollywood," *Asian American Youth: Culture, Identity, and Ethnicity*, eds. Jennifer Lee and Min Zhou (New York: Routledge, 2004), 251–68; Stephanie Greco Larson, *Media & Minorities: The Politics*

of Race in News and Entertainment (Lanham, MD: Rowman & Littlefield, 2006), 67–80; Catherine A. Luther, Carolyn Ringer Lepre, and Naeemah Clark, *Diversity in U.S. Mass Media*, 1st ed. (Malden, MA: Wiley-Blackwell, 2012), 130–51; Ashley Isola, "Yellowface, the Yellow Peril, and the Rise of the Kung Fu Master," *TCNJ Journal of Student Scholarship* XCII (2015): 1–4.

24. For more on the "model minority" myth and its impact on Asian American individuals, communities, and identity, see Wu, 59–67.

25. For more on "yellowface performances" and their role in defining and racializing Asian and Asian American identity within the US popular imagination, see Karla Rae Fuller, "Creatures of Good and Evil: Caucasian Portrayls of the Chinese and Japanese during World War II," *Classic Hollywood, Classic Whiteness*, ed. Daniel Bernardi (Minneapolis: University of Minnesotra Press, 2001), 281–300; Sean Metzger, "Charles Parsloe's Chinese Fetish: An Example of Yellowface Performance in Nineteenth-Century American Melodrama," *Theatre Journal* 56.4 (2004): 627–51; Krystyn R. Moon, *Yellowface: Creating the Chinese in American Popular Music and Performance, 1850s–1920s* (New Brunswick, NJ: Rutgers University Press, 2005); Amanda Rogers, "Asian Mutations: Yellowface from More Light to the Royal Shakespeare Company's *The Orphan of Zhao*," *Contemporary Theatre Review* 24.4 (2014): 452–66.

26. Moon, 40–42.

27. Nichola Dobson, *Historical Dictionary of Animation and Cartoons* (Lanham, MD: Scarecrow, 209), xxxvii–xxxviii.

28. Charles Solomon, "Toward a Definition of Animation," *The Art of Animation* (Los Angeles: American Film Institute, 1987), 10.

29. Georges Sifianos, "The Definition of Animation: A Letter from Norman McLaren," *Animation Journal* 3.2 (1995): 63.

30. Maureen Furniss, *Art in Motion: Animation Aesthetics*, rev. ed. (Eastleigh, UK: John Libbey, 2007), 5.

31. Paul Wells and Samantha Moore, *The Fundamentals of Animation*, 2nd ed. (London: Fairchild Books, 2016), 7.

32. Nicholas Mirzoeff, *Bodyscape: Art, Modernity, and the Ideal Figure* (London: Rougledge, 1995), 3.

33. Vicki Mayer, Miranda J. Banks, and John T. Caldwell, "Introduction: Production Studies: Roots and Routes," *Production Studies: Cultural Studies of Media Industries*, eds. Vicki Mayer, Miranda J. Banks, and John T. Caldwell (New York: Routledge, 2015), 2; John T. Caldwell, *Production Culture: Industrial Reflexivity and Critical Practice in Film and Television* (Durham, NC: Duke University Press, 2008), 2.

34. David Hesmondhalgh and Sarah Baker, *Creative Labour: Media Work in Three Cultural Industries* (London: Routledge, 2011), 7; Caldwell, 375; Jennifer Mason, "Qualitative Interviewing: Asking, Listening and Interpreting," *Qualitative Research in Action*, ed. Tim May (London: SAGE, 2002), 237.

35. Caldwell, 4, 5; Amanda D. Lotz and Horace Newcomb, "The Production of Entertainment Media," *A Handbook of Media and Communication Research: Qualitative and Quantitative Methodologies*, ed. Klaus Bruhn Jenson (New York: Routledge, 2012), 75, 79.

36. For examples of such texts, see David Rosen and Peter Hamilton, *Off-Hollywood: The Making and Marketing of Independent Films* (New York: Grove Weidenfeld, 1990); Tom Sito, *Drawing the Line: The Untold Story of the Animation Unions from Bosko to Bart Simpson* (Lexington: University Press of Kentucky, 2006); Miranda J. Banks, *The Writers: A History of American Screenwriters and Their Guild* (New Brunswick, NJ: Rutgers University Press, 2015).

37. Sito, 213, 217.

38. Paul Wells, *Animation and America* (Edinburgh, UK: Edinburgh University Press, 2002), 74; Paul Wells, "'Smarter Than the Average Art Form': Animation in the Television Era," *Prime Time Animation: Television Animation and American Culture*, eds. Carol A. Stabile and Mark Harrison (London: Routledge, 2003), 24–25.

39. Jason Mittell, "The Great Saturday Morning Exile: Scheduling Cartoons on Television's Periphery in the 1960s," *Prime Time Animation: Television Animation and American Culture*, ed. Carol A. Stabile and Mark Harrison (London: Routledge, 2003), 45–46; M. Keith Booker, *Drawn to Television: Prime-Time Animation from "The Flintstones" to "Family Guy"* (Westport, CT: Praeger, 2006), x.

40. For examples of this type of scholarship, see Adolfo Aranjuez, "'The Legend of Korra' and Minority Representation," *Screen Education* 78 (2015): 24–27; Jobia Keys, "*Doc McStuffins* and *Dora the Explorer*: Representations of Gender, Race, and Class in US Animation," *Journal of Children and Media* 10.3 (2016): 355–68.

41. Heather Hendershot, "Introduction: Nickelodeon and the Business of Fun," *Nickelodeon Nation: The History of Politics, and Economics of America's Only TV Channel for Kids*, ed. Heather Hendershot (New York: New York University Press, 2004), 9; Banet-Weiser, 63.

42. Linda Simensky, "The Early Days of Nicktoons," *Nickelodeon Nation: The History, Politics, and Economics of America's Only TV Channel for Kids*, ed. Heather Hendershot (New York: New York University Press, 2004), 93.

43. Ibid., 87–88.

44. Ibid., 102.

45. Banet-Weiser, 61.

46. Ibid., 145.

47. Ibid., 152–58.

48. Giannalberto Bendazzi, *Cartoons: One Hundred Years of Cinema Animation*, trans. Anna Taraboletti-Segre (Bloomington: Indiana University Press, 1994); Susan J. Napier, *Anime from "Akira" to "Howl's Moving Castle": Experiencing Contemporary Japanese Animation* (New York: Palgrave Macmillian, 2005); Rayna Denison, "The Global Markets of *Anime*: Miyazaki Hayao's *Spirited Away* (2001)," *Japanese Cinema: Texts and Contexts*, eds. Alastair Phillips and Julian Stringer (London: Routledge, 2007); Rayna Denison, *Anime: A Critical Introduction* (London: Bloomsbury Academic, 2015); Tze-yue G. Hu, *Frames of Anime: Culture and Image Building* (Hong Kong: Hong Kong University Press, 2010); Brian Ruh, "Adapting Anime: Transnational Media Between Japan and the United States,: (PhD diss., Indiana University, 2012) 102; Jonathan Clements, *Anime: A History* (Basingstoke, NH: Palgrave Macmillan, 2013); Ian Condry, *The Soul of Anime: Collaborative Creativity and Japan's Media Success Story* (Durham, NC: Duke University Press, 2013);

Michal Daliot-Bul and Nissim Otmazgin, *The Anime Boom in the United States: Lessons for Global Creative Industries* (Cambridge, MA: Harvard University Press, 2017).

49. Ruh, 102. The author adds: "Of course these waves are only abstract and concretized periods of time and were in reality more continuous and interrelated."

50. Daliot-Bul and Otmazgin, 112.

51. Michael Dante DiMartino and Bryan Konietzko, *Avatar: The Last Airbender—The Art of the Animated Series* (Milwaukie: Dark Horse Books, 2010), 126–29.

52. "Behind the Scenes Kung Fu Featurette" (supplementary material on DVD release of *Avatar: The Last Airbender—The Complete Book 1 Collection*), Viacom International Inc. (2006); "How *Avatar* Gets Its Kicks," *Nick Mag Presents* (Sep. 2006): 42–43; "The Essence of Bending with Bryan Konietzko and Sifu Kisu" (supplementary material on DVD release of *Avatar: The Last Airbender—The Complete Book 2 Collection*), Viacom International Inc. (2007).

53. DiMartino and Konietzko, 34–37.

CHAPTER ONE: THE VISUAL COMPONENTS OF THE ANIMATED BODYSCAPE

1. For examples of writings on blackface and yellowface, see Robert C. Toll, *Blacking Up: The Minstrel Show in Nineteenth Century America* (New York: Oxford University Press, 1974); Eric Lott, *Love and Theft: Blackface Minstrelsy and the American Working Class* (New York: Oxford University Press, 1993); Karla Rae Fuller, "Creatures of Good and Evil: Caucasian Portrayals of the Chinese and Japanese during World War II, *Classic Hollywood, Classic Whiteness*, ed. Daniel Bernardi (Minneapolis: University of Minnesota Press, 2001), 281–300; Krystyn R. Moon, *Yellowface: Creating the Chinese in American Popular Music and Performance, 1850–1920s* (New Brunswick, NJ: Rutgers University Press, 2005); Anjali Vats and LeiLani Nishime, "Containment as Neocolonial Visual Rhetoric: Fashion, Yellowface, and Karl Lagerfeld's 'Idea of China,'" *Quarterly Journal of Speech* 99.4 (2013): 423–47; Amanda Rogers, "Asian Mutations: Yellowface from *More Light* to the Royal Shakespeare Company's *The Orphan of Zhao*," *Contemporary Theatre Review* 24.4 (2014): 452–66.

2. For more on these debates concerning animation and indexicality, see Jacqueline Ristola, "Realist Film Theory and Flowers of Evil: Exploring the Philosophical Possibilities of Rotoscoped Animation," *Animation Studies Online Journal*, 3 Feb. 2018; Nea Ehrlich, "The Animated Documentary: Animation's Dual Indexicality in Mixed Realities," *Animation: Interdisciplinary Journal* 15.3 (2020): 260–75.

3. Rudolf Arnheim, *Film as Art* (London: Faber and Faber LTD, 1958), 175.

4. Paul Wells, *Animation: Genre and Authorship* (London: Wallflower, 2002), 73.

5. Jane Batkin, *Identity in Animation: A Journey into Self, Difference, Culture and the Body* (London: Routledge, 2017), 1.

6. "Commentary on Rebirth" (supplementary material on Blu-ray release of *The Legend of Korra—Book Three: Change*), Viacom International Inc. (2014).

7. Furniss, 5.

8. Paul Wells, *Understanding Animation* (London: Routledge, 1998), 25–26.

9. Scott McCloud, *Understanding Comics: The Invisible Art* (New York: HarperPerennial, 1994), 30.

10. Paul Wells, *The Animated Bestiary: Animals, Cartoons, and Culture* (New Brunswick, NJ: Rutgers University Press, 2008), 3–4.

11. Jared Gardner, "Same Difference: Graphic Alterity in the Works of Gene Luen Yang, Adrian Tomine, and Derek Kirk Kim," *Multicultural Comics: From Zap to Blue Beetle*, ed. Frederick Luis Aldama (Austin: University of Texas Press, 2010), 136.

12. McCloud, 36.

13. Annabelle Honess Roe, *Animated Documentary* (New York: Palgrave Macmillan, 2013), 108.

14. Derek Parker Royal, "Introduction: Coloring America: Multi-Ethnic Engagements with Graphic Narratives," *MELUS* 32.3 (2007): 10.

15. McCloud, 43–44.

16. Koichi Iwabuchi, *Recentering Globalization: Popular Culture and Japanese Transnationalism* (Durham, NC: Duke University Press, 2002), 28.

17. Rayna Denison, "Transcultural Creativity in Anime: Hybrid Identities in the Production, Distribution, Texts and Fandom of Japanese Anime," *Creative Industries Journal* 3.3 (2011): 226; Jane Leong, "Reviewing the 'Japaneseness' of Japanese Animation: Genre Theory and Fan Spectatorship," *Cinephile: The University of British Columbia's Film Journal* 7.1 (2011): 21.

18. Iwabuchi, 71–72.

19. Amy Shirong Lu, "What Race Do They Represent and Does Mine Have Anything to Do with It? Perceived Racial Categories of Anime Characters," *Animation: An Interdisciplinary Journal* 4.2 (2009): 169–90.

20. Terry Kawashima, "Seeing Faces, Making Races: Challenging Visual Tropes of Racial Difference," *Meridians* 3.1 (2002): 176.

21. Ueno Toshiya, "Techno-Orientalism and Media-Tribalism: On Japanese Animation and Rave Culture," *Third Text* 13.47 (1999): 97.

22. Daliot-Bul and Otmazgin, 124.

23. Ben Blacker, "Episode 154: Legend of Korra/Avatar: The Last Airbender," *Nerdist Writers Panel*, 19 Aug. 2014.

24. DiMartino and Konietzko, 24–25.

25. Edwin Zane (3 Mar. 2018), phone interview.

26. Blacker.

27. Zane.

28. "Port Wine Stain (PWS)," *The Vascular Birthmarks Foundation*, n.d.

29. Ho Wai Sun, et al., "Laser Treatment on Congenital Facial Port-Wine Stains; Long-Term Efficacy and Complication in Chinese Patients," *Lasers in Surgery and Medicine: The Official Journal of the American Society for Laser Medicine and Surgery* 30.1 (2002): 44–47; Yoo-Soo Cindy Bae, Elise Ng, and Roy G. Geronemus, "Successful Treatment of Two Pediatric Port Wine Stains in Darker Skin Types Using 595 nm Laser," *Lasers in Surgery*

and Medicine: The Official Journal of the American Society for Laser Medicine and Surgery 48.4 (2016): 339–42; Yu Wenxin, et al., "Shorter Intervals of East Asians with Port-Wine Stain with Pulsed Dye Laser Are Safe and Effective—A Prospective Side-by-Side Comparison," *Photomedicine and Laser Surgery* 36.1 (2018): 37–43.

30. DiMartino and Konietzko, 54, 67, 110.

31. Michael Dante DiMartino, Bryan Konietzko and Joaquim Dos Santos, *The Legend of Korra: The Art of the Animated Series—Book One: Air* (Milwaukie, OR: Dark Horse Books, 2013), 65; Michael Dante DiMartino, Bryan Konietzko and Joaquim Dos Santos, *The Legend of Korra: The Art of the Animated Series—Book Three: Change* (Milwaukie, OR: Dark Horse Books, 2015), 35; Michael Dante DiMartino, Bryan Konietzko and Joaquim Dos Santos, *The Legend of Korra: The Art of the Animated Series—Book Four: Balance* (Milwaukie, OR: Dark Horse Books, 2015), 44.

32. Marissa Lee, "Statement from Dao Le, Animatic Editor," Racebending.com, 31 Jul. 2009.

33. DiMartino and Konietzko, 54, 157.

34. DiMartino and Konietzko, 140; "Audio Commentary—Chapter 4: Sokka's Master" (supplementary material on DVD release of *Avatar: The Last Airbender—The Complete Book 3 Collection*), Viacom International Inc. (2008).

35. "Commentary on Reunion" (supplementary material on Blu-ray release of *The Legend of Korra—Book Four: Balance*), Viacom International Inc. (2015).

36. Sergei Eisenstein, *Eisenstein on Disney*, ed. Jay Leyda, trans. Alan Upchurch (London: Methuen, 1988), 21.

37. Wells, *Understanding*, 188, 213.

38. Batkin, 1–2.

39. Steve Tillis, "The Art of Puppetry in the Age of Media Production," *The Drama Review* 43.3 (Fall 1999): 182–95.

40. Juan Meza-Leon (21 Jul. 2018), Skype interview.

41. Olga Ulanova (22 May 2018), Google Hangouts interview.

42. Acastus, "Interview with Director Giancarlo Volpe (part 1 of 3)," *AvatarSpirit.net*, 16 Jun. 2006; "Commentary on Original Airbenders" (supplementary material on Blu-ray release of *The Legend of Korra—Book Three: Change*), Nickelodeon (2014); "The Spirit of an Episode: Original Airbenders" (supplementary material on Blu-ray release of *The Legend of Korra—Book Three: Change*), Nickelodeon (2014).

43. Michael Dante DiMartino, Bryan Konietzko, and Joaquim Dos Santos, *"The Legend of Korra": The Art of the Animated Series—Book Two: Spirits* (Milwaukie, OR: Dark Horse Books, 2014), 52, 86; DiMartino, Konietzko, and Dos Santos, *Change*, 21; "Audio Commentary—Chapter 3: The Revelation" (supplementary material on Blu-ray release of *The Legend of Korra—Book One: Air*), Viacom International Inc. (2014); "Commentary on The Southern Lights" (supplementary material on Blu-ray release of *The Legend of Korra—Book Three: Change*), Viacom International Inc. (2014); "Commentary on Night of a Thousand Stars" (supplementary material on Blu-ray release of *The Legend of Korra—Book Two: Spirits*), Viacom International Inc. (2014); "Commentary on A New Spiritual Age" (supplementary material on Blu-ray release of *The Legend of Korra—Book Two: Spirits*), Viacom International Inc. (2014).

44. DiMartino, Konietzko, and Dos Santos, *Change*, 95.

45. "Commentary on Enemy at the Gates" (supplementary material on Blu-ray release of *The Legend of Korra—Book Four: Balance*), Viacom International Inc. (2015); DiMartino, Konietzko, and Dos Santos, *Balance*, 18.

46. Acastus, "Interview with Director Giancarlo Volpe (part 3 of 3)," *AvatarSpirit.net*, 1 Jul. 2006.

47. Meza-Leon; "The Spirit of an Episode: Rebirth" (supplementary material on Blu-ray release of *The Legend of Korra—Book Three: Change*), Viacom International Inc. (2014).

48. Meza-Leon.

49. "Commentary—Reunion."

50. "Commentary on The Guide" (supplementary material on Blu-ray release of *The Legend of Korra—Book Two: Spirits*), Viacom International Inc. (2014).

51. Meza-Leon.

52. Napier, 27–34.

53. Denison, *Anime*, 3–4.

54. Hu, 137–63.

55. Stevie Suan, "Anime's Performativity: Diversity through Conventionality in a Global Media-Form," *Animation: An Interdisciplinary Journal* 12.1 (2017): 64.

56. Koji Aihara and Kentaro Takekuma, *Even a Monkey Can Draw Manga Vol. 1*, trans. Yuji Oniki (San Francisco: Viz Communications, Inc., 2002), 19; Thomas J. Wallestad, "Developing the Visual Language of Comics: The Interactive Potential of Japan's Contributions," *Hyōgen Bunka* 7 (2012): 5; Daliot-Bul and Otmazgin, 116.

57. Suan, 73.

58. "Audio Commentary—Chapter 17: Lake Laogai" (supplementary material on DVD release of *Avatar: The Last Airbender—The Complete Book 2 Collection*), Viacom International Inc. (2007).

59. Aihara and Takekuma, 19; Wallestad, 7.

60. Aihara and Takekuma, 19.

61. "Audio Commentary—Chapter 5: The Beach" (supplementary material on DVD release of *Avatar: The Last Airbender—The Complete Book 3 Collection*), Viacom International Inc. (2008).

62. Wallestad, 6.

63. "Audio Commentary—Chapter 8: When Extremes Meet" (supplementary material on Blu-ray release of *The Legend of Korra—Book One: Air*), Viacom International Inc. (2012).

64. DiMartino, Konietzko, and Dos Santos, *Spirits*, 160.

65. Suan, 70.

66. Meza-Leon. For Aang's performance, he recalled being directed to reference characters from *Time Bandits* (1981), *E.T. the Extra-Terrestrial* (1982), *The Goonies* (1985), and *Hook* (1991).

67. Ulanova.

68. "Commentary on The Ultimatum" (supplementary material on Blu-ray release of *The Legend of Korra—Book Three: Change*), Viacom International Inc. (2014).

69. DiMartino and Konietzko, 34–37; "The Making of Avatar—Inside the Korean Studios" (supplementary material on DVD release of *Avatar: The Last Airbender—The Complete Book 1 Collection*), Viacom International Inc. (2006).

70. "Commentary—New"; "Commentary on A Breath of Fresh Air" (supplementary material on Blu-ray release of *The Legend of Korra—Book Three: Change*), Viacom International Inc. (2014); "Commentary on Enter the Void" (supplementary material on Blu-ray release of *The Legend of Korra—Book Three: Change*), Viacom International Inc. (2014).

71. Hector Navarro, "Episode 1: Bryan Konietzko & Michael Dante DiMartino," *Nick Animation Podcast*, 13 May 2016.; "Audio Commentary—Chapter 20: Sozin's Comet, Part 3: Into the Inferno" (supplementary material on DVD release of *Avatar: The Last Airbender—The Complete Book 3 Collection*), Viacom International Inc. (2008); DiMartino and Konietzko, 34.

72. Blacker.

73. Ibid.

74. DiMartino and Konietzko, 34.

75. "Inside the Book of Spirits" (supplementary material on Blu-ray release of *The Legend of Korra—Book Two: Spirits*), Viacom International Inc. (2014).

76. Susan Lee MacDonald, "The INNERview #61—Yoo Jae-myung (유재명), Animation director," *The INNERview with Host Susan Lee MacDonald*, 2 May 2013. Translation by Ro Kaylin.

77. Baek Byung-yeul, "'Drawing Animation Is Our DNA,'" *The Korea Times*, 8 May 2015. No credited translator.

78. "Making—Korean." No credited translator.

79. Ibid.

80. Ibid.

81. Ibid.

82. Ibid.

83. Blacker.

84. Mark Lasswell, "Kung Fu Fightin' Anime Stars, Born in the U.S.A.," *New York Times*, 28 Aug. 2005.

85. MacDonald.

86. For more on the rise of global value chains (GVCs) and their effects on Korean animation, see Joonkoo Lee, "Three Worlds of Global Value Chains: Multiple Governance and Upgrading Paths in the Korean Animation Industry," *International Journal of Cultural Policy* 25.6 (2019): 684–700.

87. Joon-Yang Kim, "Critique of the New Historical Landscape of South Korean Animation," *Animation: An Interdisciplinary Journal* 1.1 (2006): 61–81. The first major success for South Korean animation occurred after the publication of this article, with *Leafie, A Hen in the Wild* (*Madangeul Naon Amtak*, 2011). Nevertheless, the undervaluing of Korean animation for anything other than outsourcing has persisted, as seen when one compares the massive success of the live-action *Train to Busan* (*Busanhaeng*, 2016) to the underwhelming reception of its animated sister film, *Seoul Station* (*Seoulyeok*, 2016).

88. For a more extensive account of Yoo and Studio Mir's strategies for creating and maintaining a recognizable studio brand despite not owning the intellectual property of any of their work, see Grace Han, "Musings on Mir: Finding a Name in American Animation," *Fantasy/Animation*, 27 Aug. 2021.

89. Bryan Konietzko, "Korra Crew Profile: Sylvia Filcak-Blackwolf," Tumblr, 31 Jul. 2013.

90. Kris Wimberly, "TAN—Ep43: Color Compositing Supervisor, Sylvia Filcak-Blackwolf," *The Animation Network Podcast*, 7 Mar. 2016.

91. "Commentary—Southern Lights."

92. "Audio Commentary—Episode 19: The Siege of the North—Part 1" (supplementary material on DVD release of *Avatar: The Last Airbender—The Complete Book 1 Collection*), Viacom International Inc. (2006).

93. DiMartino and Konietzko, 77.

94. Bryan Konietzko, Tumblr, 28 Jun. 2013.

95. Bryan Konietzko, Tumblr, 2 Jul. 2013.

96. DiMartino, Konietzko, and Dos Santos, *Spirits*, 13.

97. Konietzko, 2 Jul.

98. Ibid.

99. Ibid.

CHAPTER TWO: THE AURAL COMPONENTS OF THE ANIMATED BODYSCAPE

1. Toll, 161–62; Lott, 95; Joyce Flynn, "Melting Plots: Patterns of Racial and Ethnic Amalgamation in American Drama before Eugene O'Neill," *American Quarterly* 38.3 (1986): 426; Melvin Patrick Ely, *The Adventures of Amos 'n' Andy: A Social History of American Phenomenon* (Charlottesville: University Press of Virginia, 1991), 2; Michelle Hilmes, "Invisible Men: Amos 'n' Andy and the Roots of Broadcast Discourse," *Critical Studies in Mass Communication* 10.4 (1993): 308; Angela Chia-yi Pao, "False Accents: Embodied Dialects and the Characterization of Ethnicity and Nationality," *Theatre Topics* 1.1 (2004): 357.

2. Michael Newman and Angela Wu, "'Do You Sound Asian When You Speak English?' Racial Identification and Voice in Chinese and Korean Americans' English," *American Speech* 86.2 (2011): 152–78; Eric R. Kushins, "Sounding Like Your Race in the Employment Process: An Experiment on Speaker Voice, Race Identification, and Stereotyping," *Race and Social Problems* 6.3 (2014): 237–48.

3. Rick Altman, "Introduction: Four and a Half Film Fallacies," *Sound Theory, Sound Practice*, ed. Rick Altman (New York: Routledge, 1992), 40–41; Edward Branigan, "Sound and Epistemology in Film," *Journal of Aesthetics and Art Criticism* 47.4 (1989): 313.

4. Roland Barthes, *Image, Music, Text*, trans. Stephen Heath (London: Fontana, 1977).

5. David Zinder, *Body-Voice-Imagination: A Training for the Actor* (London: Routledge, 2002); Sarah Case, *The Integrated Voice: A Complete Voice Course for Actors* (London: Nick Hern Books, 2013).

6. Given the character designs previously discussed, the phenomenon of "whitewashing" is pertinent. For live-action film and television, this term refers to when a character of color is rewritten to be white. For animation, it has been expanded to describe when a white actor is cast to voice a character of color. How they came about and their effects on the construction and ascription of racialized identities require unpacking.

7. Jennie Kwan (25 Aug. 2021), Google Meet interview.

8. Acastus, "Interview with Joanna Braddy (part 1 of 2)," *AvatarSpirit.net*, 30 Nov. 2006.

9. "Commentary on Battle Zaofu" (supplementary material on Blu-ray release for *The Legend of Korra—Book Four: Balance*), Viacom International Inc. (2015).

10. Acastus, "Interview with Jessie Flower (part 1 of 2)," *AvatarSpirit.net*, 22 Dec. 2006; "Audio Commentary—Chapter 17: The Ember Island Players" (supplementary material on DVD release of *Avatar: The Last Airbender—The Complete Book 3 Collection*), Viacom International Inc. (2008); "Audio Commentary Chapter 4: The Voice in the Night" (supplementary material on Blu-ray release of *The Legend of Korra—Book One: Air*), Viacom International Inc. (2012); Hector Navarro, "Episode 46: The Legend of Korra Cast," *Nick Animation Podcast*, 20 Oct. 2017.

11. Kwan.

12. Janet Varney (20 Sep. 2017), email interview.

13. Nancy Wang Yuen, *Reel Inequality: Hollywood Actors and Racism* (New Brunswick, NJ: Rutgers University Press, 2016), 50–51.

14. Ibid., 51–57.

15. Ibid., 54.

16. Ibid., 40.

17. Ed Liu, "From Tiny Toons to Brave & Bold: Toon Zone Interviews Voice Director Andrea Romano," *Toon Zone*, 5 Aug. 2008.

18. Ibid.

19. Ibid.

20. Zane.

21. Liu, "From."

22. Varney.

23. Acastus, "Interview with Voice Director Andrea Romano (part 1 of 3)," *AvatarSpirit.net*, 12 May 2007; Liu, "From"; "Audio Commentary—Chapter 16: The Southern Raiders" (supplementary material on DVD release of *Avatar: The Last Airbender—The Complete Book 3 Collection*), Viacom International Inc. (2008).

24. Chris Hardwick, "Episode 621: Andrea Romano," *Nerdist Podcast*, 7 Jan. 2015.

25. "Commentary—Southern Raiders."

26. Lisa Granshaw, "An Oral History of Avatar: The Last Airbender: Cast Looks Back as Show Celebrates 10th Anniversary of Finale," *SYFY Wire*, 30 Jul. 2018.

27. Varney.

28. Kwan.

29. Ibid. Kwan credits this mantra to another voice director.

30. Acastus, "Voice"; "Commentary—Southern Raiders"; Hardwick.

31. Kwan.

32. Acastus, "Interview with Crawford Wilson (part 1 of 2)," *AvatarSpirit.net*, 15 Nov. 2006; Acastus, "Jessie"; "Commentary—Ember"; Varney.

33. Kwan.

34. Navarro, "1"; "Commentary—Battle."

35. Acastus, "Voice."

36. Kwan.

37. Gordon W. Allport, *The Nature of Prejudice* (Reading, MA: Addison-Wesley Publishing Company, 1954), 131–32; Donald T. Campbell, "Stereotypes and the Perception of Group Difference," *American Psychologist* 22.10 (1967): 825.

38. Here, I use "North American English" to refer to a flattened, generic US or Canadian dialect that eludes regional specificity, the type often employed by news anchors. In common parlance, it would be considered "English without an accent."

39. Eric Goldman, "IGN Interview: Jason Isaacs," *IGN*, 15 Feb. 2007.

40. "Commentary—Guide."

41. Ibid.

42. "Commentary—Battle."

43. "Commentary—Guide."

44. "Commentary on After All These Years" (supplementary material on Blu-ray release of *The Legend of Korra—Book Four: Balance*), Viacom International Inc. (2015).

45. In the first season, the character Tahno derisively refers to Korra as the "uh-vatar," mimicking the Indian pronunciation of "avatar" from the live-action film.

46. Sam Summers, "High Fantasy Meets Low Culture in *How to Train Your Dragon* (2010)," *Fantasy/Animation: Connections between Media, Mediums and Genre*, ed. Christopher Holliday and Alexander Sergeant (London: Routledge, 2018), 233–35.

47. Francis M. Agnoli, "Animating Race in 'She-Ra and the Princesses of Power,'" *Animation Studies* 2.0, 13 Jul. 2020.

48. Rosina Lippi-Green, *English with an Accent: Language, Ideology, and Discrimination in the United States* (London: Routledge, 1997), 101–3.

49. John A. Dixon, Bernice Mahoney, and Roger Cocks, "Accents of Guilt? Effects of Regional Accent, Race, and Crime Type on Attribution of Guilt," *Journal of Language and Social Psychology* 21.2 (2002): 162–68; Cheryl J. Boucher, et al., "Perceptions of Competency as a Function of Accent," *Psi Chi Journal of Psychological Research* 18.1 (2013): 27–32; Ze Wang, et al., "'You Lost Me at Hello': How and When Accent-Based Biases Are Expressed and Suppressed," *International Journal of Research in Marketing* 30.2 (2013): 185–97; Nicholas Close Subtirelu, "'She Does Have an Accent but . . .': Race and Language Ideology in Students' Evaluations of Mathematics Instructors on Ratemyprofessors.com," *Language in Society* 44.1 (2015): 35–62.

50. Homi Bhaba, "Of Mimicry and Man: The Ambivalence of Colonial Discourse," *October* 28 (1984): 126; Yuen, 10.

51. Cynthia Kwei Yung Lee, "Beyond Black and White: Racializing Asian Americans in Society Obsessed with O.J.," *Hastings Women's Law Journal* 6.2 (1995): 203.

52. Davé, "Apu's"; Loader; Hye Seung Chung, "From 'Me So Horny' to 'I'm So Ronery': Asian Images and Yellow Voices in American Cinema," *Film Dialogue*, ed. Jeff Jaeckle (New York: Wallflower, 2013): 172–91.

53. Chung, 184–86.
54. Liu, "From."
55. Chung, 173.
56. Susan Mandala, *The Language of Science Fiction and Fantasy: The Question of Style* (London: Continuum, 2010), 76, 92, 96.
57. Davé, "Apu's," 314, 317; Chung, 187.
58. Davé, *Indian*, 85–110.
59. Jean-Louis Baudry, "The Apparatus," *Camera Obscura* 1 (1976), 110.
60. Branigan, 313.
61. Baudry, 110; Altman, "Introduction" 40–43; Tom Levin, "The Acoustic Dimension: Notes on Cinema Sound, *Screen* 25.3 (1984): 56–57.
62. Michel Chion, *The Voice in Cinema*, trans. Claudia Gorbman (New York: Columbia University Press, 1999); Rick Altman, "The Material Heterogeneity of Recorded Sound," *Sound Theory, Sound Practice*, ed. Rick Atlman (New York: Routledge, 1992): 14–31.
63. Michel Chion, *Audio-Vision: Sound on Screen*, trans. Claudia Gorbman (New York: Columbia University Press, 1994), 5.
64. Mary Ann Doane, "The Voice in the Cinema: The Articulation of Body and Space," *Yale French Studies* 60 (1980): 33–34.
65. Ibid., 37.
66. Rick Altman, "Moving Lips: Cinema as Ventriloquism," *Yale French Studies* 60 (1980): 67, 69, 73.
67. William Johnson, "The Liberation of Echo: A New Hearing for Film Sound," *Film Quarterly* 38.4 (1985): 3; Branigan, 311.
68. Johnson, 3.
69. Gianluca Sergi, "Actors and the Sound Gang," *Screen Acting*, ed. Alan Lovell and Peter Krämer (London: Routledge, 1999), 36.
70. Pamela Robertson Wojcik, "The Sound of Film Acting," *Journal of Film and Video* 58.1/2 (2006): 80.
71. Starr A. Marcello, "Performance Design: An Analysis of Film Acting and Sound Design," *Journal of Film and Video* 58.1/2 (2006): 60, 62.
72. "Commentary—Battle."
73. "Commentary—Southern Raiders."
74. Kwan; "Commentary—Voice."
75. Ed Liu, "Toon Zone News Interviews Bryan Konietzko & Mike DiMartino on 'Avatar the Last Airbender,'" *Toon Zone*, 22 Apr. 2008.
76. "Commentary—Southern Raiders."
77. "Audio Commentary—Chapter 2: A Leaf in the Wind" (supplementary material on Blu-ray release of *The Legend of Korra—Book One: Air*), Viacom International Inc. (2012).
78. Kwan.
79. "Commentary—Southern Raiders."
80. "Commentary—Enemy."
81. Joe Bevilacqua, "Celebrity Voice Actors: The New Sound of Animation," *Animation World Magazine* 4.1 (1999); Marcello.

82. Richard Dyer, *Heavenly Bodies: Film Stars and Society* (London: Routledge, 2004), 4–5.

83. Martin Shingler, "Fasten Your Seatbelts and Prick Up Your Ears: The Dramatic Voice in Film," *Scope: An Online Journal of Film Studies* 5 (2006). Shingler cites David Bromwich on James Stewart, Vicky Lowe on Robert Donat, and Philip Kemp on Claude Rains as examples.

84. Colleen Montgomery, "Pixarticulation: Vocal Performance in Pixar Animation," *Music, Sound, and the Moving Image* 10.1 (2016): 10–14; Rayna Denison, "Star-Spangled Ghibli: Star Voices in the American Versions of Hayao Miyazaki's Films," *Animation: An Interdisciplinary Journal* 3.2 (2008): 137–38.

85. Bevilacqua; Marcello, 63–64; Martin Barker, "Introduction," *Contemporary Hollywood Stardom*, eds. Thomas Austin and Martin Barker (London: Arnold, 2003), 20; Paul Wells, "To Affinity and Beyond: Woody, Buzz and the New Authority," *Contemporary Hollywood Stardom*, ed. Thomas Austin and Martin Barker (London: Arnold, 2003), 94; Christopher Holliday, *The Computer-Animated Film: Industry, Style and Genre* (Edinburgh: Edinburgh University Press, 2018), 153–54.

86. Tanine Allison, "Blackface, *Happy Feet*: The Politics of Race in Motion Capture and Animation," *Special Effects: New Histories/Theories/Contexts*, eds. Dan North, Bob Rehak, and Michael Duffy (London: Palgrave, 2015), 114–15.

87. Some long-running shows with iconic characters rather than high-profile celebrity voice actors have also played major roles in mainstream discussions of race and animation, most notably *The Simpsons* and *Family Guy*.

CHAPTER THREE: THE NARRATIVE COMPONENTS OF THE ANIMATED BODYSCAPE

1. W. R. Irwin, *Game of the Impossible: A Rhetoric of Fantasy* (Urbana: University of Illinois Press, 1977); Rosemary Jackson, *Fantasy: The Literature of Subversion* (London: Methuen, 1981); Kathryn Hume, *Fantasy and Mimesis: Responses to Reality in Western Literature* (New York: Methuen, 1984).

2. Irwin, 9, 189.

3. Jackson, 8, 19–20, 42–43.

4. Hume, 20.

5. George Slusser and Eric S. Rapkins, "Introduction: Shadows of the Magic Lamp," *Shadows of the Magic Lamp: Fantasy and Science Fiction in Film*, eds. George Slusser and Eric S. Rabkin (Carbondale: Southern Illinois University Press, 1985), vii; Kenneth von Gunden, *Flights of Fancy: The Great Fantasy Films* (Jefferson, NC: McFarland, 2001), vii.

6. Christopher Holliday and Alexander Sergeant, "Introduction: Approaching Fantasy/Animation," *Fantasy/Animation: Connections between Media, Mediums and Genres*, eds. Christopher Holliday and Alexander Sergeant (New York: Routledge, 2018), 2, 6.

7. James O. Young, *Cultural Appropriation and the Arts* (Oxford, UK: Blackwell, 2008), 6–7.

8. Richard A. Rogers, "From Cultural Exchange to Transculturation: A Review and Reconceptualization of Cultural Appropriation," *Communication Theory* 16 (2006): 477.

9. Desmond and Emirbayer, *Race*, 310–12.

10. Ibid., 312–14.

11. Aaron Ehasz (10 May 2018), Google Hangout interview.

12. Tim Hedrick (21 Sep. 2018), email interview; Tim Hedrick (24 Sep. 2018), email interview.

13. DiMartino and Konietzko, 122.

14. Harish Johari, *Chakras: Energy Centers of Transformation* (Rochester, VT: Destiny Books, 2000), 1; The Editors of Encyclopædia Britannica, "Chakra," *Encyclopædia Britannica Online* (Encyclopædia Britannica, Inc., 4 Sep. 2018).

15. Johari, 2; John A. Grimes, *A Concise Dictionary of India Philosophy: Sanskrit Terms Defined in English* (Albany: State University of New York Press, 1996), 100–101, 265, 390.

16. Johari, 2; Grimes, 390.

17. For consistency and clarity, I refer to the real-world concept as "qi" and the *Avatar* version as "chi."

18. The Editors of Encyclopædia Britannica, "Qi," *Encyclopædia Britannica* (10 Aug. 2018).

19. Brian Kennedy and Elizabeth Guo, *Chinese Martial Arts Training Manuals: A Historical Survey* (Berkeley, CA: Blue Snake Books, 2005), 15, 20, 26–33; Lu Shengli, *Combat Techniques of Taiji, Xingyi, and Bagua: Principles and Practices of Internal Martial Arts*, trans. Zhang Yun and Susan Darley (Berkeley, CA: Blue Snake Books, 2006), 37–38; Alexandra Ryan, "Globalisation and the 'Internal Alchemy' of Chinese Martial Arts: The Transmission of Taijiquan to Britain," *East Asia Science, Technology and Society: An International Journal* 2.4 (2008): 527; Peter Allan Lorge, *Chinese Martial Arts from Antiquity to the Twenty-First Century* (Cambridge: Cambridge University Press, 2011), 10–11, 201; Wang Guangxi, *Chinese Kung Fu*, trans. Han Huizhi, Wang Wenliang, and Kang Jin (Cambridge: Cambridge University Press, 2012), 6; Hsiao-Hung Chang, "The Unbearable Lightness of Globalization: On the Transnational Flight of *Wuxia* Film," *Cinema Taiwan: Politics, Popularity and State of the Arts*, eds. Darrell William Davis and Ru-Shou Robert Chen (London: Routledge, 2007), 96–98.

20. Johari, 2; Grimes, 239.

21. Otherwise credited as "Acupuncturist," his name is only revealed on his business card with the logogram 郭 (Guō).

22. "Commentary on Old Wounds" (supplementary material on Blu-ray release of *The Legend of Korra—Book Three: Change*), Viacom International Inc., 2014.

23. Roberta A. Bivins, *Acupuncture, Expertise and Cross-Cultural Medicine* (Basingstoke, UK: Palgrave, 2000), 1, 197.

24. Bivins, 13; The Editors of Encyclopædia Britannica, "Acupuncture," *Encyclopædia Britannica* (20 Aug. 2018).

25. Bivins, 5, 10, 13.

26. "Commentary—Lake"; Hedrick (21 Sep.).

27. Wen-hsin Yeh, "Dai Li and the Liu Geqing Affair: Heroism in the Chinese Secret Service during the War of Resistance," *Journal of Asian Studies* 48.3 (1989): 345.

28. Frederic E. Wakeman, *Spymaster: Dai Li and the Chinese Secret Service* (Oakland: University of California Press, 2003), xiii, 4.

29. Yeh, 346.

30. Hedrick (24 Sep.).

31. "Audio Commentary—Chapter 12: The Journey to Ba Sing Se, Part 1: The Serpent's Pass" (supplementary material on DVD release of *Avatar: The Last Airbender—The Complete Book 2 Collection*), Viacom International Inc. (2007); "Commentary—Old."

32. "Commentary—Southern Lights"; "Commentary on The Earth Queen" (supplementary material on Blu-ray release of *The Legend of Korra—Book Three: Change*), Viacom International Inc. (2014); Ehasz; Hedrick (21 Sep.); Pilar Allesandra, 526; "The Adventures of Katie Mattila," *On the Page*, 6 Oct. 2017.

33. "Audio Commentary—Episode 20: The Siege of the North—Part 2" (supplementary material on DVD release of *Avatar: The Last Airbender—The Complete Book 1 Collection*), Viacom International Inc. (2006); "Commentary—Southern Lights"; "Commentary—Earth Queen"; "Commentary—Old"; Blacker; Allesandra; Ehasz; Hedrick (21 Sep.).

34. Blacker. In our interview, Ehasz credited his mentors Bill Oakley and Josh Weinstein of *Mission Hill* (The WB, 1999–2000; Cartoon Network, 2002) for teaching him this process; they had, in turn, learned it from their time on *The Simpsons*.

35. "Commentary—Earth Queen"; Blacker.

36. Ehasz.

37. Allesandra.

38. Ehasz; Hedrick (21 Sep.).

39. Ehasz.

40. "Commentary—Southern Lights."

41. Ehasz.

42. "Commentary—When."

43. Hedrick (21 Sep.).

44. Ehasz; Allesandra.

45. "Commentary—Southern Lights."

46. Ehasz.

47. Ehasz; Hedrick (21 Sep.).

48. "Commentary—Lake"; "Audio Commentary—Chapter 18: The Earth King" (supplementary material on DVD release of *Avatar: The Last Airbender—The Complete Book 2 Collection*), Viacom International Inc. (2007).

49. Young, 9.

50. Yuen, 57–60.

51. Ehasz.

52. Mary Louise Pratt, *Imperial Eyes: Travel Writing and Transculturation* (London: Routledge, 1992), 6.

53. Kim Soyoung, "Genre as Contact Zone: Hong Kong Action and Korean *Hwalkuk*," *Hong Kong Connections: Transnational Imagination in Action Cinema*, eds. Meaghan Morris, Siu Leung Li, and Stephen Chan Ching-kiu (Durham, NC: Duke University Press, 2005), 101; Caldwell, *Production*, 108.

54. Blacker; Allesandra; Ehasz; Hedrick (21 Sep.).

55. Zane.
56. Ibid.
57. Brandon Ancil, "Did the 'Airbender' adaptation ever have a chance?," *CNN*, 1 Jul. 2010.
58. Catherine A. Luther, Carolyn Ringer Lepre, and Naeemah Clark, *Diversity in U.S. Mass Media*, 1st ed. (Malden, MA: Wiley-Blackwell, 2012), 148–49.
59. Zane.
60. Ehasz; Hedrick (21 Sep.).
61. For an example of this practice, consider appendix F for *The Lord of the Rings* (1954–55), in which author J. R. R. Tolkien metatextually maintains he had translated a preexisting text into English.
62. Braj B. Kachru, ed., *The Other Tongue: English across Cultures* (Urbana: University of Illinois Press, 1982); Farzad Sharifian, ed., *English as an International Language: Perspectives and Pedagogical Issues* (Bristol, UK: Multilingual Matters, 2009); Vaughan Rapatahana and Pauline Bunce, eds., *English Language as Hydra: Its Impacts on Non-English Language Cultures* (Bristol, UK: Multilingual Matters, 2012).
63. Braj B. Kachru, "World Englishes: Agony and Ecstasy," *Journal of Aesthetic Education* 30.2 (Summer 1996): 138.
64. Ibid., 138.
65. Mandala, 76, 92, 96.

CHAPTER FOUR: VISUAL WORLDBUILDING AND THE ANIMATED BODYSCAPE

1. Ehasz.
2. Desmond and Emirbayer, *Race*, 314.
3. Mirzoeff, 158–59.
4. Jean Fisher, "In Search of the 'Inauthentic': Disturbing Signs in Contemporary Native American Art," *Art Journal* 51.3 (1992): 44–45.
5. Ibid., 45–46.
6. Edward W. Said, *Orientalism*, 25th Anniversary Ed. (New York: Vintage Books, 1994), 1–2.
7. Furniss, 66.
8. Francis M. Agnoli, "Building the Transcultural Fantasy World of Avatar," *Animation Studies Online Journal*, 24 Jul. 2019.
9. Elsa Garagarza (7 Mar. 2018), email interview.
10. Elsa Garagarza (6 Apr. 2018), email interview.
11. Emily Tetri (27 Mar. 2018), email interview.
12. DiMartino, Konietzko, and Dos Santos, *Spirits*, 62; "Commentary on Beginnings: Part 2" (supplementary material on Blu-ray release of *The Legend of Korra—Book Two: Spirits*), Viacom International Inc. (2014).
13. Angela Sung (17 Feb. 2018), Skype interview.

14. DiMartino and Konietzko, 86, 132; "Audio Commentary—Chapter 14: City of Walls and Secrets" (supplementary material on DVD release of *Avatar: The Last Airbender—The Complete Book 2 Collection*), Viacom International Inc. (2007); "Commentary—Sokka's"; "Commentary—Beach"; "Audio Commentary—Chapter 12: The Western Air Temple" (supplementary material on DVD release of *Avatar: The Last Airbender—The Complete Book 3 Collection*), Viacom International Inc. (2008); DiMartino, Konietzko and Dos Santos, *Change*, 154.

15. Sung.

16. Sam Kaden Lai, "Episode 59: Growing Up Avatar-American," *Imaginary Worlds*, 8 Feb. 2017.

17. Emily Tetri (10 Mar. 2019), email interview.

18. "Commentary on Civil Wars: Part 2" (supplementary material on Blu-ray release of *The Legend of Korra—Book Two: Spirits*), Viacom International Inc. (2014).

19. Evan Miller, "The Gallery: Elsa Garagarza," *Anime News Network*, 31 Jan. 2009.

20. Garagarza (7 Mar.).

21. Tom Dankiewicz (19 Feb. 2018), email interview.

22. Chris Oatley, "Interview with 'Korra' and 'Dreamworks' Artist, Frederic William Stewart: Artcast #95," *The Oatley Academy ArtCast*, 2 Jun. 2017.

23. Ibid.

24. "Making—Korean." No credited translator.

25. Dankiewicz.

26. DiMartino and Konietzko, 52.

27. Dankiewicz.

28. DiMartino, Konietzko, and Dos Santos, *Change*, 169.

29. Garagarza (7 Mar.).

30. Dankiewicz.

31. Sung.

32. E. Miller.

33. Dankiewicz.

34. DiMartino and Konietzko, 61.

35. Garagarza (7 Mar.).

36. Ibid.

37. "Commentary—Beach."

38. DiMartino and Konietzko, 156.

39. DiMartino, Konietzko, and Santos, *Air*, 55.

40. DiMartino, Konietzko, and Dos Santos, *Air*, 38, 60; DiMartino, Konietzko and Dos Santos, *Change*, 48; Tasha Robinson, "*Legend of Korra*'s Michael Dante DiMartino and Joaquim Dos Santos," *The A.V. Club*, 13 Apr. 2012.

41. "Audio Commentary—Episode 18: The Waterbending Master" (supplementary material on DVD release of *Avatar: The Last Airbender—The Complete Book 1 Collection*), Viacom International Inc. (2006); "Commentary—Lake."

42. "Commentary on the Metal Clan" (supplementary material on Blu-ray release of *The Legend of Korra—Book Three: Change*), Viacom International Inc. (2014).

43. DiMartino, Konietzko and Dos Santos, *Change*, 71.

44. Bevis Hillier, *Art Deco of the 20s and 30s* (London: Studio Vista, 1968), 13; The Editors of Encyclopædia Britannica, "Art Deco," *Encyclopædia Britannica Online* (Encyclopædia Britannica, Inc., 25 Oct. 2018).

45. Alastair Duncan, *Art Deco* (London: Thames and Hudson, 1988), 8; Michael Windover, *Art Deco: A Mode of Mobility* (Quebec City: Presses de l'Université du Québec, 2012), 2; Anthony Robins, *New York Art Deco: A Guide to Gotham's Jazz Age Architecture* (Albany, NY: Excelsior Editions, 2017), 5.

46. Windover, 263–64; Robins, 2.

47. Windover, 7, 30.

48. Duncan, 180; John Alff, "Art Deco: Gateway to Indian Modernism," *Architecture + Design* 8.6 (1991): 60–61; Windover 11, 20.

49. Duncan, 8.

50. "Commentary—Metal."

51. Bevis Hillier and Stephen Escritt, *Art Deco Style* (London: Phaidon, 1997), 188; Windover, 160.

52. Hillier 40, 52; Duncan, 6, 8; Alff, 58; Carla Breeze, *American Art Deco: Architecture and Regionalism* (New York: W. W. Norton, 2003), 13–14; Bridget Elliott, "Art Deco in a Tomb: Reanimating Egypt in Modern(ist) Visual Culture," *South Central Review* 25.1 (2008): 114–35; Windover, 5; Robins, 4.

53. Hillier, 52; Elliott, 115.

54. Windover, 36.

55. Duncan, 184; Breeze, 13.

56. Alff; Hillier and Escritt, 205–6; Windover 159–201; Ageeth Sluis, *Deco Body, Deco City: Female Spectacle and Modernity in Mexico City, 1900-1939* (Lincoln: University of Nebraska Press, 2016); Xu Lingna and Dai Zeyu, "Regaining the Sense of Being a Shanghainese: A Study of the Revival of Art Deco as an Apparatus of Cultural Memory from an Intercultural Perspective," *Intercultural Communication Studies* 20.1 (2011): 234–48.

57. Sung.

58. DiMartino and Konietzko, 26; Eduardo Vasconcellos, "Interview: Avatar's Bryan Konietzko and Michael Dante DiMartino," *IGN* (6 Sep. 2007); Blacker. Regarding *The Lord of the Rings*, while the wizards do not use wands, the scope and limitations of their magic is undefined within the text. Therefore, the cocreators' original point still stands.

59. "How"; "Essence"; DiMartino and Konietzko, 113, 124; "Nickelodeon: The Last Airbender: Legend of Korra Martial Arts Reference Demo—Fusion Comics," *Vimeo* (9 Aug. 2011).

60. "Behind."

61. Siu Leung Li, "Kung Fu: Negotiating Nationalism and Modernity," *Cultural Studies* 15.3/4 (2001): 522; Leon Hunt, *Kung Fu Cult Masters: From Bruce Lee to Crouching Tiger* (London: Wallflower, 2003), 22, 29–35.

62. S. L. Li: 522; Hunt, 39–41

63. Kennedy and Guo. 78.

64. Kennedy and Guo, 78–80; Ryan 528; Lu S., 11; Wang G., 8–9.

65. Kennedy and Guo, 83–84; Lorge, 206.

66. Kennedy and Guo, 84.

67. Wang G., 12–13.

68. Hunt, 29; Kennedy and Guo, 80–83.

69. Hunt, 15; Gina Marchetti, "Martial Arts, North and South: Liu Jialang's Vision of Hung Gar in Shaw Brothers Films," *EnterText* 6.1 (2006) 75.

70. "In Their Elements," *Nick Mag Presents* (Sep. 2006): 6; DiMartino and Konetizko, 26.

71. Hunt, 6–7; H.-h. Chang, 97–98.

72. Kin-Yan Szeto, *The Martial Arts Cinema of the Chinese Diaspora: Ang Lee, John Woo, and Jackie Chan in Hollywood* (Carbondale: Southern Illinois Press, 2011), 20; Stephen Teo, *Chinese Martial Arts Cinema: The Wuxia Tradition* (Edinburgh: Edinburgh University Press, 2016), 8.

73. Hunt, 3, 6–7; Szeto, 20.

74. Hunt, 39–41; H.-h. Chang, 97–98.

75. H.-h. Chang; Hunt; S. L. Li: 515–42; Lorge; Marchetti; Ryan; Szeto; Teo; Meaghan Morris, Siu Leung Li, and Stephen Chan Ching-kiu, eds., *Hong Kong Connections: Transnational Imagination in Action Cinema* (Durham, NC: Duke University Press, 2005); David West, *Chasing Dragons: An Introduction to the Martial Arts Film* (London: I. B. Tauris, 2006); D. S. Farrer and John Whalen-Bridge, eds., *Martial Arts as Embodied Knowledge: Asian Traditions in a Transnational World* (Albany: SUNY Press, 2011); Tim Trausch, ed., *Chinese Martial Arts Media Culture: Global Perspectives* (London: Rowman & Littlefield International, 2018).

76. Lu Zhouziang, Qi Zhang, and Fan Hong, "Projecting the 'Chineseness': Nationalism, Identity and Chinese Martial Arts Films," *International Journal of the History of Sport* 31.3 (2014): 320–35; Teo.

77. Kim S., 101.

78. Navarro, "1."

79. Navarro, "1"; Vasconcellos; Lasswell; DiMartino and Konietzko, 26.

80. "How": 43.

81. AKA: *Taiji* or 太极拳 (Tài jí quán).

82. "Behind"; "Essence."

83. Lu S., 64–71.

84. "How": 43; "Behind"; "Essence."

85. AKA: *Hungar, Hung Ga, Hung Ga Kuen,* or 洪家 (Hóng jiā).

86. "Behind"; "Essence."

87. Marchetti, 77.

88. S. L. Li, 522; Hunt, 15, 23; Marchetti, 75.

89. AKA: 南派螳螂 (Nán pài táng láng).

90. "Avatar Spirits" (supplementary material on DVD release of *Avatar: The Last Airbender—The Complete Book 1 Collection (Collector's Edition)*), Viacom International Inc. (2010); DiMartino and Konietzko, 162; Minister Faust, "Sifu Kisu on Martial Arts Mastery and Designing + Choreographing the Bending of Avatar the Last Airbender (MF Galaxy 069)," *MF Galaxy*, 14 Mar. 2016.

91. D. S. Farrer, "Coffee-Shop Gods: Chinese Martial Arts of the Singapore Diaspora," *Martial Arts as Embodied Knowledge: Asian Traditions in a Transnational World,*

eds. D. S. Farrer and John Whalen-Bridge (Albany: SUNY Press, 2011), 221; D. S. Farrer, "Becoming-animal in the Chinese Martial Arts," *Living Beings: Perspectives on Interspecies Engagements*, ed. Penelope Dransart (London: Bloomsbury, 2013), 150.

92. "How": 43.
93. AKA: 北少林 (Běi shào lín).
94. "Behind"; "Essence."
95. Hunt, 29.
96. Lorge, 195, 206.
97. Faust.
98. AKA: *Zhāquán* or 查拳 (Chá quán).
99. "Essence"; Gene Ching, "Kisu on The Legend of Korra," *Kung Fu Magazine*, n.d.; Faust.
100. Kennedy and Guo, 293.
101. AKA: 八卦掌 (Bāguà zhǎng).
102. "Behind"; "Essence."
103. "Behind"; Kennedy and Guo, 10.
104. Lorge, 206.
105. "Essence."
106. AKA: Hsing-I, Hsing Yi, or 形意拳 (Xíng yì quán).
107. "Essence"; Acastus, "Interview with Sifu Kisu" (part 2 of 3), *AvatarSpirit.net*, 12 Oct. 2006.
108. Lorge, 206.
109. Lu S., 85.
110. Kennedy and Guo, 12.
111. Kennedy and Guo; Lu S.; William Acevedo and Mei Cheung, "A Historical Overview of Mixed Martial Arts in China," *Journal of Asian Martial Arts* 19.3 (2010): 31–45; Lorge.
112. Hunt, 30; Kim S., 108.
113. T. Robinson.
114. Seth Robinson, "Joaquim Dos Santos Ready to Tell THE LEGEND OF KORRA," *Newsarama*, 10 Apr. 2012.
115. Jake Huang (31 Oct. 2018), Google Hangouts interview.
116. Ibid.
117. S. Robinson; Charles Webb, "Interview: Paging, Dr. Fight! A Chat with 'Legend of Korra' Art Director and Co-Executive Producer Joaquim Dos Santos," *MTV*, 23 Apr. 2012; Huang.
118. Christopher John Farley, "'The Legend of Korra' Creators Answer Your Questions," *Wall Street Journal*, 22 Jun. 2012.
119. Raúl Sánchez García and Dominic Malcolm, "Decivilizing, Civilizing, or Informalizing? The International Development of Mixed Martial Arts," *International Review for the Sociology of Sport* 45.1 (2010): 40, 43–46.
120. AKA: 截拳道 (Jié quán dào).
121. Acevedo and Cheung, 31; Stacey Howard Bishop, Paul La Bounty, and Michael Devlin, "Mixed Martial Arts: A Comprehensive Review," *Journal of Sport and Human Performance* 1.1 (2013): 28.

122. Marc Wickert, "Dana White and the Future of the UFC," *Fight Times*, 1 Oct. 2004.

123. "Essence"; Brad Curran, "Interview with Sifu Kisu," *Kung-Fu Kingdom*, 6 Oct. 2015; Faust; Huang.

124. Huang.

125. Acastus, "Interview with Sifu Kisu (part 1 of 3)," *AvatarSpirit.net*, 5 Oct. 2006; "Commentary—Enter"; Ed Liu, "Toon Zone Interviews Joaquim Dos Santos on Directing 'Avatar,'" *Toon Zone*, 22 Jul. 2008; Ulanova.

126. Meza-Leon.

127. Ulanova.

128. Ibid.

129. "Essence"; Curran; Faust; Liu, "Interviews"; Huang.

130. "Spirit—Breath."

131. "Commentary—Enter."

132. Acastus, "Director 3"; Liu, "Interviews"; Meza-Leon; "Spirit—Breath"; Ulanova.

133. "Essence."

134. Huang.

135. Hunt, 35–39.

136. Meza-Leon.

137. Ibid.

138. "Making—Korean." No credited translator.

139. Ulanova.

140. Huang.

141. Allison, 114–15.

142. The character's namesake, actor Mako Iwamatsu, used the kanji 誠 (Makoto) and the katakana マコ (Ma ko).

143. Siu-Leung Lee (30 Jan. 2018), email interview.

144. Siu-Leung Lee (31 Jan. 2018), email interview.

145. S.-L. Lee (30 Jan.).

146. "Commentary—Journey."

147. Siu-Leung Lee (13 Feb. 2018), email interview.

148. DiMartino and Konietzko, 126.

149. Ibid., 126.

150. S.-L. Lee (31 Jan.).

151. DiMartino and Konietzko, 126.

152. S.-L. Lee (31 Jan.); DiMartino and Konietzko, 127; "Fire Nation's Most Wanted," *Nick Mag Presents* (Sep. 2006): 48.

153. DiMartino and Konietzko, 126. These sixteen eras are (1) 氤武 (yáng wǔ), (2) 淳泰 (chún tài), (3) 圫元 (zhī yuán), (4) 烔裕 (jiǒng yù), (5) 氤隆 (yáng lóng), (6) 溢文 (yì wén), (7) 培治 (péi zhì), (8) 焜德 (kūn dé), (9) 氳貞 (yūn zhēn), (10) 渦明 (rú míng), (11) 堯平 (yáo píng), (12) 煬崇 (yáng chóng), (13) 氛安 (fēn ān), (14) 漳順 (zhāng shùn), (15) 垣正 (yuán zhèng), and (16) 焯光 (chāo guāng).

154. Garagarza (6 Apr.); Sung.

155. S.-L. Lee (31 Jan.).

156. "Commentary—Journey."

157. S.-L. Lee (31 Jan.).
158. DiMartino, Konietzko and Dos Santos, *Spirits*, 76.
159. S.-L. Lee (30 Jan.).
160. Lasswell.

CHAPTER FIVE: AURAL WORLDBUILDING
AND THE ANIMATED BODYSCAPE

1. Claudia Gorbman, *Unheard Melodies: Narrative Film Music* (Bloomington: Indiana University Press, 1987), 5–6.
2. Gianluca Sergi, "In Defence of Vulgarity: The Place of Sound Effects in the Cinema," *Scope: An Online Journal of Film Studies* 5 (2006).
3. Janet K. Halfyard, "Introduction: Finding Fantasy," *The Music of Fantasy Cinema*, ed. Janet K. Halfyard (Sheffield, UK: Equinox, 2012), 8.
4. James Buhler, *Theories of the Soundtrack* (New York: Oxford University Press, 2019), 190–91.
5. Ronald Radano and Philip V. Bohlman, eds., *Music and the Racial Imagination* (Chicago: University of Chicago Press, 2000).
6. Buhler, 194–95.
7. Mark Brownrigg, "Hearing Place: Film Music, Geography and Ethnicity," *International Journal of Media and Cultural Politics* 3.3 (2007): 312.
8. Acastus, "Music Interview with the Track Team (part 1 of 3)," *AvatarSpirit.Net*, 26 Jul. 2006; Acastus, "Music Interview with the Track Team (part 2 of 3)," *AvatarSpirit.Net*, 5 Aug. 2006; Mike Brennan, "The Music of 'Avatar: The Last Airbender,'" *Soundtrack*, 7 Apr. 2008; Marissa Lee, "Interview with the Track Team: The Musicians behind *The Legend of Korra*," Racebending.com, 27 Mar. 2012.
9. Brownrigg: 309.
10. Janice Esther Tulk, "An Aesthetic of Ambiguity: Musical Representation of Indigenous Peoples in Disney's *Brother Bear*," *Drawn to Sound: Animation Film Music and Sonicity*, ed. Rebecca Coyle (London: Equinox, 2010), 130.
11. Buhler, 192–93.
12. Brownrigg: 308.
13. "Commentary on Light in the Dark" (supplementary material on Blu-ray release of *The Legend of Korra—Book Two: Spirits*), Nickelodeon (2014); Brennan; M. Lee, "Interview"; Hector Navarro, "Episode 30: Jeremy Zuckerman & Bryan Konietzko," *Nick Animation Podcast*, 27 Jan. 2017.
14. Brennan.
15. "Audio Commentary—Chapter 6: The Avatar and the Firelord" (supplementary material on DVD release of *Avatar: The Last Airbender—The Complete Book 3 Collection*), Viacom International Inc. (2008); "Avatar Spirits"; Acastus, "Music 2"; Brennan.
16. Li Xiaoxiang, *Origins of Chinese Music*, trans. Wong Huey Khey (Singapore: Asiapac Books Pte, 2007), 80; Jin Jie, *Chinese Music* (Cambridge, UK: Cambridge University Press 2010), 64.

17. Li X., 82; Jin, 64–65.

18. Jin, 64–65.

19. Acastus, "Music 2."

20. Li X., 45–46.

21. "Commentary—Avatar"; "Avatar Spirits"; Acastus, "Music 2"; Acastus, "Music Interview with the Track Team (part 3 of 3), *AvatarSpirit.Net*, 12 Aug. 2006. While Armenia is technically located in West Asia, it is more commonly associated with the Middle East than with South or East Asia.

22. Acastus, "Music 3."

23. Andy Nercessian, *The Duduk and National Identity in Armenia* (Lanham, MD: Scarecrow, 2001), 3.

24. Paul Berliner, *The Soul of Mbira: Music and Traditions of the Shona People of Zimbabwe* (Chicago: University of Chicago Press, 1978).

25. "Commentary—Avatar"; "Commentary on Operation: Beifong" (supplementary material on Blu-ray release of *The Legend of Korra—Book Four: Balance*), Viacom International Inc. (2015).

26. Acastus, "Music 3."

27. M. Lee, "Interview."

28. Joel Cornah, "Jeremy Zuckerman Interview," *Sci Fi Fantasy Network*, 16 Jan. 2016.

29. AKA: 茉莉花 (*Mò lì huā*).

30. M. Lee, "Interview."

31. Brownrigg: 310–11.

32. Jin, 81–82.

33. Acastus, "Music 1"; M. Lee, "Interview"; Cornah.

34. Brownrigg: 310.

35. M. Lee, "Interview."

36. "Acastus, "Music 1."

37. Brennan.

38. Joanna R. Smolko, "Southern Fried Foster: Representing Race and Place through Music in Looney Tunes Cartoons" *American Music* 30.3 (2012): 353.

39. For more on this history, see Dena J. Epstein, "The Folk Banjo: A Documentary History," *Ethnomusicology* 19.3 (1975): 347–71; Karen Linn, *The Half-Barbaric Twang: The Banjo in American Popular Culture* (Urbana: University of Illinois Press, 1994); Cecilia Conway, *African Banjo Echoes in Appalachia: A Study of Folk Traditions* (Knoxville: University of Tennessee Press, 1995).

40. "Audio Commentary—Chapter 18: Sozin's Comet, Part 1: The Phoenix King" (supplementary material on DVD release of *Avatar: The Last Airbender—The Complete Book 3 Collection*), Viacom International Inc. (2008); Brennan; "Avatar Spirits."

41. Brennan.

42. Ibid.

43. "Audio Commentary—Chapter 20: The Crossroads of Destiny" (supplementary material on DVD release of *Avatar: The Last Airbender—The Complete Book 2 Collection*), Viacom International Inc. (2007); Brennan.

44. Brennan.

45. Kaya Savas, "Composer Interview: Jeremy Zuckerman," *Film.Music.Media*, 11 Oct. 2013.

46. Acastus, "Music 3"; Brennan; M. Lee, "Interview"; Cornah; Navarro, "30."

47. Acastus, "Music 3"; Brennan.

48. "Commentary on Beginnings: Part 1" (supplementary material on Blu-ray release of *The Legend of Korra—Book Two: Spirits*), Viacom International Inc. (2014); "Commentary—Beginnings 2."

49. "Audio Commentary—Chapter 6: And the Winner Is. . . ." (supplementary material on Blu-ray release of *The Legend of Korra—Book One: Air*), Viacom International Inc. (2012).

50. Goldmark, 77–106.

51. Buhler, 191–92.

52. E. Taylor Atkins, *Blue Nippon: Authenticating Jazz in Japan* (Durham, NC: Duke University Press, 2001); Alyn Shipton, *A New History of Jazz*, rev. ed. (New York: Continuum, 2007), 290–91; Peter Keppy, "Southeast Asia in the Age of Jazz: Locating Popular Culture in the Colonial Philippines and Indonesia," *Journal of Southeast Asia Studies* 44.3 (2013): 444–64; Eugene Marlow, *Jazz in China: From Dance Hall Music to Individual Freedom of Expression* (Jackson: University Press of Mississippi, 2018).

53. Loren Kajikawa, "The Sound of Struggle: Black Revolutionary Nationalism and Asian American Jazz," *Jazz/Not Jazz*, eds. Daniel Goldmark, Charles Hiroshi Garrett, and David Andrew Ake (Berkeley: University of California Press, 2012), 209.

54. "KorraScope Interviews Jeremy Zuckerman," *YumChunks*, 21 Apr. 2014; Cornah; Navarro, "30"; "Commentary—And."

55. Shipton, 24–31; Gary Giddins and Scott DeVeaux, *Jazz* (New York: W. W. Norton, 2009), 67; Ted Gioia, *The History of Jazz*, 2nd ed. (Oxford, UK: Oxford University Press, 2011), 20.

56. Shipton, 71–78, 443–51.

57. "Republic City Dispatch #51: Audio Bending with Jeremy Zuckerman and Benjamin Wynn," *Republic City Dispatch*, 19 Jan. 2015.

58. Navarro, "30."

59. "Republic City Dispatch #29: Sound of Book 2 w/Jeremy Zuckerman and Benjamin Wynn," *Republic City Dispatch*, 3 Feb. 2014; "Commentary—Light"; Savas.

60. "Commentary—And"; "Commentary—Beginnings 2"; "Commentary—Light"; "Commentary—Metal"; "Commentary—Operation"; "KorraScope"; Navarro "30."

61. Cristina Chang, "Las Vegas Musician Helping Preserve Chinese Folk Music, Instruments," *Las Vegas Sun* (12 Aug. 2012).

62. "Audio Commentary—Episode 17: The Northern Air Temple" (supplementary material on DVD release of *Avatar: The Last Airbender—The Complete Book 1 Collection*), Viacom International Inc. (2006); "Commentary—Avatar"; "Commentary—Beginnings 1"; "Inside"; Acastus, "Music 1"; Brennan; Michal Schick, "SeptBender Interview: Jeremy Zuckerman Discusses Music-Bending on 'The Legend of Korra,'" *Hypable*, 23 Sep. 2013; Savas; "KorraScope."

63. Steve Tushar (22 Jun. 2018), Skype interview.

64. Taberham, 143–45.

65. "Commentary—Northern"; "Commentary—Avatar."
66. Vanessa Theme Ament, *The Foley Grail: The Art of Performing Sound for Film, Games, and Animation*, 2nd ed. (New York: Focal, 2014), 86.
67. Ibid., 34–39.
68. Ibid., 39–40, 76–81.
69. "The Making of Avatar—Inside the Sound Studios" (supplementary material on DVD release of *Avatar: The Last Airbender—The Complete Book 1 Collection*), Viacom International Inc. (2006).
70. "Commentary on The Terror Within" (supplementary material on Blu-ray release of *The Legend of Korra—Book Three: Change*), Viacom International Inc. (2014).
71. third ear audio, Tumblr, 9 Mar. 2013.
72. third ear audio, Tumblr, 11 Mar. 2013.
73. "Commentary—Terror."
74. Ibid.
75. third ear audio, Tumblr, 9 Jul. 2013.
76. "Audio Commentary—Chapter 9: Out of the Past" (supplementary material on Blu-ray release of *The Legend of Korra—Book One: Air*), Viacom International Inc. (2012).
77. "Making—Sound"; "Commentary—Terror."
78. "Audio Commentary—Chapter 10: The Day of Black Sun, Part 1: The Invasion" (supplementary material on DVD release of *Avatar: The Last Airbender—The Complete Book 3 Collection*), Viacom International Inc. (2008).
79. "Commentary—Terror."
80. Brennan.
81. Tushar (22 Jun.).
82. Brennan; third ear audio, Tumblr, 3 May 2013.
83. Brennan.
84. Steve Tushar (28 Apr. 2019), email interview.
85. "Commentary—Northern"; "Commentary—Avatar"; "Making—Sound."
86. Tushar (22 Jun.); Tushar (28 Apr.).
87. Taberham, 136–40.
88. Brennan.
89. "Commentary—Beginnings 1."
90. Tushar (22 Jun.).
91. "Commentary—Beginnings 1."
92. Ibid.
93. Tushar (22 Jun.).
94. Ibid.

BIBLIOGRAPHY

Acevedo, William, and Mei Cheung. "A Historical Overview of Mixed Martial Arts in China." *Journal of Asian Martial Arts* 19.3 (2010): 31–45.

Andreeva, Nellie. "'Family Guy': Arif Zahir Replaces Mike Henry as Cleveland Brown on Fox Animated Series." *Deadline Hollywood*, 25 Sep. 2020. Accessed 23 Jan. 2022.

Aranjuez, Adolfo. "'The Legend of Korra' and Minority Representation." *Screen Education* 78 (2015): 24–27.

Agnoli, Francis M. "Animating Race in 'She-Ra and the Princesses of Power.'" *Animation Studies* 2.0, 13 July 2020.

Agnoli, Francis M. "Building the Transcultural Fantasy World of Avatar." *Animation Studies Online Journal* 24 Jul. 2019.

Aihara, Koji, and Kentaro Takekuma. *Even a Monkey Can Draw Manga Vol. 1.* Trans. Yuji Oniki. San Francisco, CA: Viz Communications, Inc., 2002.

Alff, John. "Art Deco: Gateway to Indian Modernism." *Architecture + Design* 8.6 (1991): 57–63.

Allison, Tanine. "Blackface, *Happy Feet*: The Politics of Race in Motion Capture and Animation." *Special Effects: New Histories/Theories/Contexts*. Eds. Dan North, Bob Rehak, and Michael S. Duffy. London: Palgrave, 2015. 114–26.

Allport, Gordon W. *The Nature of Prejudice*. Reading, MA: Addison-Wesley, 1954.

Altman, Rick. "Introduction: Four and a Half Film Fallacies." *Sound Theory, Sound Practice*. Ed. Rick Altman. New York: Routledge, 1992. 35–45.

Altman, Rick. "The Material Heterogeneity of Recorded Sound." *Sound Theory, Sound Practice*. Ed. Rick Altman. New York: Routledge, 1992. 14–31.

Altman, Rick. "Moving Lips: Cinema as Ventriloquism." *Yale French Studies* 60 (1980): 67–79.

Ament, Vanessa Theme. *The Foley Grail: The Art of Performing Sound for Film, Games, and Animation.* 2nd ed. New York: Focal Press, 2014.

Andreasen, Robin O. "The Cladistic Race Concept: A Defense." *Biology and Philosophy* 19 (2004): 425–42.

Andreasen, Robin O. "The Meaning of 'Race': Folk Conceptions and the New Biology of Race." *Journal of Philosophy* 102.2 (Feb. 2005): 94–106.

Andreasen, Robin O. "A New Perspective on the Race Debate." *British Journal for the Philosophy of Science* 49 (1998): 199–225.

Andreasen, Robin O. "Race: Biological Reality or Social Construct?" *Philosophy of Science* 67 (2000): S653–S666.

Arnheim, Rudolf. *Film as Art*. London: Faber and Faber LTD, 1958.

Atkins, E. Taylor. *Blue Nippon: Authenticating Jazz in Japan*. Durham, NC: Duke University Press, 2001.

Bae, Yoo-Soo Cindy, Elise Ng, and Roy G. Geronemus. "Successful Treatment of Two Pediatric Port Wine Stains in Darker Skin Type Using 595 nm Laser." *Lasers in Surgery and Medicine: The Official Journal of the American Society for Laser Medicine and Surgery* 48.4 (2016): 339–42.

Banet-Weiser, Sarah. *Kids Rule! Nickelodeon and Consumer Citizenship*. Durham, NC: Duke University Press, 2007.

Banks, Miranda J. *The Writers: A History of American Screenwriters and Their Guild*. New Brunswick, NJ: Rutgers University Press, 2015.

Barkan, Elazar. *The Retreat of Scientific Racism: Changing Concepts of Race in Britain and the United States between the World Wars*. Cambridge, UK: Cambridge University Press, 1992.

Barker, Martin. "Introduction." *Contemporary Hollywood Stardom*. Eds. Thomas Austin and Martin Barker. London: Arnold, 2003. 1–24.

Barthes, Roland. *Image, Music, Text*. Trans. Stephen Heath. London: Fontana Press, 1977.

Batkin, Jane. *Identity in Animation: A Journey into Self, Difference, Culture, and the Body*. London: Routledge, 2017.

Baudry, Jean-Louis. "The Apparatus." *Camera Obscura* 1 (1976): 104–26.

Bendazzi, Giannalberto. *Cartoons: One Hundred Years of Cinema Animation*. Trans. Anna Taraboletti-Segre. Bloomington: Indiana University Press, 1994.

Berliner, Paul. *The Soul of Mbira: Music and Traditions of the Shona People of Zimbabwe*. Chicago: University of Chicago Press, 1978.

Bevilacqua, Joe. "Celebrity Voice Actors: The New Sound of Animation." *Animation World Magazine* 4.1 (1999).

Bhaba, Homi. "Of Mimicry and Man: The Ambivalences of Colonial Discourse." *October* 28 (1984): 125–33.

Bishop, Stacy Howard, Paul La Bounty, and Michael Devlin. "Mixed Martial Arts: A Comprehensive Review." *Journal of Sport and Human Performance* 1.1 (2013): 28–42.

Bivins, Roberta A. *Acupuncture, Expertise and Cross-Cultural Medicine*. Basingstoke, UK: Palgrave, 2000.

Blackmon, Samantha. "Pickanninnies and Pixels: On Race, Racism and Cuphead at E3." *NYMG*, 17 Jun. 2015. Accessed 23 Jan. 2022.

Bogle, Donald. *Toms, Coons, Mulattoes, Mammies, and Bucks: An Interpretive History of Blacks in American Films, Updated and Expanded Fifth Edition*. New York: Bloomsbury, 2016.

Booker, M. Keith. *Drawn to Television: Prime-Time Animation from "The Flintstones" to "Family Guy."* Westport, CT: Praeger, 2006.

Boucher, Cheryl J., et al., "Perceptions of Competency as a Function of Accent." *Psi Chi Journal of Psychological Research* 18.1 (2013): 27–32.

Brace, C. Loring. *"Race" Is a Four-Letter Word: The Genesis of the Concept.* Oxford, UK: Oxford University Press, 2005.
Branigan, Edward. "Sound and Epistemology in Film." *Journal of Aesthetics and Art Criticism* 47.4 (1989): 311–24.
Breeze, Carla. *American Art Deco: Architecture and Regionalism.* W. W. Norton, 2003.
Brownrigg, Mark. "Hearing Place: Film Music, Geography and Ethnicity." *International Journal of Media and Cultural Politics* 3.3 (2007): 307–23.
Buhler, James. *Theories of the Soundtrack.* New York: Oxford University Press, 2019.
Burguera, Xavier Fuster. "Muffled Voices in Animation. Gender Roles and Black Stereotypes in Warner Bros. Cartoons: From Honey to Babs Bunny." *Bulletin of the Transilvania University of Braşov* 4.2 (2011): 65–76.
Caldwell, John T. *Production Culture: Industrial Reflexivity and Critical Practice in Film and Television.* Durham, NC: Duke University Press, 2008.
Campbell, Donald T. "Stereotypes and the Perception of Group Difference." *American Psychologist* 22.10 (1967): 817–29.
Case, Sarah. *The Integrated Voice: A Complete Voice Course for Actors.* London: Nick Hern Books, 2013.
Chaney, Michael A. "Coloring Whiteness and Blackvoice Minstrelsy: Representations of Race and Place in *Static Shock*, *King of the Hill*, and *South Park*." *Journal of Popular Film and Television* 31.4 (2004): 167–84.
Chang, Hsiao-hung. "The Unbearable Lightness of Globalization: On the Transnational Flight of *Wuxia* Film." *Cinema Taiwan: Politics, Popularity and State of the Arts.* Eds. Darrell William Davis and Ru-Shou Robert Chen. London: Routledge, 2007. 95–107.
Cheng, Anne Anlin. *Ornamentalism.* New York, NY: Oxford University Press, 2019.
Chion, Michel. *Audio-Vision: Sound on Screen.* Trans. Claudia Gorbman. New York: Columbia University Press, 1994.
Chion, Michel. *The Voice in Cinema.* Trans. Claudia Gorbman. New York: Columbia University Press, 1999.
Chung, Hye Seung. "From 'Me So Horny' to 'I'm So Ronery': Asian Images and Yellow Voices in American Cinema." *Film Dialogue.* Ed. Jeff Jaeckle. New York: Wallflower, 2013: 172–91.
Clements, Jonathan. *Anime: A History.* Basingstoke, NH: Palgrave Macmillan, 2013.
Cohen, Karl. "Racism and Resistance: Black Stereotypes in Animation." *Animation Journal* 4.2 (1996): 43–68.
Cole, Yussef. "Cuphead and the Racist Spectre of Fleischer Animation." *Unwinnable*, 10 Nov. 2017. Accessed 23 Jan. 2022.
Condry, Ian. *The Soul of Anime: Collaborative Creativity and Japan's Media Success Story.* Durham, NC: Duke University Press, 2013.
Conway, Cecilia. *African Banjo Echoes in Appalachia: A Study of Folk Traditions.* Knoxville: University of Tennessee Press, 1995.
Daliot-Bul, Michal, and Nissim Otmazgin. *The Anime Boom in the United States: Lessons for Global Creative Industries.* Cambridge, MA: Harvard University Press, 2017.

Davé, Shilpa. "Apu's Brown Voice: Cultural Inflection and South Asian Accents." *East Main Street: Asian Popular Culture*. Eds. Shilpa Davé, LeiLani Nishime, and Tasha G. Oren. New York: New York University Press, 2005: 313–36.

Davé, Shilpa. *Indian Accents: Brown Voice and Racial Performance in American Television and Film*. Champaign: University of Illinois Press, 2013.

Denison, Rayna. *Anime: A Critical Introduction*. London: Bloomsbury, 2015.

Denison, Rayna. "The Global Markets of *Anime*; Miyazaki Hayao's *Spirited Away* (2001)." *Japanese Cinema: Texts and Contexts*. Eds. Alastair Phillips and Julian Stringer. London: Routledge, 2007.

Denison, Rayna. "Star-Spangled Ghibli: Star Voices in the American Versions of Hayao Miyazaki's Films." *Animation: An Interdisciplinary Journal* 3.2 (2008): 129–46.

Denison, Rayna. "Transcultural Creativity in Anime: Hybrid Identities in the Production, Distribution, Texts and Fandom of Japanese Anime." *Creative Industries Journal* 3.3 (2011): 221–35.

Desmond, Matthew, and Mustafa Emirbayer. *Race in America*. New York: W. W. Norton, 2006.

Desmond, Matthew, and Mustafa Emirbayer, "What Is Racial Domination?" *Du Bois Review: Social Science Research on Race* 6.2 (2009): 335–55.

Desta, Yohana. "*The Simpsons* Still Doesn't Understand the Problem with Apu." *Vanity Fair*, 9 Apr. 2018. Accessed 23 Jan. 2022.

Dixon, John A., Berenice Mahoney, and Roger Cocks. "Accents of Guilt? Effects of Regional Accent, Race, and Crime Type on Attributions of Guilt." *Journal of Language and Social Psychology* 21.2 (2002): 162–68.

Doane, Mary Ann. "The Voice in the Cinema: The Articulation of Body and Space." *Yale French Studies* 60 (1980): 33–50.

Dobson, Nichola. *Historical Dictionary of Animation and Cartoons*. Lanham, MD: Scarecrow, 2009.

Duncan, Alastair. *Art Deco*. London: Thames and Hudson, 1988.

Dyer, Richard. *Heavenly Bodies: Film Stars and Society*. 2nd ed. London: Routledge, 2004.

Editors of Encyclopædia Britannica, The. "Acupuncture." *Encyclopædia Britannica Online*. Encyclopædia Britannica, Inc., 20 Aug. 2018. Accessed 4 Mar. 2019.

Editors of Encyclopædia Britannica, The. "Art Deco." *Encyclopædia Britannica Online*. Encyclopædia Britannica, Inc., 25 Oct. 2018. Accessed 20 Feb. 2019.

Editors of Encyclopædia Britannica, The. "Chakra." *Encyclopædia Britannica Online*. Encyclopædia Britannica, Inc., 4 Sep. 2018. Accessed 4 Mar. 2019.

Editors of Encyclopædia Britannica, The. "Qi." *Encyclopædia Britannica Online*. Encyclopædia Britannica, Inc., 10 Aug. 2018. Accessed 4 Mar. 2019.

Ehrlich, Nea. "The Animated Document: Animation's Dual Indexicality in Mixed Realities." *Animation: An Interdisciplinary Journal* 15.3 (2020): 260–75.

Eisenstein, Sergei. *Eisenstein on Disney*. Ed. Jay Leyda. Trans. Alan Upchurch. London: Methuen, 1988.

Elliott, Bridget. "Art Deco in a Tomb: Reanimating Egypt in Modern(ist) Visual Culture." *South Central Review* 25.1 (2008): 114–35.

Ely, Melvin Patrick. *The Adventures of Amos 'n' Andy: A Social History of an American Phenomenon*. Charlottesville: University of Virginia Press, 1991.

Farrer, D. S. "Becoming-animal in the Chinese Martial Arts." *Living Beings: Perspectives on Interspecies Engagements*. Ed. Penelope Dransart. London: Bloomsbury, 2013. 145–65.

Farrer, D. S. "Coffee-Shop Gods: Chinese Martial Arts of the Singapore Diaspora." *Martial Arts as Embodied Knowledge: Asian Traditions in a Transnational World*. Eds. D. S. Farrer and John Whalen-Bridge. Albany: SUNY Press, 2011. 203–37.

Farrer, D. S., and John Whalen-Bridge, eds. *Martial Arts as Embodied Knowledge: Asian Traditions in a Transnational World*. Albany: SUNY Press, 2011.

Fisher, Jean. "In Search of the 'Inauthentic': Disturbing Signs in Contemporary Native American Art." *Art Journal* 51.3 (1992): 44–50.

Flynn, Joyce. "Melting Plots: Patterns of Racial and Ethnic Amalgamation in American Drama before Eugene O'Neill." *American Quarterly* 38.3 (1986): 417–38.

Fuller, Karla Rae. "Creatures of Good and Evil: Caucasian Portrayals of the Chinese and Japanese during World War II." *Classic Hollywood, Classic Whiteness*. Ed. Daniel Bernardi. Minneapolis: University of Minnesota Press, 2001. 281–300.

Furniss, Maureen. *Art in Motion: Animation Aesthetics*. Rev. ed. Eastleigh, UK: John Libbey, 2007.

García, Raúl Sánchez, and Dominic Malcolm. "Decivilizing, Civilizing, or Informalizing? The International Development of Mixed Martial Arts." *International Review for the Sociology of Sport* 45.1 (2010): 39–58.

Gardner, Jared. "Same Difference: Graphic Alterity in the Works of Gene Luen Yang, Adrian Tomine, and Kirk Kim." *Multicultural Comics: From Zap to Blue Beetle*. Ed. Frederick Luis Aldama. Austin: University of Texas Press, 2010. 132–47.

Gillespie, Michael Boyce. *Film Blackness: American Cinema and the Idea of Black Film*. Durham, NC: Duke University Press, 2016.

Goldmark, Daniel. *Tunes for 'Toons: Music and the Hollywood Cartoon*. Berkeley: University of California Press, 2005.

Gorbman, Claudia. *Unheard Melodies: Narrative Film Music*. Bloomington: Indiana University Press, 1987.

Gould, Stephen Jay. *The Mismeasure of Man*. New York: W. W. Norton, 1996.

Grimes, John A. *A Concise Dictionary of Indian Philosophy: Sanskrit Term Defined in English*. Albany: State University of New York Press, 1996.

Halfyard, Janet K. "Introduction: Finding Fantasy." *The Music of Fantasy Cinema*. Ed. Janet K. Halfyard. Sheffield, UK: Equinox, 2012. 1–15.

Han, Grace. "Musings on Mir: Finding a Name in American Animation." *Fantasy/Animation*, 27 Aug. 2021. Accessed 22 Feb. 2022.

Hendershot, Heather. "Introduction: Nickelodeon and the Business of Fun." *Nickelodeon Nation: The History, Politics, and Economics of America's Only TV Channel for Kids*. Ed. Heather Hendershot. New York: New York University Press, 2004. 1–12.

Hesmondhalgh, David, and Sarah Baker. *Creative Labour: Media Work in Three Cultural Industries*. London: Routledge, 2011.

Hillier, Bevis. *Art Deco of the 20s and 30s*. London: Studio Vista, 1968.
Hillier, Bevis, and Stephen Escritt. *Art Deco Style*. London: Phaidon, 1997.
Hilmes, Michelle. "Invisible Men: *Amos 'n' Andy* and the Roots of Broadcast Discourse." *Critical Studies in Media Communication* 10.4 (1993): 301–21.
Ho Wai Sun, et al., "Laser Treatment on Congenital Facial Port-Wine Stains: Long-Term Efficacy and Complication in Chinese Patients." *Lasers in Surgery and Medicine: The Official Journal of the American Society for Laser Medicine and Surgery* 30.1 (2002): 44–47.
Holliday, Christopher. *The Computer-Animated Film: Industry, Style and Genre*. Edinburgh: Edinburgh University Press, 2018.
Holliday, Christopher, and Alexander Sergeant. "Introduction: Approaching Fantasy/Animation." *Fantasy/Animation: Connections between Media, Mediums and Genres*. Eds. Christopher Holliday and Alexander Sergeant. New York: Routledge, 2018.
Hu, Tze-yue G. *Frames of Anime: Culture and Image-Building*. Hong Kong: Hong Kong University Press, 2010.
Hume, Kathryn. *Fantasy and Mimesis: Responses to Reality in Western Literature*. New York: Methuen, 1984.
Hunt, Leon. *Kung Fu Cult Masters: From Bruce Lee to Crouching Tiger*. London: Wallflower, 2003.
Irwin, W. R. *Game of the Impossible: A Rhetoric of Fantasy*. Urbana: University of Illinois Press, 1977.
Isola, Ashley. "Yellowface, the Yellow Peril, and the Rise of the Kung Fu Master." *TCNJ Journal of Student Scholarship* XCII (2015): 1–4.
Iwabuchi, Koichi, Stephen Muecke, and Mandy Thomas. "Introduction: Siting Asian Cultural Flows." *Rogue Flows: Trans-Asian Cultural Traffic*. Eds. Koichi Iwabuchi, Stephen Muecke, and Mandy Thomas. Hong Kong: Hong Kong University Press, 2004. 1–10.
Jackson, Rosemary. *Fantasy: The Literature of Subversion*. London: Routledge, 1981.
Jin Jie. *Chinese Music*. Cambridge, UK: Cambridge University Press, 2010.
Johari, Harish. *Chakras: Energy Centers of Transformation*. Rochester, VT: Destiny Books, 2000.
Johnson, William. "The Liberation of Echo: A New Hearing for Film Sound." *Film Quarterly* 38.4 (1985): 2–12.
Jung, E. Alex. "Raphael Bob-Waksberg, In Good Faith: The *BoJack Horseman* creator on Times Up, Bad Men, and His Apology Tour." *Vulture*, 20 Sep. 2018. Accessed 23 Jan. 2022.
Kachru, Braj B. "World Englishes: Agony and Ecstasy." *Journal of Aesthetic Education* 30.2 (1996): 135–55.
Kachru, Braj B., ed. *The Other Tongue: English across Cultures*. Urbana: University of Illinois Press, 1982.
Kajikawa, Loren. "The Sound of Struggle: Black Revolutionary Nationalism and Asian American Jazz." *Jazz/Not Jazz*. Eds. Daniel Goldmark, Charles Hiroshi Garrett, and David Andrew Ake. Berkeley: University of California Press, 2012. 190–216.
Kang, Inkoo. "*BoJack Horseman*'s Raphael Bob-Waksberg Talks about Coming to Terms with the 'Original Sin' of the Show's All-White Cast." *Slate*, 12 Sep. 2018. Accessed 23 Jan. 2022.

Katz, Daniel, and Kenneth Braly. "Racial Stereotypes of One Hundred College Studies." *Journal of Abnormal and Social Psychology* 28.3 (1933): 280–90.

Kawashima, Terry. "Seeing Faces, Making Races: Challenging Visual Tropes of Racial Difference." *Meridians* 3.1 (2002): 161–90.

Kennedy, Brian, and Elizabeth Guo. *Chinese Martial Arts Training Manuals: A Historical Survey*. Berkeley, CA: Blue Snake Books, 2005.

Keppy, Peter. "Southeast Asia in the Age of Jazz: Locating Popular Culture in the Colonial Philippines and Indonesia." *Journal of Southeast Asia Studies* 44.3 (2013): 444–64.

Keveney, Bill. "'The Simpsons' exclusive: Matt Groening (mostly) remembers the show's record 636 episodes." *USA Today*, 27 Apr. 2018. Accessed 23 Jan. 2022.

Keys, Jobia. "Doc McStuffins and Dora the Explorer: Representations of Gender, Race, and Class in US Animation." *Journal of Children and Media* 10.3 (2016): 355–68.

Kim, Joon-Yang. "Critique of the New Historical Landscape of South Korean Animation." *Animation: An Interdisciplinary Journal* 1.1 (2006): 61–81.

Kim Soyoung. "Genre as Contact Zone: Hong Kong Action and Korean *Hwalkuk*." *Hong Kong Connections: Transnational Imagination in Action Cinema*. Eds. Meaghan Morris, Siu Leung Li, and Stephen Chan Ching-kiu. Durham, NC: Duke University Press, 2005. 97–110.

King, C. Richard, Mary K. Bloodsworth-Lugo, and Carmen R. Lugo-Lugo, eds. Animated Representations of Blackness [Special Issue], *Journal of African American Studies* 14.4 (2010).

Klein, Hugh, and Kenneth S. Shiffman. "Race-Related Content of Animated Cartoons." *Howard Journal of Communication* 17 (2006): 163–82.

Kotlarz, Irene. "The Birth of a Notion." *Screen* 24.2 (1982): 21–29.

Kushins, Eric R. "Sounding Like Your Race in the Employment Process: An Experiment on Speaker Voice, Race Identification, and Stereotyping." *Race and Social Problems* 6.3 (2014): 237–48.

LaPiere, Richard T. "Types-Rationalizations of Group Antipathy." *Special Forces* 15.2 (1936): 232–54.

Larson, Stephanie Greco. *Media & Minorities: The Politics of Race in News and Entertainment*. Lanham, MD: Rowman & Littlefield, 2006.

Lee, Cynthia Kwei Yung. "Beyond Black and White: Racializing Asian Americans in Society Obsessed with OJ." *Hastings Women's Law Journal* 6.2 (1995): 165–207.

Lee, Joonkoo. "Three Worlds of Global Value Chains: Multiple Governance and Upgrading Paths in the Korean Animation Industry." *International Journal of Cultural Policy* 25.6 (2019): 684–700.

Lehman, Christopher P. *The Colored Cartoon: Black Presentation in American Animated Short Films, 1907–1954*. Amherst: University of Massachusetts Press, 2007.

Leong, Jane. "Reviewing the 'Japaneseness' of Japanese Animation: Genre Theory and Fan Spectatorship." *Cinephile: The University of British Columbia's Film Journal* 7.1 (2011): 20–25.

Levin, Tom. "The Acoustic Dimension: Notes on Cinema Sound." *Screen* 25.3 (1984): 55–68.

Levinson, Daniel J., and R. Nevitt Sanford. "A Scale for the Measurement of Anti-Semitism." *Journal of Psychology* 17.2 (1944): 339–70.

Li, Siu Leung. "Kung Fu: Negotiating Nationalism and Modernity. *Cultural Studies* 15.3/4 (2001): 515–42.

Li Xiaoxiang. *Origins of Chinese Music*. Trans. Wong Huey Khey. Singapore: Asiapac Books Pte, 2007.

Linn, Karen. *The Half-Barbaric Twang: The Banjo in American Popular Culture*. Urbana: University of Illinois Press, 1994.

Linneaus, Carl. *Systema Naturae*. 10th ed., vol. 1. 1758.

Lippi-Green, Rosina. *English with an Accent: Language, Ideology, and Discrimination in the United States*. London: Routledge, 1997.

Lippmann, Walter. *Public Opinion*. New York: Harcourt, Brace and Company, 1922.

Loader, Alison [Reiko]. "We're Asian, More Expected of Us: Representation, the Model Minority, & Whiteness on *King of the Hill*." *Animated Studies* 5 (2010).

Lorge, Peter Allan. *Chinese Martial Arts from Antiquity to the Twenty-First Century*. Cambridge: Cambridge University Press, 2011.

Lott, Eric. *Love and Theft: Blackface Minstrelsy and the American Working Class*. New York: Oxford University Press, 1993.

Lotz, Amanda D., and Horace Newcomb. "The Production of Entertainment Media." *A Handbook of Media and Communication Research: Qualitative and Quantitative Methodologies*. Ed. Klaus Bruhn Jenson. New York: Routledge, 2012. 71–86.

Lu, Amy Shirong. "What Race Do They Represent and Does Mine Have Anything to Do with It? Perceived Racial Categories of Anime Characters." *Animation: An Interdisciplinary Journal* 4.2 (2009): 169–90.

Lu Shengli. *Combat Techniques of Taiji, Xingyi, and Bagua: Principles and Practices of Internal Martial Arts*. Trans. Zhang Yun and Susan Darley. Berkeley, CA: Blue Snake Books, 2006.

Luther, Catherine A., Carolyn Ringer Lepre, and Naeemah Clark. *Diversity in U.S. Mass Media*. Malden, MA: Wiley-Blackwell, 2012.

Lu Zhouziang, Qi Zhang, and Fan Hong. "Projecting the 'Chineseness': Nationalism, Identity and Chinese Martial Arts Films." *International Journal of the History of Sport* 31.3 (2014): 320–35.

Mandala, Susan. *The Language of Science Fiction and Fantasy: The Question of Style*. London: Continuum, 2010.

Marcello, Starr A. "Performance Design: An Analysis of Film Acting and Sound Design." *Journal of Film and Video* 58.1/2 (2006): 59–70.

Marchetti, Gina. "Martial Arts, North and South: Liu Jialiang's Vision of Hung Gar in Shaw Brothers Films." *EnterText* 6.1 (2006): 74–110.

Marlow, Eugene. *Jazz in China: From Dance Hall Music to Individual Freedom of Expression*. Jackson: University Press of Mississippi, 2018.

Mason, Jennifer. "Qualitative Interviewing: Asking, Listening and Interpreting." *Qualitative Research in Action*. Ed. Tim May. London: SAGE, 2002. 225–41.

Mayer, Vicki, Miranda J. Banks, and John T. Caldwell. "Introduction: Production Studies: Roots and Routes." *Production Studies: Cultural Studies of Media Industries*. Eds. Vicki Mayer, Miranda J. Banks, and John T. Caldwell. New York: Routledge, 2009. 1–12.

McCloud, Scott. *Understanding Comics: The Invisible Art*. New York: HarperPerennial, 1994.

Metzger, Sean. "Charles Parsloe's Chinese Fetish: An Example of Yellowface Performance in Nineteenth-Century American Melodrama." *Theatre Journal* 56.4 (2004): 627–51.

Mirzoeff, Nicholas. *Bodyscape: Art, Modernity, and the Ideal Figure*. London: Routledge, 1995.

Mittell, Jason. "The Great Saturday Morning Exile: Scheduling Cartoons on Television's Periphery in the 1960s." *Prime Time Animation: Television Animation and American Culture*. Eds. Carol A. Stabile and Mark Harrison. London: Routledge, 2003. 33–54.

Montgomery, Colleen. "Pixarticulation: Vocal Performance in Pixar Animation." *Music, Sound, and the Moving Image* 10.1 (2016): 1–23.

Moon, Krystyn R. *Yellowface: Creating the Chinese in American Popular Music and Performance, 1850s–1920s*. New Brunswick, NJ: Rutgers University Press, 2005.

Morris, Meaghan, Siu Leung Li, and Stephen Chan Ching-kiu, eds. *Hong Kong Connections: Transnational Imagination in Action Cinema*. Durham, NC: Duke University Press, 2005.

Napier, Susan J. *Anime from "Akira" to "Howl's Moving Castle": Experiencing Contemporary Japanese Animation*. New York: Palgrave Macmillan, 2005.

Nercessian, Andy. *The Duduk and National Identity in Armenia*. Lanham, MD: Scarecrow, 2001.

Neupert, Richard. "Trouble in Watermelon Land: George Pal and the Little Jasper Cartoons." *Film Quarterly* 55.1 (2001): 14–26.

Newman, Michael, and Angela Wu. "'Do You Sound Asian When You Speak English?' Racial Identification and Voice in Chinese and Korean Americans' English." *American Speech* 86.2 (2011): 152–78.

Ngai, Sianne. "'A Foul Lump Started Making Promises in My Voice': Race, Affect, and the Animated Subject." *American Literature* 74.3 (2002): 571–601.

Pao, Angela Chia-yi. "False Accents: Embodied Dialects and the Characterization of Ethnicity and Nationality." *Theatre Topics* 14.1 (2004): 353–72.

Pedersen, Erik. "Watchdog Group Chides Laika for 'White-Washing' 'Kubo and the Two Strings.'" *Deadline*, 23 Aug. 2016. Accessed 23 Jan. 2022.

Petski, Denise. "'Central Park': Emmy Raver-Lampman Joins Apple Series in Recasting for Mixed-Race Character Originally Voiced by Kristen Bell." *Deadline Hollywood*, 24 Jul. 2020. Accessed 23 Jan. 2022.

Petski, Denise. "'The Simpsons': The New Voice of Hank Azaria's Carl Is Revealed." *Deadline Hollywood*, 24 Sep. 2020. Accessed 23 Jan. 2022.

Porter, Rick. "'Big Mouth,' 'Central Park' to Recast Jenny Slate, Kristen Bell with Black Actors for Biracial Characters." *Hollywood Reporter*, 24 Jun. 2020. Accessed 23 Jan. 2022.

Porter, Rick. "'The Simpsons' to Recast Characters of Color, 'Family Guy' Actor Stops Voicing Black Role." *Hollywood Reporter*, 26 Jun. 2020. Accessed 23 Jan. 2022.

"Port Wine Stain (PWS)." *The Vascular Birthmarks Foundation*, n.d. Accessed 4 Mar. 2019.

Pratt, Mary Louis. *Imperial Eyes: Travel Writing and Transculturation*. London: Routledge, 1992.

Radano, Ronald, and Philip V. Bohlman, eds. *Music and the Racial Imagination*. Chicago: University of Chicago Press, 2000.

Rahman, Abid. "'The Simpsons' Addresses Apu Stereotype Controversy." *Hollywood Reporter*, 8 Apr. 2018. Accessed 23 Jan. 2022.

Rao, Sonia. "'The Simpsons' and 'Big Mouth' Are Recasting Nonwhite Roles. But It's About More Than Finding the Right Voices." *Washington Post*, 2 Jul. 2020. Accessed 23 Jan. 2022.

Rapatahana, Vaughan, and Pauline Bunce, editors. *English Language as Hydra: Its Impacts on Non-English Language Cultures*. Bristol, UK: Multilingual Matters, 2012.

Ristola, Jacqueline. "Realist Film Theory and Flowers of Evil: Exploring the Philosophical Possibilities of Rotoscoped Animated." *Animation Studies Online Journal*, 3 Feb. 2018.

Robins, Anthony. *New York Art Deco: A Guide to Gotham's Jazz Age Architecture*. Albany: Excelsior Editions, 2017.

Roe, Annabelle Honess. *Animated Documentary*. New York: Palgrave Macmillan, 2013.

Rogers, Amanda. "Asian Mutations: Yellowface from More Light to the Royal Shakespeare Company's the Orphan of Zhao." *Contemporary Theatre Review* 24.4 (2014): 452–66.

Rogers, Richard A. "From Cultural Exchange to Transculturation: A Review and Reconceptualization of Cultural Appropriation." *Communication Theory* 16 (2006): 474–503.

Rose, Steve. "Wes Anderson's Isle of Dogs: Loving Homage to Japan or Cultural Appropriation?" *The Guardian*, 26 Mar. 2018. Accessed 23 Jan. 2022.

Rosen, David, and Peter Hamilton. *Off-Hollywood: The Making and Marketing of Independent Films*. New York: Grove Weidenfeld, 1990.

Ruh, Brian. "Adapting Anime: Transnational Media Between Japan and the United States." PhD diss., Indiana University, 2012.

Ryan, Alexandra. "Globalisation and the 'Internal Alchemy' in Chinese Martial Arts: The Transmission of Taijiquan to Britain." *East Asia Science, Technology and Society: An International Journal* 2.4 (2008): 525–43.

Said, Edward W. *Orientalism*. 25th Anniversary Ed. New York: Vintage Books, 1994.

Sammond, Nicholas. *Birth of an Industry: Blackface Minstrelsy and the Rise of American Animation*. Durham, NC: Duke University Press, 2015.

Sergi, Gianluca. "Actors and the Sound Gang." *Screen Acting*. Eds. Alan Lovell and Peter Krämer. London: Routledge, 1999. 126–37.

Sergi, Gianluca. "In Defence of Vulgarity: The Place of Sound Effects in the Cinema." *Scope: An Online Journal of Film Studies* 5 (2006).

Sharifian, Farzad, ed. *English as an International Language: Perspectives and Pedagogical Issues*. Bristol, UK: Multilingual Matters, 2009.

Shingler, Martin. "Fasten Your Seatbelts and Prick Up Your Ears: The Dramatic Voice in Film." *Scope: An Online Journal of Film Studies* 5 (2006).

Shipton, Alyn. *A New History of Jazz*. Rev. ed. New York: Continuum, 2007.

Sifianos, Georges, "The Definition of Animation: A Letter from Norman McLaren." *Animation Journal* 3.2 (1995): 62–66.

Simensky, Linda. "The Early Days of Nicktoons." *Nickelodeon Nation: The History, Politics, and Economics of America's Only TV Channel for Kids*. Ed. Heather Hendershot. New York: New York University Press, 2004. 87–107.

Sito, Tom. *Drawing the Line: The Untold Story of Animation Unions from Bosko to Bart Simpson*. Lexington: University Press of Kentucky, 2006.

Sluis, Ageeth. *Deco Body, Deco City: Female Spectacle and Modernity in Mexico City, 1900–1939*. Lincoln: University of Nebraska Press, 2016.

Slusser, George, and Eric S. Rankins. "Introduction: Shadows of the Magic Lamp." *Shadows of the Magic Lamp: Fantasy and Science Fiction in Film*. Eds. George Slusser and Eric S. Rankin. Carbondale: Southern Illinois University Press, 1985. vii–xvii.

Smedley, Audrey, and Brian D. Smedley. *Race in North America: Origin and Evolution of a Worldview*. 4th ed. Boulder, CO: Westview Press, 2012.

Smolko, Joanna R. "Southern Fried Foster: Representing Race and Place through Music in Looney Tunes Cartoons." *American Music* 30.3 (2012): 344–72.

Solomon, Charles. "Toward a Definition of Animation." *The Art of Animation*. Los Angeles: American Film Institute, 1988. 9–12.

Spivak, Gayatri Shakravorty. "Can the Subaltern Speak?" *Marxism and the Interpretation of Culture*. Eds. Cary Nelson and Lawrence Grossberg. Urbana: University of Illinois Press, 1988. 271–313.

Street, Mikelle. "The 'Kubo and the Two Strings' Controversy Proves Whitewashing Is More Complicated Than You Think." *Complex*, 23 Aug. 2016. Accessed 23 Jan. 2022.

Suan, Stevie. "Anime's Performativity: Diversity through Conventionality in the Global Media-Form." *Animation: An Interdisciplinary Journal* 12.1 (2017): 62–79.

Subtirelu, Nicholas Close. "'She Does Have an Accent but . . .': Race and Language Ideology in Students' Evaluations of Mathematics Instructors on Ratemyprofessors.com." *Language in Society* 44.1 (2015): 35–62.

Summers, Sam. "High Fantasy Meets Low Culture in *How to Train Your Dragon* (2010)." *Fantasy/Animation: Connections between Media, Mediums and Genres*. Eds. Christopher Holliday and Alexander Sergeant. London: Routledge, 2018. 227–42.

Szeto, Kin-Yan. *The Martial Arts Cinema of the Chinese Diaspora: Ang Lee, John Woo, and Jackie Chan in Hollywood*. Carbondale: Southern Illinois Press, 2011.

Taberham, Paul. "A General Aesthetics of American Sound Design." *Animation: An Interdisciplinary Journal* 13.2 (2018): 131–47.

Teo, Stephen. *The Asian Cinema Experience: Styles, Spaces, Theory*. London: Routledge, 2013.

Tillis, Steve. "The Art of Puppetry in the Age of Media Production." *The Drama Review* 43.3 (Fall 1999): 182–95.

Toll, Robert C. *Blacking Up: The Minstrel Show in Nineteenth Century America*. New York: Oxford University Press, 1974.

Trausch, Tim, ed., *Chinese Martial Arts Media Culture: Global Perspectives* (London: Rowman & Littlefield International, 2018).

Tulk, Janice Esther. "An Aesthetic of Ambiguity: Musical Representation of Indigenous Peoples in Disney's *Brother Bear*." Ed. Rebecca Coyle. London: Equinox, 2010. 120–37.

Turchiano, Danielle. "'Big Mouth': Ayo Edebiri to Replace Jenny Slate as Missy (EXCLUSIVE)." *Variety*, 28 Aug. 2020. Accessed 23 Jan. 2022.

Ueno Toshiya. "Techno-Orientalism and Media Tribalism: On Japanese Animation and Rave Culture." *Third Text* 13.47 (1999): 95–106.

Vasconcellos, Eduardo. "Interview: Avatar's Bryan Konietzko and Michael Dante DiMartino." *IGN*, 6 Sep. 2007. Accessed 8 Mar. 2018.

Vats, Anjali, and LeiLani Nishime. "Containment as Neocolonial Visual Rhetoric: Fashion, Yellowface, and Karl Lagerfeld's 'Idea of China.'" *Quarterly Journal of Speech* 99.4 (2013): 423–47.

Viruet, Pilot. "The Creator Of 'BoJack Horseman' Doesn't Want to Ignore Animation's Diversity Problem Anymore." *UPROXX*, 30 Jan. 2018. Accessed 23 Jan. 2022.

von Gunden, Kenneth. *Flights of Fancy: The Great Fantasy Films*. Jefferson, NC: McFarland, 2001.

Wakeman, Frederic E. *Spymaster: Dai Li and the Chinese Secret Service*. Oakland: University of California Press, 2003.

Wang, Ze, et al., "'You Lost Me at Hello': How and When Accent-Based Biases Are Expressed and Suppressed." *International Journal of Research in Marketing* 30.2 (2013): 185–96.

Wang Guangxi. *Chinese Kung Fu*. Trans. Han Huizhi, Wang Wenliang, and Kang Jin. Cambridge: Cambridge University Press, 2012.

Wells, Paul. *The Animated Bestiary: Animals, Cartoons, and Culture*. New Brunswick, NJ: Rutgers University Press, 2008.

Wells, Paul. *Animation: Genre and Authorship*. London: Wallflower, 2002.

Wells, Paul. *Animation and America*. Edinburgh, UK: Edinburgh University Press, 2002.

Wells, Paul. "'Smarter Than the Average Art Form': Animation in the Television Era." *Prime Time Animation: Television Animation and American Culture*. Eds. Carol A. Stabile and Mark Harrison. London: Routledge, 2003. 15–32.

Wells, Paul. "To Affinity and Beyond: Woody, Buzz and the New Authority." *Contemporary Hollywood Stardom*. Eds. Thomas Austin and Martin Barker. London: Arnold, 2003. 90–102.

Wells, Paul. *Understanding Animation*. London: Routledge, 1998.

Wells, Paul, and Samantha Moore. *The Fundamentals of Animation*. 2nd ed. London: Fairchild Books, 2016.

West, David. *Chasing Dragons: An Introduction to the Martial Arts Film*. London: I. B. Tauris, 2006.

Wickert, Marc. "Dana White and the Future of UFC." *Fight Times*, 1 Oct. 2004. Accessed 20 Mar. 2019.

Wojcik, Pamela Robertson. "The Sound of Film Acting." *Journal of Film and Video* 58.1/2 (2006): 71–83.

Wu, Frank H. *Yellow: Race in American beyond Black and White*. New York: Basic Books, 2003.

Xu Lingna and Dai Zeyu. "Regaining the Sense of Being a Shanghainese: A Study of the Revival of Art Deco as an Apparatus of Cultural Memory from an Intercultural Perspective." *Intercultural Communication Studies* 20.1 (2011): 234–48.

Yeh, Wen-hsin. "Dai Li and the Liu Geqing Affair: Heroism in the Chinese Secret Service during the War of Resistance." *Journal of Asian Studies* 48.3 (1989): 545–62.

Windover, Michael. *Art Deco: A Mode of Mobility*. Quebec City: Presses de l'Université du Québec, 2012.

Young, James O. *Cultural Appropriation and the Arts*. Chichester, UK: Wiley-Blackwell, 2010.

Yu Wenxin, et al. "Shorter Intervals of East Asians with Port-Wine Stains with Pulsed Dye Laser Are Safe and Effective—A Prospective Side-by-Side Comparison." *Photomedicine and Laser Surgery* 36.1 (2018): 37–43.

Yuen, Nancy Wang. "Performing Race, Negotiating Identity: Asian American Professional Actors in Hollywood." In *Asian American Youth: Culture, Identity, and Ethnicity*. Ed. Jennifer Lee and Min Zhou. New York: Routledge, 2004. 251–68.

Yuen, Nancy Wang. *Reel Inequality: Hollywood Actors and Racism*. New Brunswick, NJ: Rutgers University Press, 2016.

Zinder, David. *Body-Voice-Imagination: A Training for the Actor*. London: Routledge, 2002.

OTHER SOURCES

Acastus. "Interview with Crawford Wilson (part 1 of 2)." *AvatarSpirit.net*, 15 Nov. 2006. Accessed 20 Dec. 2017.
Acastus. "Interview with Director Giancarlo Volpe (part 1 of 3)." *AvatarSpirit.net*, 16 Jun. 2006. Accessed 20 Dec. 2017.
Acastus. "Interview with Director Giancarlo Volpe (part 3 of 3)." *AvatarSpirit.net*, 1 Jul. 2006. Accessed 20 Dec. 2017.
Acastus. "Interview with Jessie Flower (part 1 or 2)." *AvatarSpirit.net*, 22 Dec. 2006. Accessed 20 Dec. 2017.
Acastus. "Interview with Joanna Braddy (part 1 of 2)." *AvatarSpirit.net*, 30 Nov. 2006. Accessed 20 Dec. 2017.
Acastus. "Interview with Sifu Kisu (part 1 of 3)." *AvatarSpirit.net*, 5 Oct. 2006. Accessed 20 Dec. 2017.
Acastus. "Interview with Sifu Kisu (part 2 of 3)." *AvatarSpirit.net*, 12 Oct. 2006. Accessed 20 Dec. 2017.
Acastus. "Music Interview with the Track Team (part 1 of 3)." *AvatarSpirit.net*, 26 Jul. 2006. Accessed 20 Dec. 2017.
Acastus. "Music Interview with the Track Team (part 2 of 3)." *AvatarSpirit.net*, 5 Aug. 2006. Accessed 20 Dec. 2017.
Acastus. "Music Interview with the Track Team (part 3 of 3)." *AvatarSpirit.net*, 12 Aug. 2006. Accessed 20 Dec. 2017.
Acastus. "Interview with Voice Director Andrea Romano (part 1 of 3)." *AvatarSpirit.net*, 12 May 2007. Accessed 20 Dec. 2017.
Allesandra, Pilar. "526: The Adventures of Katie Mattila." *On The Page*, 6 Oct. 2017.
Ancil, Brandon. "Did the 'Airbender' adaptation ever have a chance?" *CNN*, 1 Jul. 2010.
"Audio Commentary—Chapter 2: A Leaf in the Wind" (supplementary material on Blu-ray release of *The Legend of Korra—Book One: Air*). Viacom International Inc., 2012.
"Audio Commentary—Chapter 3: The Revelation" (supplementary material on Blu-ray release of *The Legend of Korra—Book One: Air*). Viacom International Inc., 2012.
"Audio Commentary—Chapter 4: Sokka's Master" (supplementary material on DVD release of *Avatar: The Last Airbender—The Complete Book 3 Collection*). Viacom International Inc., 2008.
"Audio Commentary—Chapter 4: The Voice in the Night" (supplementary material on Blu-ray release of *The Legend of Korra—Book One: Air*). Viacom International Inc., 2012.

"Audio Commentary—Chapter 5: The Beach" (supplementary material on DVD release of *Avatar: The Last Airbender—The Complete Book 3 Collection*). Viacom International Inc., 2008.

"Audio Commentary—Chapter 6: And the Winner Is . . ." (supplementary material on Blu-ray release of *The Legend of Korra—Book One: Air*). Viacom International Inc., 2012.

"Audio Commentary—Chapter 6: The Avatar and the Firelord" (supplementary material on DVD release of *Avatar: The Last Airbender—The Complete Book 3 Collection*). Viacom International Inc., 2008.

"Audio Commentary—Chapter 8: When Extremes Meet" (supplementary material on Blu-ray release of *The Legend of Korra—Book One: Air*). Viacom International Inc., 2012.

"Audio Commentary—Chapter 9: Out of the Past" (supplementary material on Blu-ray release of *The Legend of Korra—Book One: Air*). Viacom International Inc., 2012.

"Audio Commentary—Chapter 10: The Day of Black Sun, Part 1: The Invasion" (supplementary material on DVD release of *Avatar: The Last Airbender—The Complete Book 3 Collection*). Viacom International Inc., 2008.

"Audio Commentary—Chapter 12: The Journey to Ba Sing Se, Part 1: The Serpent's Pass" (supplementary material on DVD release of *Avatar: The Last Airbender—The Complete Book 2 Collection*). Viacom International Inc., 2007.

"Audio Commentary—Chapter 12: The Western Air Temple" (supplementary material on DVD release of *Avatar: The Last Airbender—The Complete Book 3 Collection*). Viacom International Inc., 2008.

"Audio Commentary—Chapter 14: City of Walls and Secrets" (supplementary material on DVD release of *Avatar: The Last Airbender—The Complete Book 2 Collection*). Viacom International Inc., 2007.

"Audio Commentary—Chapter 16: The Southern Raiders" (supplementary material on DVD release of *Avatar: The Last Airbender—The Complete Book 3 Collection*). Viacom International Inc., 2008.

"Audio Commentary—Chapter 17: Lake Laogai" (supplementary material on DVD release of *Avatar: The Last Airbender—The Complete Book 2 Collection*). Viacom International Inc., 2007.

"Audio Commentary—Chapter 17: The Ember Island Players" (supplementary material on DVD release of *Avatar: The Last Airbender—The Complete Book 3 Collection*). Viacom International Inc., 2008.

"Audio Commentary—Chapter 18: Sozin's Comet, Part 1: The Phoenix King" (supplementary material on DVD release of *Avatar: The Last Airbender—The Complete Book 3 Collection*). Viacom International Inc., 2008.

"Audio Commentary—Chapter 18: The Earth King" (supplementary material on DVD release of *Avatar: The Last Airbender—The Complete Book 2 Collection*). Viacom International Inc., 2007.

"Audio Commentary—Chapter 20: Sozin's Comet, Part 3: Into the Inferno" (supplementary material on DVD release of *Avatar: The Last Airbender—The Complete Book 3 Collection*). Viacom International Inc., 2008.

"Audio Commentary—Chapter 20: The Crossroads of Destiny" (supplementary material on DVD release of *Avatar: The Last Airbender—The Complete Book 2 Collection*). Viacom International Inc., 2007.

"Audio Commentary—Episode 17: The Northern Air Temple" (supplementary material on DVD release of *Avatar: The Last Airbender—The Complete Book 1 Collection*). Viacom International Inc., 2006.

"Audio Commentary—Episode 18: The Waterbending Master" (supplementary material on DVD release of *Avatar: The Last Airbender—The Complete Book 1 Collection*). Viacom International Inc., 2006.

"Audio Commentary—Episode 19: The Siege of the North—Part 1" (supplementary material on DVD release of *Avatar: The Last Airbender—The Complete Book 1 Collection*). Viacom International Inc., 2006.

"Audio Commentary—Episode 20: The Siege of the North—Part 2" (supplementary material on DVD release of *Avatar: The Last Airbender—The Complete Book 1 Collection*). Viacom International Inc., 2006.

"Avatar Spirits" (supplementary material on DVD release of *Avatar: The Last Airbender—The Complete Book 1 Collection (Collector's Edition)*). Viacom International Inc., 2010.

Baek Byung-yeul. "'Drawing animation is our DNA.'" *The Korean Times*, 8 May 2015. Accessed 30 Jul. 2018.

"Behind the Scenes Kung Fu Featurette" (supplementary material on DVD release of *Avatar: The Last Airbender—The Complete Book 1 Collection*). Viacom International Inc., 2006.

Blacker, Ben. "Episode 154: Legend of Korra/Avatar: The Last Airbender." *Nerdist Writers Panel*, 19 Aug. 2014. Accessed 10 Sep. 2018.

Brennan, Mike. "The Music of Avatar: The Last Airbender." *Soundtrack*, 7 Apr. 2008. Accessed 10 Aug. 2018.

Chang, Christina. "Las Vegas musician helping preserve Chinese folk music, instruments." *Las Vegas Sun*, 12 Aug. 2012. Accessed 10 Aug. 2018.

Ching, Gene. "Kisu on The Legend of Korra." *Kung Fu Magazine*, n.d. Accessed 30 Jul. 2018.

"Commentary on A Breath of Fresh Air" (supplementary material on Blu-ray release of *The Legend of Korra—Book Three: Change*). Viacom International Inc., 2014.

"Commentary on A New Spiritual Age" (supplementary material on Blu-ray release of *The Legend of Korra—Book Two: Spirits*). Viacom International Inc., 2014.

"Commentary on After All These Years" (supplementary material on Blu-ray release of *The Legend of Korra—Book Four: Balance*). Viacom International Inc., 2015.

"Commentary on Battle Zaofu" (supplementary material on Blu-ray release of *The Legend of Korra—Book Four: Balance*). Viacom International Inc., 2015.

"Commentary on Beginnings: Part 1" (supplementary material on Blu-ray release of *The Legend of Korra—Book Two: Spirits*). Viacom International Inc., 2014.

"Commentary on Beginnings: Part 2" (supplementary material on Blu-ray release of *The Legend of Korra—Book Two: Spirits*). Viacom International Inc., 2014.

"Commentary on Civil Wars: Part 2" (supplementary material on Blu-ray release of *The Legend of Korra—Book Two: Spirits*). Viacom International Inc., 2014.

"Commentary on Enemy at the Gates" (supplementary material on Blu-ray release of *The Legend of Korra—Book Four: Balance*). Viacom International Inc., 2015.
"Commentary on Enter the Void" (supplementary material on Blu-ray release of *The Legend of Korra—Book Three: Change*). Viacom International Inc., 2014.
"Commentary on Light in the Dark" (supplementary material on Blu-ray release of *The Legend of Korra—Book Two: Spirits*). Viacom International Inc., 2014.
"Commentary on Night of a Thousand Stars" (supplementary material on Blu-ray release of *The Legend of Korra—Book Two: Spirits*). Viacom International Inc., 2014.
"Commentary on Old Wounds" (supplementary material on Blu-ray release of *The Legend of Korra—Book Three: Change*). Viacom International Inc., 2014.
"Commentary on Operation: Beifong" (supplementary material on Blu-ray release of *The Legend of Korra—Book Four: Balance*). Viacom International Inc., 2015.
"Commentary on Original Airbenders" (supplementary material on Blu-ray release of *The Legend of Korra—Book Three: Change*). Viacom International Inc., 2014.
"Commentary on Rebirth" (supplementary material on Blu-ray release of *The Legend of Korra—Book Three: Change*). Viacom International Inc., 2014.
"Commentary on Reunion" (supplementary material on Blu-ray release of *The Legend of Korra—Book Four: Balance*). Viacom International Inc., 2015.
"Commentary on The Earth Queen" (supplementary material on Blu-ray release of *The Legend of Korra—Book Three: Change*). Viacom International Inc., 2014.
"Commentary on The Guide" (supplementary material on Blu-ray release of *The Legend of Korra—Book Two: Spirits*). Viacom International Inc., 2014.
"Commentary on The Metal Clan" (supplementary material on Blu-ray release of *The Legend of Korra—Book Three: Change*). Viacom International Inc., 2014.
"Commentary on The Southern Lights" (supplementary material on Blu-ray release of *The Legend of Korra—Book Two: Spirits*). Viacom International Inc., 2014.
"Commentary on The Terror Within" (supplementary material on Blu-ray release of *The Legend of Korra—Book Three: Change*). Viacom International Inc., 2014.
"Commentary on The Ultimatum" (supplementary material on Blu-ray release of *The Legend of Korra—Book Three: Change*). Viacom International Inc., 2014.
Cornah, Joel. "Jeremy Zuckerman Interview." *Sci Fi Fantasy Network*, 16 Jan. 2016. Accessed 10 Aug. 2018.
Curran, Brad. "Interview with Sifu Kisu." *Kung-Fu Kingdom*, 6 Oct. 2015. Accessed 30 Jul. 2017.
Dankiewicz, Tom. Email interview. 19 Feb. 2018.
DiMartino, Michael Dante, and Bryan Konietzko. *Avatar: The Last Airbender—The Art of the Animated Series*. Milwaukie, OR: Dark Horse Books, 2010.
DiMartino, Michael Dante, Bryan Konietzko, and Joaquim Dos Santos. *The Legend of Korra: The Art of the Animated Series—Book Four: Balance*. Milwaukie, OR: Dark Horse Books, 2015.
DiMartino, Michael Dante, Bryan Konietzko, and Joaquim Dos Santos. *The Legend of Korra: The Art of the Animated Series—Book One: Air*. Milwaukie, OR: Dark Horse Books, 2013.

DiMartino, Michael Dante, Bryan Konietzko, and Joaquim Dos Santos. *The Legend of Korra: The Art of the Animated Series—Book Three: Change*. Milwaukie, OR: Dark Horse Books, 2015.

DiMartino, Michael Dante, Bryan Konietzko, and Joaquim Dos Santos. *The Legend of Korra: The Art of the Animated Series—Book Two: Spirits*. Milwaukie, OR: Dark Horse Books, 2014.

Ehasz, Aaron. Google Hangout interview. 10 May 2018.

"Essence of Bending with Bryan Konietzko and Sifu Kisu, The" (supplementary material on DVD release of *Avatar: The Last Airbender—The Complete Book 2 Collection*). Viacom International Inc., 2007.

Farley, Christopher John. "The Legend of Korra Creators Answer Your Questions." *Wall Street Journal*, 22 Jun. 2012. Accessed 20 Mar. 2019.

Faust, Minister. "Sifu Kisu on Martial Arts Mastery and Designing—Choreographing the Bending of Avatar the Last Airbender (MF Galaxy 069)." *MF Galaxy*, 14 Mar. 2016. Accessed 30 Jul. 2018.

"Fire Nation's Most Wanted." *Nick Mag Presents* (Sep. 2006): 48.

Garagarza, Elsa. Email interview. 7 Mar. 2018.

Garagarza, Elsa. Email interview. 6 Apr. 2018.

Goldman, Eric. "IGN Interview: Jason Isaacs." *IGN*, 15 Feb. 2007. Accessed 20 Dec. 2017.

Granshaw, Lisa. "An Oral History of Avatar: The Last Airbender: Cast Looks Back as Show Celebrates 10th Anniversary of Finale." *SYFY Wire*, 30 Jul. 2018. Accessed 1 Apr. 2019.

Hardwick, Chris. "Episode 621: Andrea Romano." *Nerdist Podcast*, 7 Jan. 2015. Accessed 20 Dec. 2017.

Hedrick, Tim. Email interview. 21 Sep. 2018.

Hedrick, Tim. Email interview. 24 Sep. 2018.

"How *Avatar* Gets Its Kicks." *Nick Mag Presents* (Sep. 2006): 42–43.

Huang, Jake. Google Hangouts interview. 31 Oct. 2018.

"In Their Elements." *Nick Mag Presents* (Sep. 2006): 26–27.

"Inside the Book of Spirits" (supplementary material on Blu-ray release of *The Legend of Korra—Book Two: Spirits*). Viacom International Inc., 2014.

Konietzko, Bryan. "Korra Crew Profile: Sylvia Filcak-Blackwolf." Tumblr, 31 Jul. 2013. Accessed 8 Mar. 2018.

Konietzko, Bryan. Tumblr, 28 Jun. 2013. Accessed 18 Apr. 2018.

Konietzko, Bryan. Tumblr, 2 Jul. 2013. Accessed 18 Apr. 2018.

"KorraScope Interviews Jeremy Zuckerman." *YumChunks*, 21 Apr. 2014. Accessed 10 Aug. 2018.

Kwan, Jessie. Google Meet interview. 25 Aug. 2021.

Lasswell, Mark. "Kung Fu Fightin' Anime Stars, Born in the U.S.A." *New York Times*, 28 Aug. 2005. Accessed 8 Mar. 2018.

Lee, Marissa. "Interview with the Track Team: The musicians behind The Legend of Korra." Racebending.com, 27 Mar. 2012. Accessed 10 Aug. 2018.

Lee, Marissa. "Statement from Dao Le, Animatic Editor." Racebending.com, 31 Jul. 2009. Accessed 11 Mar. 2019.

Lee, Siu-Leung. Email interview. 30 Jan. 2018
Lee, Siu-Leung. Email interview. 31 Jan. 2018.
Lee, Siu-Leung. Email interview. 13 Feb. 2018.
Liu, Ed. "From Tiny Toons to Brave & Bold: Toon Zone Interviews Voice Director Andrea Romano." *Toon Zone*, 5 Aug. 2008. Accessed 20 Dec. 2017.
Liu, Ed. "Toon Zone Interviews Joaquim Dos Santos on Directing 'Avatar.'" *Toon Zone*, 22 Jul. 2008. Accessed 30 Jul. 2018.
Liu, Ed. "Toon Zone News Interviews Bryan Konietzko & Mike DiMartino on 'Avatar the Last Airbender.'" *Toon Zone*, 22 Apr. 2008. Accessed 20 Dec. 2017.
MacDonald, Susan Lee. "The INNERview #61—Yoo Jae-myung (유재명), Animation director." *The INNERview with Host Susan Lee MacDonald*, 2 May 2013. Accessed 30 Jul. 2018.
"Making of Avatar, The—Inside the Korean Studios" (supplementary material on DVD release of *Avatar: The Last Airbender—The Complete Book 1 Collection*), Viacom International Inc., 2006.
"Making of Avatar, The—Inside the Sound Studios" (supplementary material on DVD release of *Avatar: The Last Airbender—The Complete Book 1 Collection*), Viacom International Inc., 2006.
Meza-Leon, Juan. Skype interview. 21 Jul. 2018.
Miller, Evan. "The Gallery: Elsa Garagarza." *Anime News Network*, 31 Jan. 2009. Accessed 20 Dec. 2017.
Navarro, Hector. "Episode 1: Bryan Konietzko & Michael Dante DiMartino." *Nick Animation Podcast*, 13 May 2016. Accessed 20 Dec. 2017.
Navarro, Hector. "Episode 30: Jeremy Zuckerman & Bryan Konietzko." *Nick Animation Podcast*, 27 Jun 2017. Accessed 20 Dec. 2017.
Navarro, Hector. "Episode 46: The Legend of Korra Cast." *Nick Animation Podcast*, 20 Oct. 2017. Accessed 20 Dec. 2017.
"Nickelodeon: The Last Airbender: Legend of Korra Martial Arts Reference Demo—Fusion Comics." *Vimeo*, 9 Aug. 2011. Accessed 19 Apr. 2017.
Oatley, Chris. "Interview with 'Korra' and 'Dreamworks' Artist, Frederic William Stewart: Arcast #95." *The Oatley Academy Artcast*, 2 Jun. 2017. Accessed 8 Mar. 2018.
Robinson, Seth. "Joaquim Dos Santos Ready to Tell THE LEGEND OF KORRA." *Newsarama*, 10 Apr. 2012. Accessed 30 Jul. 2018.
Robinson, Tasha. "*Legend of Korra*'s Michael Dante DiMartino and Joaquim Dos Santos." *The A.V. Club*, 13 Apr. 2012. Accessed 30 Jul. 2018.
Savas, Kaya. "Composter Interview: Jeremy Zuckerman." *Film.Music.Media*, 11 Oct. 2013. Accessed 10 Aug. 2018.
Schick, Michal. "SeptBender Interview: Jeremy Zuckerman Discusses Music-Bending on 'The Legend of Korra.'" *Hypable*, 23 Sep. 2013. Accessed 10 Aug. 2018.
"Spirit of an Episode, The: Original Airbenders" (supplementary material on Blu-ray release of *The Legend of Korra—Book Two: Spirits*). Viacom International Inc., 2014.
"Spirit of an Episode, The: Rebirth" (supplementary material on Blu-ray release of *The Legend of Korra—Book Two: Spirits*). Viacom International Inc., 2014.
Sung, Angela. Skype interview. 17 Feb. 2018.

Tetri, Emily. Email interview. 27 Mar. 2018.
Tetri, Emily. Email interview. 10 Mar. 2019.
third ear audio. Tumblr, 9 Mar. 2013. Accessed 10 Aug. 2018.
third ear audio. Tumblr, 11 Mar. 2013. Accessed 10 Aug. 2018.
third ear audio. Tumblr, 3 May 2013. Accessed 10 Aug. 2018.
third ear audio. Tumblr, 9 Jul. 2013. Accessed 10 Aug. 2018.
Tushar, Steve. Email interview. 28 Apr. 2019.
Tushar, Steve. Skype interview. 22 Jun. 2018.
Ulanova, Olga. Google Hangouts interview. 22 May 2018.
Varney, Janet. Email interview. 20 Sep. 2017.
Webb, Charles. "Interview: Paging, Dr. Fight! A Chat With 'Legend of Korra' Art Director and Co-Executive Producer Joaquim Dos Santos." *MTV*, 23 Apr. 2012. Accessed 30 Jul. 2018.
Wimberly, Kris. "TAN—Ep43: Color Compositing Supervisor, Sylvia Filcak-Blackwolf." *The Animation Network Podcast*, 7 Mar. 2016. Accessed 8 Mar. 2018.
Zane, Edwin. Phone interview. 3 Mar. 2018.

INDEX

References to figures are in **bold**.

abstraction, 69, 85, 139; definition of, 10, 22; sound effects, 130
accents, 9, 55–60; Asian, 58; in *Avatar*, 57–60; in *Korra*, 58–60; in media, 9, 58
Acevedo, William, 104
acupuncture, 73–74, 76, 83
Age of Enlightenment, 5
Aihara, Koji, 35
Alazraqui, Carlos, 57
Allison, Tanine, 65, 108
Altman, Rick, 61, 65
Ament, Vanessa Theme, 125
American Dragon: Jake Long, 15
Angilirq, Paul Apak, 87
animated bodyscape, 10, 12, 15, 18; aural components of, 49–67; aural worldbuilding and, 115–32; definition of, 12, 32; iconicity, 12, 22, 25, 32, 68, 133, 135; indexical elements, 20; linking, 35; narrative components, 17, 68–84, 133; nonindexicality, 12, 20, 22, 32, 45, 133–35; plasmaticity, 12, 37, 45, 62, 68, 133, 135; racialized identities, 15, 45, 47, 61, 66, 68, 133; visual components of, 20–48; visual worldbuilding and, 85–114
animation, 17, 20, 77–78; 1920s and 1930s, 32; 1952–1988, 13; application of color, 39–43; Asian representation in, 3; audience demographics, 13; aural components, 11, 12; Black representation in, 3, 14; cinematic, 10; computer, 32, 86; core qualities of, 20; creating meaning in, 137–41; definition of, 9–10; Golden Age of, 3; hyperrealist, 22, 32, 138–39; iconicity, 12, 21, 39, 47; indication, 40; Japanese, 14, 24–25, 31, 37, 130, 134; Korean, 42–43, 154n87; Latino representation in, 14; mainstream television, 19, 22, 49, 134; motion capture, 20, 50, 108, 109, 135; nonindexicality, 12, 21, 39, 47; outsourcing, 39–43; plasmaticity, 12, 21, 39, 47, 134; primetime, 13; racialized identities in, 10, 12, 13, 19, 20, 21, 32, 48; rotoscoping, 20, 108–9, 135; shorts, 13; stop-motion, 20, 32, 135; television, 11; whitewashing, 65, 66, 156n6
anime, 34, 141; conventions, 15, 38, 130; cultural identity of, 34, 37; cultural imperialism of, 34; specificity in, 24–25
Aniston, Jennifer, 38
Aoki, Guy, 80
Arnheim, Rudolf, 20
art deco, 95–97, 112, 122
Art in Motion: Animation Aesthetics (Furniss), 9
Asians: accents in media, 58; birthmarks specific to, 26–27, 47, 139; -coded characters, 28, 30, 31, 59, 60; exoticism of, 9; model minority status, 8–9, 60; racialized identity, 8–9, 56, 76, 78, 85, 88; referents, 80, 95–96, 107; representation in animation, 3, 45; signifiers, 8, 14,

25–26, 35, 68, 73, 74, 80, 85, 94, 109, 130, 137–39; voice over actors, 52, 64
Atanarjuat: The Fast Runner, 87
Atkins, E. Taylor, 122
Attack on Titan, 24–25; Mikasa Ackerman, 25
Attack on Titan: Junior High, 25
Automated Dialogue Replacement (ADR), 63
aural components, 11, 17, 49–67, 139; accents, 55–60; building blocks, 50, 55, 61–63, 67; cinematic sound, 61–62; "cyborg" voice, 61; dialects, 55, 58, 110; dialogue tracks, 50, 54, 62–63, 136; dubbing, 136; ensemble recording, 54; environmental sounds, 127–28; indexability, 135; *le grain* of voice, 49; line readings, 50, 55, 135, 139–40; linguistic profiling, 49; multiple readings, 55; music, 68, 115–32; production process, 49–50, 135; pronunciation, 56–57; racialized identities, 17–18, 49, 50, 53, 55, 67, 74, 76, 81, 132, 135; recording, 20, 54–61, 135, 142; sound editing, 50, 61–68, 121, 135–36; sound effects, 125–31; synchronization, 61–67; vocal casting, 49–54, 67; vocal coaches, 49; vocal performance, 11, 17, 74, 77, 83, 115, 135; voice actors, 50–54, 76; voice director, 54–55, 135; worldbuilding, 115–32
authenticity, 85–86, 88, 97, 104, 113, 120; archival, 86, 98–106, 107, 117; cinematic, 107; corporeal, 86, 98, 106–9, 124–25, 132; cultural, 15
A.V. Club, 104
Avatar: The Last Airbender, 9, 12, 13, 14–15, 68–69; Aang, 15, 35, **36**, 38, 39, 41–42, 46, 60, 63, 71–72, 74, 129, 134, 136, 142; accents and dialects in, 57–60; Air Nomads, 15, 59, 71, 100, 103; airbending, 100, 103–4, 128; animals in, 69; animation outsourcing, 39, 40; architecture in, 89–90, 92–93; art book, 35, 39–40, 46, 95, 110–12, 140; Aunt Wu, 59; authenticity in, 86; Avatar, 15; "The Avatar State," 59; Azula, 15, 35, 74, 102–3, 129; Ba Sing Se, 74–75, 137; Ba Sing Se bureaucrats, 60; "Bato of the Water Tribe," 28; BG, 87, 88–90; "Bitter Work," 100–104; "The Blind Bandit," 60, 101, 119; bloodbending, 128; "The Boiling Rock, Part 1," 28, **29**, 78; "The Boy in the Iceberg," **26**; calligraphy, 82, 109–10, 112; casting, 50–52, 78; "The Cave of Two Lovers," 129; chakras in, 71–73, 76, 78; Chan, 35, **36**, 129; choreography, 98–100, 102–5, 113–14; "City of Walls and Secrets," 28, 60, 74–75; "The Crossroads of Destiny," 39, 134; cultural consultant, 16, 26–27, 47, 53, 80, 84, 103, 137, 139; Dai Li, 74–76, 78, 83, 137; "The Deserter," 59; dialogue tracks, 62–63; directors, 33–34, 37, 52–55; "The Drill," 81, 110; "The Earth King," 81; Earth Kingdom, 15, 25, 71, 100; earthbending, 100–102, 128; Eastern Air Temple, 71–72; Fire Nation, 15, 25–26, 88, 90, 94, 100–103, 118–19, 137; Fire Sage, 89–90, 93; firebending, 73, 100, 102–3, 128, 137; "The Firebending Masters," 92–93; Foaming Mouth Guy, 41–42, 47; Foggy Swamp Tribe, 57, 120; "The Fortune Teller," 59; General Sung, 81–82; guest actors, 53, 78; Guo, 74, 76, 83; "The Guru," 60, 71–72; Guru Pathik, 60, 71–73, 76, 83; home video release, 39, 97; Iroh, 15, 51, 59, 100–104, 136; Jeong Jeong, 59; Joo Dee, 28, 35, 60, 75; June, 28; Katara, 15, 38, 39, 44, 46, 47, 82, 109, 129, 134; King Bumi, 44; "The King of Omashu," 44; "Lake Laogai," 35, **36**; language as a neutral object in, 82–83; Li, 59; "The Library," 111; Lin, 74; live action film, 28, 56–57, 80; Lo, 59; logograms, 82, 110–11, 167n153; Long Feng, 74, 81; Mayor Tong, 60; Monk Gyatso, 59; music, 115–32; "Nightmares and Daydreams," 60, 74; North American English in, 55–57, 60, 81–83, 83, 138; Ozai, 15, 93, 97; "The Painted Lady," 93; Pakku, 38–39, 134; Piandao, 30, 33, 134; pilot, 39, 40; Pirate Barker, 28, **29**; pirates, 28; production narratives, 79, 80, 86, 97–98, 104; puns, 81; Queen Hou-Tang, 75; "Rebel Spirit," 81; recording sessions,

55; referents, 69, 70, 84, 88–90, 93–94, 103; "The Serpent's Pass," 60, 82, 111; "The Siege of the North, Part 1," 45; skin tones in, 44; Sokka, 15, 54–55, 63, 81, 129; "Sokka's Master," 30; sound effects, 125–31; "The Southern Air Temple," 56, 59; star personas, 66; "The Storm," 59, 93, 129; storyboards, 33–35, 37, 42, 106; Sun Warrior ruins, 92–94; Suki, 50, 64; "The Swamp," 57, 120; Toph Bei Fong, 15, 74, 101–2, 119–20, 143; topography, 88–89; Warden, 28, **29**; "The Warriors of Kyoshi," 41–42; Water Tribe, 15, 100, 133; waterbending, 100–101, 120; "The Waterbending Master," 38–39, 44, 134; "The Waterbending Scroll," 28, **29**; "The Winter Solstice, Part 1," 89–90; writers and writing process, 70, 71, 77–78, 80, 82; Yue, 50; Zhao, 55, 66; Zuko, 15, 25–27, 45, 47, 51, 66, 100, 104, 139
Azaria, Hank, 4, 52

background (BG), 86–97, 136; designs, 77, 86; lighting, 88; painting, 86, 88, 136; production of, 87; research, 87–88
Baldi, Enzo, 92–93
Baldwin, Greg, 59, 63, 136
Banet-Weiser, Sarah, 3, 13, 14
Barthes, Roland, 49
Basco, Dante, 51, 53–54, 56, 64, 66
Bassett, William H., 57
Batkin, Jane, 21, 32
Baudry, Jean-Louis, 61
Bell, Kristen, 4
Bendazzi, Giannalberto, 14
Bennett, Jeff, 57
Bernier, François, 5
Bian, Christine, 28
Big Mouth, 4; Missy Foreman-Greenwaldon, 4
"Birth of a Notion, The" (Kotlarz), 3
Bivins, Robert E., 74
Black/Blackness: 1930s and 1940s representation in cartoons, 3; audiences, 24; commodification of, 3; jazz as a signifier, 122–23, 131; as a racial minority in US animation, 3; racialized identity, 30, 108; signifiers of, 120, 122–23; vocal performances, 4
blackface, 23
Bloodsworth-Lugo, Mary K., 3
Blum, Steve, 31
Blumenbach, Johann Friedrich, 5
bodyscape, definition, 10
Bodyscape: Art, Modernity, and the Ideal Figure (Mirzoeff), 10
Bogle, Donald, 7
Bohlman, Philip V., 115
BoJack Horseman, 4
Booker, M. Keith, 13
Braddy, Johanna, 50–51
Branigan, Edward, 61
Brother Bear, 116
Brown, Clancy, 60
"brown voice," 4, 58, 60, 140
Brownrigg, Mark, 116, 120
Bue, Jevon, 92
Buhler, James, 115, 122
Buonarroti, Michelangelo, 39, 134
Bureau of Investigation and Statistics, 75

cable TV, 13
Caldwell, John T., 12, 79
calligraphy, 82, 83, 86, 109–12
Caplan, Lizzy, 4
Carano, Gina, 105, 134
celebrity casting/star personas, 139–40; voice, 50, 65–66; white as nonwhite characters in animation, 4, 53, 65–66
Central Park, 4; Molly Tillerman, 4
chakras, 71–73, 76, 83; chi/*qi* and, 72–73, 160n17
Chan, Jackie, 106
Chan, May, 78
character design, 4, 17, 18, 21–32, 41, 83; definition of, 21; iconicity, 21–32, 39; local colors, 21, 134; model sheets, 21, 39, 134; racialized identity, 22, 25–27, 39, 76; real-world contexts, 26–27; signifiers, 23, 27, 74; simplification, 22, 23; stick figures, 22–23, 25, 27; villain designs, 24–26, 103, 137

Cheng, Anne Anlin, 7–8
Cheung, Mei, 104
Chiang Kai-shek, 75
Chin, Tsai, 59
Chion, Michel, 61
Chung, Hye Seung, 4, 58–59
civil rights movement, 6
Civil War, 6
Clements, Jonathan, 14
CNN, 80
Coleman, Eric, 25–26
colonialism, 5, 85–86; photography, 86
color: correction, 45; dials, 44, 45, 46, 47; finished episodes, 44, 45; iconicity, 43–47; lighting conditions, 44, 46; local colors, 43, 45–46, 134; model sheet, 43, 47, 134; plasmaticity, 43–47; skin tone, 43, 44, 45
Condry, Ian, 14
Confucianism, 73
contact zone, 79, 84, 99
Cowboy Bebop, 31, 33–34
Crunchyroll, 14
cultural appropriation, 18, 71, 79, 95–96; antiracist, 69–70; content appropriation, 69; definition, 69; effects of, 69–70; motif appropriation, 69; object appropriation, 69; racist, 69–70; style appropriation, 69; subject appropriation, 78, 80
cultural markers, 8–9, 24–25, 49, 68, 133
cultural signifiers: fighting styles, 102; language, 81–83
Cuphead, 4
Cuphead Show!, The, 4
Cuvier, Georges, 5

Dacey, Maryanne, 52
Dai Li, 75, 137
Daliot-Bul, Michal, 14, 15, 25
Dankiewicz, Tom, 88, 89, 91, 93
Danzig, Mac, 105
Daoism, 73
Dark Horse, 140
Davé, Shilpa, 4, 58
de Gobineau, Joseph Arthur, 5
Deitch, Gene, 10

DeLisle, Grey, 64
Deliverance, 120
Denison, Rayna, 14, 24, 34, 65
DeSena, Jack, 54–55, 63–64
Desmond, Matthew, 5, 69, 85
digital filmmaking, 61
DiMartino, Michael Dante, 15–17, 40–42, 50, 55–56, 71, 76, 87, 90, 93, 97, 104, 128
Disney, 22, 58, 116
Diversity in U. S. Mass Media, 80
Doane, Mary Ann, 61
Dobson, Nichola, 9
Dos Santos, Joaquim, 17, 33, 107
Doug, 13
DR Movie, 16, 39, 43
Dragon Ball Z, 15, 24
DreamWorks, 14
Dyer, Richard, 65

East West Players, 52
Eco, Umberto, 22
Edebiri, Ayo, 4
Egyptomania, 96
Ehasz, Aaron, 15, 17, 70–71, 76–80, 84–85, 142, 161n34
Eisen, Zach Taylor, 62–63, 136, 142
Eisenstein, Sergei, 32
Elliot, Bridget, 96
Emirbayer, Mustafa, 5, 69, 85
E.T. the Extra-Terrestrial, 153n66
eugenics, 6

Fairly OddParents, The, 13
Family Guy, 4, 159n87
fantasmatic body, 61, 64
fantasy, 4, 8, 14, 25, 68–69; definition, 68; fantasification process, 70–76, 114, 136; film and, 69; high, 69–70, 136; "lens of inspiration," 71; mimesis and, 83, 85, 115, 117, 120, 127; positioning culture, 71; worldbuilding, 18, 67, 80, 84
FCC, 13
fight choreography, 97–109, 113–14; archival authenticity, 98–109; historical referents, 98–106; wushu, 97–99

Filcak-Blackwolf, Sylvia, 44
film music, 115; composing, 116–25; instrumentation, 117–22, 124, 128, 131; racialized identity of, 115–17, 119
Fischer, Takayo, 59
Fisher, Jean, 86
FLCL, 130
Flintstones, The, 13
Flower, Jessie, 50, 55, 64, 66–67
Foley, 125, 132; definition of, 125–27; three categories of, 126
Fowler, Mark, 13
Fundamentals of Animation, The (Wells, Moore), 10
Funimation, 14
Furniss, Maureen, 9, 10, 22, 85–86, 112

Gabriel, Seychelle, 50, 51, 63, 142
Garagarza, Elsa, 87–88, 91–94, 111, 142
Gardner, Jared, 23
George, Brian, 60
Ghostrider: Spirit of Vengeance, 128
Glover, Savion, 108
Goldmark, Daniel, 122
Goofy Movie, A, 24
Goonies, The, 153n66
Gorbman, Claudia, 115
Great Hypostyle Hall, 93
Grimes, John A., 72
Gu, Woo Sung, 28
Guisetti, Vincent, 126
Guo, Elizabeth, 98, 102–4, 106

Halfyard, Janet K., 115
Hamilton, Joshua, 17
Han, Grace, 43
Hanna-Barbera, 129–30
Happy Feet, 108–9
Harmandir Sahib, 94
Harry Potter film franchise, 66, 97; *Harry Potter and the Deathly Hallows: Part 1*, 128
Heche, Anne, 57
Heck, Colin, 38, 46
Heder, Jon, 66, 140

Hedrick, Tim, 17, 71, 75–78, 80
Hendershot, Heather, 13
Henry, Mike, 4
Hi Hi Puffy AmiYumi, 15
Higgins, John Michael, 55, 64
Hillier, Bevis, 96
Himmler, Heinrich, 75
Hinduism, 72, 73
Hitler, Adolf, 6
Holocaust, 6
Homo sapien classifications, 5
Hong, James, 59
Hong Kyoung Pyo, 41
Hook, 153n66
Horiuchi, Glenn, 123
House of Flying Daggers, 38–39, 134
How to Train Your Dragon, 57–58
Hu, Tze-yue G., 14, 34
Huang, Jake, 17, 104–8
Hulu, 14
Hume, Kathryn, 68, 85, 112
Hunt, Leon, 98, 104
hyperrealism, 22, 125, 130

I Ching, 103
Ichioka, Yuji, 6
identity construction, 21–22
Imaginary Worlds, 87
imperialism, 69; language and, 82–83
Indianicity, 86
Inside Job, 4
Integrated Services Digital Network (ISDN), 63
intelligence quotient (IQ) tests, 6
Irwin, W. R., 68
Isaacs, Jason, 55–56, 66
Isle of Dogs, 4
Ito, Lance, 58
Iwabuchi, Koichi, 24
Iwamatsu, Mako, 51, 53–54, 56, 59, 63, 136

Jackie Chan Adventures, 15
Jackson, Rosemary, 68, 71
"Jasmine Flower," 119–20

jazz, 131; Asian appropriation of, 123–24; as a Black signifier, 122–23; Dixieland, 123; instrumentation, 122–23, 131; ragtime, 123
Jeet Kune Do, 105
Jeong Hoon, 41
Jeong Sang Woong, 89
Jin Jie, 119
JM Animation, 16, 28, 39–43, 89
Johari, Harish, 72
Johnson, William, 61–62
Juntong, 75

Kachru, Braj B., 82
Kajikawa, Loren, 123
Kamp Koral: SpongeBob's Under Years, 14
Kawashima, Terry, 25
Kennedy, Brian, 98, 102–5
Keppy, Peter, 122
Kettle, Jeff, 126
Khan, Genghis, 102
Ki, Yoon Young, 25
Kim, Hye Jung, 45
Kim, Jae Woon, 28
Kim, Joon-Yang, 43
Kim Soyoung, 79, 99, 104
King, C. Richard, 3
Kirwan, Kevin, 45
Kisu, Sifu, 16–17, 30, 33, 97, 100–103, 105, 107–8, 134
Klein, Hugh, 3
Knox, Robert, 5
Konietzko, Bryan, 15, 17, 21, 25–28, 30, 33–34, 39–41, 45–47, 50, 55–57, 63, 71, 77, 87–88, 90–97, 100, 104, 107, 110–12, 122, 126, 128, 142
Korra. See *Legend of Korra, The*
Kotlarz, Irene, 3
Kubo and the Two Strings, 4
Kung Fu Panda: Legends of Awesomeness, 14
Kwan, Jennie, 50–51, 54–55, 63–64, 142

Labourne, Geraldine "Gerry," 13
Lamarr, Phil, 60
Lang, Herbert, 86
Las Vegas Sun, 124
Lau Kar-leung, 101

Le, Dao, 28, 30
Leafie, A hen in the Wild, 154n87
Lee, Bruce, 105
Lee, Cynthia Kwei Yung, 58
Lee, Dae-Woo, 35, 38
Lee, Siu-Leung, 15–17, 110–12, 142
Legend of Korra, The, 4–5, 9, 12, 38, 57, 68; accents and dialects in, 58–60; acupuncture in, 73–74, 76, 78; "After All These Years," 57; Ahna, **31**; Air Nation, 16, 93; Air Nomads, 90; Air Temple Island, **91**; airbending, 105; Amon, 16; animation outsourcing, 39, 41; architecture in, 88, 90, **91**, 93–96; art book, 112, 140; Asami Sato, 16, 50–51; assistant director, 32–33; authenticity in, 86; Avatar, 16; Baatar Jr., 33; Baraz, **31**, 33; "The Beach," 35, **36**, 93, 129; "Beginnings," 122, 130; Beifong Estate, 96; BG, 88–89, 90, 93–94, 96; Bolin, 16, 38, 105; "A Breath of Fresh Air," 107; Bumi, 46; calligraphy, 109; casting, 50–52, 78; chi blockers, 72–73; choreography, 98, 99, 104–5, 107, 113–14; colorists, 44; commentary tracks, 126; "The Coronation," 28; "Darkness Falls," 35, **37**, 46, 129; dialogue tracks, 62–63, 136; directors, 33, 35, 37; Earth Empire, 16, 31; Earth Kingdom, 16, 94, 101; "Enemy at the Gate," 33; Equalist doorman, 28; Eska, 66, 139; General Iroh, 66; guest characters, 35, 57; Guo, 60; Ikki, 35, **37**, 129; Korra, 16, 35, 44–45, 47, 50, 53, 63, 105–6, 109, 134, 143; Kuvira, 16, 50; Kuvira supporters, 28; Kya, 35, **37**, 45–47; language as a neutral object in, 82–83; "A Leaf in the Wind," 105; Lin Beifong, 73, 78; Mako, 16, 82, 105, 109; Metal Clan, 94–96, 112; "The Metal Clan," **96**; model sheets, 33–35; music, 115–32; North American English in, 83, 138; Northern Water Tribe, 16, 44, 94; "Old Wounds," 60, 66–67, 73; pro-bending, 105, 114; producers, 33; production narratives, 39–40, 80, 86, 94; puns, 81–82; "Rebel Spirit," 34; "Rebirth," 28; referents, 69, 70, 73, 84, 88, 94–96, 101;

Republic City, 94, 104–5; "The Reunion," 31; "The Revelation," 28; Ryu, 28, 66, 140; Shiro Shinobi, 57; skin tones in, 44–46; sound effects, 125–31; "The Southern Lights," 45; Southern Water Tribe, 16; Spirit World, 130–31; "The Stakeout," 81; star personas, 66; storyboards, 34–38; Suyin Beifong, 57, 67, 73, 95, 97; Tenzin, 16, 35, **37**, 46, 66, 105, 129; "The Terror Within," 82, 126; Tonraq, 16; "Turning the Tides," 66; "The Ultimatum," 38; Unalaq, 16; "Venom of the Red Lotus," 90, **91**; Verrick, 34, 55; Water Tribe, 34, 88; "When Extremes Meet," 35, **37**, 129; writers and writing process, 77, 82; Zaheer, 16, 107; Zaofu, 73, 95–97; Zhao, 55, 66; Zuko, 38
Lehman, Christopher P., 3
Leong, Jane, 24
Levi, Antonia, 34
Li, Siu Leung, 98
Li Xiaoxiang, 117
linguistic profiling, 58
Linnaeus, Carl, 5–6
Lippi-Green, Rosina, 58
Lippmann, Walter, 7, 22
Liu, Celia, 117, 124
live-action productions, 3, 20, 56–57, 85; aural components, 49; indexical, 20; racialized, 5, 21
Loader, Alison Reiko, 4, 58
logograms, 82, 110
Looney Tunes, 24, 120
Lord of the Rings, The, 97, 162n61
Lorge, Peter Allan, 102, 104
Lu, Amy Shirong, 24, 141
Lu Shengli, 100, 104
Lugo-Lugo, Carmen R., 3
Luttrell, Jenna, 80

Mandala, Susan, 59
manga, 25; notations, 34
manpu, 34–35, 38, 47, 129, 134; appropriation of, 35; black/white eyes, 37; steam, 35, 129; tears and sweat, 35; veins, 35

Marcello, Starr A., 62
Marlow, Eugene, 122
martial arts: Bagua, 98, 103–4, 107; Buddhism, 98, 102; Chaquan, 102–3; Chinese, 16; Chow Gar, 101; Chu Gar, 101; cinematic, 99–100; hard, 98; Hung Gar, 101–2; kung fu, 99–100, 102, 104, 108; northern system, 98–100, 102–3, 137; Praying Mantis, 101; Shaolin, 98, 100, 102–3, 137; Tai Chi, 98, 100–103; Xingyi, 98, 103–4
Maruyama, Karen, 60
Mattila, Katie, 17, 73, 76
McCloud, Scott, 23–24
McLaren, Norman, 10
Media Action Network for Asian Americans (MANAA), 16, 80
Meza-Leon, Juan, 32–34, 38, 106–8
mimesis, 22, 38, 67, 68, 98, 107, 121, 129–30, 133, 138; definition of, 10; false, 128–29; fantasy and, 83, 85, 115, 117, 120, 127
minstrelsy, 3, 58
Mirzoeff, Nicholas, 10, 11, 85–86
Mission Hill, 161n34
Mittell, Jason, 13
mixed martial arts (MMA), 105, 106, 122, 134
model minority, 8–9
Moi Animation, 16, 39, 43
Monsters vs. Aliens, 14
Montgomery, Colleen, 65
Montgomery, Lauren, 17, 34, 46
Moon, Krystyn R., 9
Moore, Samantha, 10
Morse, Robert, 57
Mueller, Angela Song, 28, 30, 33
mukokuseki, 24

Nakauchi, Paul, 60
Napier, Susan J., 14, 34
Napoleon Dynamite, 66
narrative components, 68–84; fantastification process, 70–76; writing process and the writers' room, 76–81, 136
Native American artwork, 86
Natural Architecture (Rocca), 87

Nercessian, Andy, 118
Netflix, 14
New York Times, 42, 112
Nick Animation Podcast, 124
Nickelodeon, 13–15, 25–26, 28, 40, 45, 50, 52, 55, 76, 97; brand identity, 3, 14; Clearance Department, 75; executives, 55, 80, 84; history of animation department, 13–14; inclusivity and diversity at, 14
Nickelodeon Animation Studio, 42, 78, 89, 109; as a "contact zone," 79–80, 84
Nickelodeon Magazine, 100, 111
Nicktoons, 14

Oakley, Bill, 161n34
Oh, Seung Hyun, 28, 30, 34, 41, 92, 108
online fandom, 66, 140
Ono, Kenji, 35, 38
"Orient, the," 86
Original Dixieland Jazz Band, 123
Other, the, 22–24; accents and, 58, 60
Otmazgin, Nissim, 14–15, 25
Own Race Projection (ORP), 24, 141
Oz the Great and Powerful, 66, 131

"Paramount Decision," 13
paraxial areas, 68–69, 71
Parker, Trey, 59
Parks and Recreation, 66
Patrick Star Show, The, 14
Patriot, The, 66
Penguins of Madagascar, The, 14
Peter Pan, 66
phrenology, 6
Pieta (Buonarroti), 39, 134
Pixar films, 65
planetary productions cultures model, 11–12, 80, 141–43
Plaza, Aubrey, 66, 139
Poitras, Gilles, 34
Pokémon, 15
police brutality, 4
port wine stains, 27
power dynamics: cultural dominance, 69; cultural exchange, 69; cultural exploitation, 69; cultural representation, 79; transculturation, 69, 79, 95, 120
Powerpuff Girls, The, 15, 130
Pratt, Mary Louise, 79, 99

QuickTime, 107

race: absence of markers, 24–25, 28; construction, 3; definition of, 5–7; discourse, 3; folk understandings of, 5; holistic approach to analysis of, 4; stereotypes, 7, 22; taxonomies, 5–6
Racebending.com, 119
racialized identities, 6–10, 12–14, 17, 19, 25–26, 68, 76, 78, 81, 85, 108–9, 133, 137; in animation, 10, 12–13, 15, 19–20, 32, 45, 47–48; development of, 22; sound and, 17–18, 49, 61, 66–67, 74, 76, 85
racism: caricatures, 3; colorblind, 51, 78; corporate, 3; holistic approach to analysis of, 4; justifications for, 6; scientific, 6; studies of, 7
Radano, Ronald, 115
Raimi, Sam, 66
Raver-Lampman, Emmy, 4
Reagan, Ronald, 13
Red vs. Blue, 62
Reel Inequality: Hollywood Actors and Racism (Yuen), 51
referents, 31, 38, 79, 84–85, 87, 93–94, 106, 137, 138; footage and corporal authenticity, 106–9; historical, 98–106
Ren & Stimpy Show, The, 13
Ri, Lee Joo, 41
Rinaldi, William, 28
Rise of the Teenage Mutant Ninja Turtles, 14
Robbins, Brian, 14
Rocca, Alessandro, 87
Rodrigues, Sifu Manuel, 101
Roe, Annabelle Honess, 23
Rogers, Richard A., 69
Romano, Andrea, 17, 52–55, 59
Royal, Derek Parker, 23
Rugrats, 13–14

Ruh, Brian, 14
Ryu, Ki Hyun, 17, 28, 34, 35, 38, 41–42, 46, 66

Said, Edward W., 86
Sailor Moon, 14
Saltair Pavilion, 94
Sammond, Nicholas, 3
Samurai Champloo, 16; Mugen, 31
Samurai Jack, 15; Jack, 59
Sanskrit, 72–73
Saturday morning cartoons, 13
Scannell, Herb, 13–14
Screen Actors Guild (SAG), 52
Seinfeld, 60
Seoul Station, 154n87
Sergi, Gianluca, 62, 115
Shaolin Soccer, 99
Shaw Brothers, 101
She-Ra and the Princesses of Power, 58
Shiffman, Kenneth S., 3
Shimono, Sab, 59
Shipton, Alyn, 122
Simensky, Linda, 13
Simmons, J. K., 66
Simpson, O. J., 58
Simpsons, The, 4, 159n87, 161n34; Apu, 52; guest stars on, 65
Sito, Tom, 13
Slate, Jenny, 4
slavery, 6
Smolko, Joanna R., 120
Solomon, Charles, 9
Spider-Man, 66
Spivak, Gayatri Chakravorty, 7
SpongeBob SquarePants, 13
square boxes, 7
Stewart, Frederic William, 89
Stewart, Mark Allan, 57
storyboarding, 17, 39–41, 47, 68, 77, 134; art department/artists, 33–34, 38, 68, 78; *Avatar*, 33–35, 37, 42, 106; credits, 33; fight scenes, 107–8; first drafts, 106; *Korra*, 34–38; plasmaticity and, 32–41; selection of models, 38
Strong, Tara, 59

Studio Ghibli, 65
Studio Mir, 17, 39–40, 43
Studio Pierrot, 17, 39
Studio Reve, 39
Suan, Stevie, 34–35, 37–38
Sullivan, Owen, 107
Sung, Angela, 87, 91, 96, 111
System Naturae (Linnaeus), 5

Taberham, Paul, 115, 125
Takekuma, Kentaro, 35
Tanchum, Aran, 125, 126
Team America: World Police, 59
Technicolor India, 39
Teen Titans, 15
Teenage Mutant Ninja Turtles, 14
Tetri, Emily, 87, 88
Time Bandits, 153n66
Tin House, 39
Tom, Lauren, 60
Track Team, 15, 17
Train to Busan, 154n87
transculturation, 69, 79, 95, 120
Tulk, Janice Esther, 116
Tumblr, 46, 47
Tushar, Steve, 125, 128, 130–31, 142
Tutankhamen, 96

Ueno Toshiya, 25
Ulanova, Olga, 32–33, 38, 106–8
Ultimate Fighting Championship (UFC), 105
Umphries, Jeremy, 105
United States v. Paramount Pictures, Inc., 13

Varney, Janet, 50, 51, 53–55, 63
Vascular Birthmarks Foundation, 27
visual components, 61, 68; of animated bodyscape, 20–48; animatics, 39–41; character design and iconicity, 21–32; color, iconicity, and plasmaticity, 43–47; exposure sheets, 40–41; logograms, 57, 110; markers, 24–25, 49; outsourcing animation, 39–43; signifiers, 21, 38, 53, 133; storyboarding and plasmaticity,

32–41; timing sheets, 40, 41; worldbuilding, 85–114
Volpe, Giancarlo, 33, 92, 107

Wakeman, Frederic E., 75
Wallestad, Thomas J., 35
Wang, Hong, 124
Wang Guangxi, 98
Weinstein, Josh, 161n34
Wells, Paul, 10, 13, 19–23, 32, 125
White, Dana, 105
white supremacists, 6
Whitman, Mae, 64
Wile E. Coyote, 129
Williams, Zelda, 50, 57
Wilson, Crawford, 55
Windover, Michael, 95
Wojcik, Pamela Robertson, 62
Wong, Francis, 123
Wong, Miken Lee, 28
World War II, 6
worldbuilding: aural, 115–32; fantasy, 18, 67, 80, 84, 86; fight choreography, 97–109; visual, 85–114
writers' room, 76–81; collaboration in, 78–79, 81, 84, 93; episode pitches, 77; production culture, 76; "room punch," 77
writing, 70, 76–81, 83, 136; authenticity in, 85; fantasification process, 70–76; feedback, 77, 80; language as a signifier in, 81–83; outline, 77, 80; premise, 77–78, 80; process, 80, 85, 142, 161n34; retreats, 76; script, 77–78, 80
Wudang systems: Bagua, 98, 103–4, 107; Tai Chi, 98, 100–103; Xingyi, 98, 103–4

wushu, 99; Buddhism, 98, 102; Chaquan, 102, 103; Chow Gar, 101; Chu Gar, 101; cinematic, 99–100; hard, 98; Hung Gar, 101–2; kung fu, 99–100, 102, 104, 108; northern system, 98–100, 102–3, 137; Praying Mantis, 101; Shaolin, 98, 100, 102–3, 137; signifiers, 99; soft, 98; southern system, 98–99, 101; Taekwondo and, 104; Taoism, 98, 102, 103; Wudang, 98; *wuxia*, 38–39, 99, 134
Wynn, Benjamin, 15, 121, 125–31

Xiaolin Showdown, 15; Omi, 59

Yang, Lisa, 28
Yangtze River, 89
Yeh, Wen-hsin, 75
Yellow Crane Temple, 89–90, 93
"yellow voice," 4, 58–60, 140
yellowface, 9, 23
Yoo, Jae-myung, 40–43, 63, 142
Young, James O., 69
Young, Keone, 59
YouTube, 106–7
Yuen, Nancy Wang, 51, 78

Zahir, Arif, 4
Zane, Edwin, 16, 26–27, 47, 53, 80, 84, 103, 137, 139
Zarghami, Cyma, 14
Zemeckis, Robert, 65
Zieff, Rick, 57
Zuckerman, Jeremy, 15, 116–25
Zurcher, Lauren, 90
Zwyer, Melchior, 33, 107

ABOUT THE AUTHOR

Francis M. Agnoli is an independent scholar who specializes in the areas of race, identity, and animation studies. He earned his doctorate at the University of East Anglia, where he first developed the concept of the animated bodyscape. His previous work has been published in *Animation: An Interdisciplinary Journal*, the online journal *Animation Studies*, and the edited collection *Fantasy/Animation: Connections between Media, Mediums and Genres*. He is also the editor on a forthcoming collection of essays on the *Avatar* television franchise.

www.ingramcontent.com/pod-product-compliance
Lightning Source LLC
Chambersburg PA
CBHW021821220426
43663CB00029B/352